Wills *and* Aministrations

of

SOUTHAMPTON COUNTY

VIRGINIA

1775-1800

(Volume #2)

Compiled By:

Blanche Adams Chapman

Please direct all correspondence and orders to:

www.southernhistoricalpress.com
or
SOUTHERN HISTORICAL PRESS, Inc.
PO BOX 1267
375 West Broad Street
Greenville, SC   29601
southernhistoricalpress@gmail.com

ISBN #0-89308-883-8

Printed in the United States of America

CLAUD, Joshua.   Dec. 22, 1775.   Estate appraised
by Joshua Nicholson, Amos Harris and John Barrow.
   R.   Jan. 11, 1776   Page 144

BYNUM, Elizabeth.   March 10, 1774.   Estate appraised
by Jacob Newsum, Nathan Harris and John Drake.
   R.   Feb. 8, 1776   Page 144

AVERY, Richard.   Leg.- son Joel; son Thomas; son
Edward the part of estate already paid for him to John
Wilkinson; daughter Martha; son Etheldred when twenty
one; wife Fortune; daughter Elizabeth Avery.
   Ex. Howell Edmunds.
   D.   July 27, 1773   R.   Feb. 8, 1776
   Wit. David Edmunds Sr., David Edmunds, Jr.,
         Benjamin Turner   Page 145

IVY, Henry.   Account estate. 1774.
Audited by James Ridley and Joshua Nicholson
Exs. Henry Ivy and Robert Ivy
   R.   Feb. 8, 1776   Page 146

BYNUM, Elizabeth.   Account Current. Ex., John
Wilkinson. Paid the heirs of William Bynum as per ac-
count, returned by Elizabeth Bynum.
   Audited by John Thomas Blow and John Crafford.
   R.   Feb. 8, 1776   Page 147

JOHNSON, John.   Appraisal estate by Benjamin Griffin,
Hardy Doyel and John Worrell.   R. April 11, 1776
                                             Page 148

STEPHENSON, Elizabeth.   Estate account.   Ex.,
William Stephenson.   Audited by Simon Boykin, John
Clayton and John Summerell.   R. May 9, 1776
                                             Page 148

HARRISON, Samuel.   Parish of St. Luke. Leg.- wife
Amima; son Joseph; son William when twenty one; to my

children Olive, Rebecca, Elizabeth, Anne, Joseph,
Charlotte, Solomon, Harmon, Hannah Richardson and Mary.
Ex., Edward Lundy and Joshua Nicholson.
D. March 19, 1775   R. May 9, 1776
Wit. James Lundy Jr., Moses Harris, Joel Atkinson,
    William Morgan   Page 149

Vasser, Lydia. Parish of St. Luke. Leg.- son Jesse
land purchased of Nicholas Gurley, when of age; daughter
Anne; daughter Mary; daughter Elizabeth; daughter Margaret.
Ex., son-in-law Robert Carr.
D. Oct. 10, 1773   May 9, 1776
Wit. George Gurley, Abraham Mitchell, William Edwards.
                                            Page 150

TAYLOR, Lucy. Leg.- daughter Mary Mason Taylor; daugh-
ter Martha; son Robert; daughter Ann Brown.
Exs, brother-in-law Henry Taylor, son-in-law William Brown
D. April 5, 1776   R. July 11, 1776
Wit. Temperance Taylor, Henry Taylor.   Page 151

RIDLEY, Nathaniel. Leg.- wife Sarah; son Mathew
when of age, reversion to nephew Nathaniel the son of Day
Ridley; negroes to be divided among the children of Day
Ridley, his son Nathaniel excepted, Ann Holliday and
Pamelia Coffield.
Exs., wife Sarah and brothers Day and Thomas Ridley.
D. Jan. 7, 1776   R. July 11, 1776
Wit. Jeremiah Drew, Faith Lane, James Ridley.
                                            Page 152

GLOVER, George.   May 29, 1776. Estate appraised by
John Crenshaw, James Story, Philemon Hatfield.
R. July 11, 1776   Page 153

Evans, Benjamin. June 21, 1776. Estate appraised by
Arthur Foster, Enos James, William Francis.
R. Sept. 12, 1776   Page 154

WRAY, William.   Inventory. May 26, 1775
Anne Wray, Extx.   R. Oct. 10, 1776   Page 155

STEPHENSON, Ann.   Inventory 1774
Martha Clary, Extx.   R. Oct. 10, 1776   Page 155

DAY, Edmund.   July 19, 1776   Estate appraised by

John Thomas Blow, John Taylor and William Miller
  R. Oct. 10, 1776   Page 155

JOYNER, Bridgman. Leg.- wife Mary, plantation bought of
Jesse Council; nephew Lewis Joyner; to Jacob the son of
Jacob Joyner; brother Jacob Joyner; brother Jesse Joyner.
Friends Jacob Beale, James Fowler and Absalom Tallaugh to
divide my estate Ex., brother Jacob Joyner.
  D. July 26, 1776   R. Nov. 14, 1776
Wit. J. Denson, Jacob Beale, Absalom Tallough.
                                          Pa

BAILEY, Robert. Estate appraised by Henry Davis and
Joel Davis.   R. Nov. 14, 1775   Page 157

DAVIS, Thomas, Jr. Leg.- daughter Anne; son Phillip;
daughter Elizabeth; wife Hannah.
Ex., son Phillip Davis.
D. Sept. 17, 1776   R. Nov. 14, 1776
Wit. Edwin Davis, Sally Riggan   Page 158

WESTBROOK, Elias. Leg.- Aunt Amey Foster and uncle
Moses Foster.
Ex., uncle Moses Foster.
D. July 9, 1776   R. Jan. 9, 1777
Wit. John Simmons, Joshua Fort.   Page 159

BOWERS, William. Leg.- son Britain; daughter Middey
Exs., Jacob Turner and son Randolph Bowers.
D. Dec. 18, 1776   R. Jan 9, 1777
Wit. Randolph Bowers, William Barmer, Jacob Turner.
                                   Page 159

TAYLOR, Etheldred. St. Luke's Parish. Leg.- cousin
Charles Taylor, son of my brother John Taylor
Ex., brother John Taylor
D. April 15, 1776   R. Jan 9, 1777
Caveat entered by James Taylor.
Wit. Batt Peterson, John Peterson.   Page 160

MERCER, Robert   Inventory   Jan 9, 1777
Ex., Joseph Holleman   Page 161

4

KINNEBREW, Ann. Leg.- son Edwin; son Lot; granddaugh-
ter Prissy Kinnebrew. Ex., friend Benjamin Blunt.
D. Nov. 12, 1776   R. Jan 9, 1777
Wit. Mary Bittle, Benjamin Blunt.   Page 161

JOHNSON, Jesse. Estate appraised by John Mitchel,
William Branch, John Coll (?)   Adm. Samuel Cooper
R. Jan. 9, 1777   Page 162

BARROW, John. Leg.- oldest son William; son Daniel;
son John; granddaughter Phoeba Hill Barrow; daughter Anne
Kinnebrew; daughter Hannah Pitman; daughter Martha Frizzell
Exs. son John Barrow and Benjamin Turner
D. John Blake, Henry Stephenson, Lucy Stephenson
D. July 29, 1776   R. Jan. 9, 1777   Page 162
Inventory. March 13, 1777   Page 166

JARRELL, Thomas. Estate appraised by William Miller,
Richard Blow, William Thomas.   R. Feb. 13, 1777
                                                 Page 163

JOYNER, Bridgman. Estate appraised by David Wright,
John Joyner and Etheldred Drake. R. Feb. 13, 1777
                                                 Page 164

KINNEBREW, Lot. Inventory.   Feb. 13, 1777
                                                 Page 163

CLAUD, Joshua. Of St Luke's Parish. Leg. My estate
to my sister Phoebe Lundy's children.
Exs., brother-in-law Byrd Lundy and Drury Lundy.
D. Nov. 20, 1775   R. Feb. 13, 1777
Wit. Edward Harris, Edward Lundy, Solomon Harrison.
                                                 Page 165

GAY, Edmund. Leg. Elizabeth Scott, daughter of John
Scott; Godson Edmund Blunt; children of my deceased bro-
ther Thomas Gay; to my brothers and sister,- John Gay;
Charles Gay; Mary Barker, William Gay and Jonathan Gay
Ex., friend William Scott.
D. Oct. 31, 1774   R. May 9, 1776
Wit. William Scott, James Moore, Richard Johnston,
        Jacob Randolph   Page 165

POPE, Joseph. **Estate appraised by Thomas Edmunds,**
Richard Blow and Edmund Gay.   R. March 12, 1777
Page 167

DELK, Joseph.   Estate Account. 1774
Audited by William Miller and John Taylor.
R. March 13, 1777
Page 168

DAVIS, Thomas Jr.   Estate appraised by Richard Wren,
Charles Briggs and John Cobb.   R. March 13, 1777 Page 168

WESTBROOK, Thomas.   Parish of St Luke.   Leg.- wife
Hellen; son Henry; son Thomas; daughter Lucy Hunt; daughter
Hellen Speed, plantation I had of James Speed; grandson
Benjamin Speed; daughter Martha Judkins.
Exs., Wife Hellen and son Henry Westbrook.
D. Aug. 25, 1775   R. May 8, 1777
Wit. John Simmons, Sr., Susannah Simmons, Benjamin Lewis.
Page 169

FOWLER, James.   Of Nottoway Parish.   Leg.- **son William;**
son James; my land to be divided by **William Williams, Jonas**
Edwards and David Wright.   Wife Sarah Fowler.
Ex., son William Fowler.
D. Feb. 23, 1777   R. May 8, 1777
Wit. Christian Johnson, Martha Johnson, Thomas Williams
Page 169

HALE, Joseph.   Estate appraised by **John Gardner, Samuel**
Sandiford, James Chappell   D. Feb. 13, 1777
Elizabeth Hale, Admtx.   R. May 8, 1777   Page 170

HARGRAVE, Michael.   Estate appraised by **John Powell,**
William Vaughan, Samuel Kindred.   R. May 8, 1777   Page 171

HARRISON, William .   Legs.- brother Henry (provided he
pay a certain amount to brothers Benjamin, Richard and
Nathaniel), reversion of bequest to his son Henry; sister
Sarah McLemore.
Exs., brothers Henry and Richard Harrison.
D. June 4, 1777   R. June 12, 1777
Wit. John Sturgeon, Simon Harris, Celia Sturgeon.
Page 172

6

POPE, William. Leg.- daughter Christian; son
Willian; my gun at Andrew Pope to be given Thomas Pope
at twenty one; Hezekiah Pope; my hand mill at my son
John Pope is to be used by Andrew, Jesse, William and
John Pope; estate to be sold and the money equally di-
vided between my sons and daughters, viz.- John, William,
Hardy, Jesse and Andrew; daughters, Christian, Ann and
Martha Pope (widow); daughter Alice Newton.
  Exs., sons William and Andrew Pope
  D. July 8, 1776   R. June 12, 1777
  Wit. Thomas Edmunds, Benjamin Blunt, John Porter,
        Samuel Edmunds   Page 173

JOYNER, William. Leg.- wife Ann; son William; son
William; son Lawrence; son Jethro; Ann Joyner, daughter
of my brother Lewis Joyner.
  Exs., sons William, Lawrence and Jethro Joyner.
  D. Dec. 31, 1776   R. July 11, 1777
  Wit. R. Kello, Micajah Griffin, Charles Council
                                          Page 174

CATHAN, John. Account estate. W. Gwaltney, Adm.
Audited by Henry Briggs and Abraham Mitchell
  R. Aug. 14, 1777   Page 175

LITTLE, John. Account estate. Orphan William Little
in account with Lucy Turner, Admtx of Simon Turner, his
guardian.   R. Aug. 14, 177
  Audited by William Blunt and John Sturgeon (or Stringer)
                                          Page 175

Kinnebrew, Ann. Estate appraised by John Kirby and
Kirby Brittle.   R. Aug. 14, 1777   Page 175

VASSER, Lydia. Estate appraised by Henry Briggs,
William Thomas, Abram Mitchell.
  D. June 3, 1776   R. Aug. 13, 1777   Page 176

ATKINSON, Timothy. Parish of Nottoway. Leg.- wife
Elizabeth; son Timothy; daughter Holland; daughter Sally;
daughter Patty; daughter Mary; daughter Betty Atkinson.
  Ex. son Timothy Atkinson
  D. Jan. 27, 1777   R. Sept. 11, 1777

Wit. William Urquhart, John Clayton, Benjamin Britt

Page 178

DREWRY, Thomas. Leg.- wife Elizabeth, reversion to all my children. Extx., wife Elizabeth Drewy
D. April 9, 1777   R. Sept. 11, 1777
Wit. John Davis, Jacob Joyner, Robert Hasty   Page 179

AVORY, Richard. Estate appraised by Jacob Turner, John Powell and David Edmunds.
D. Feb. 16, 1776   R. Sept. 11, 1777   Page 179

JOYNER, William. Estate appraised by Mathew Charles, Henry Joyner, Joseph Mountfortt   R. Sept. 11, 1777
Page 180

EDMUNDS, Mary. Leg.- son Howell; son William, son John; son Samuel at twenty one; to Charles, son of Henry Edmunds; daughter Sarah; daughter Mary Nicholson; daughter Martha Myrick; grandchildren Edmunds and Susan Myrick at age; daughter Lucy Nicholson; granddaughter Sarah and Lucy daughters of Howell Edmunds; granddaughter Elizabeth, Mary, Lucy and Martha, daughters of Stephen Williamson; to Etheldred son of Thomas Edmunds.
Exs., sons William and Samuel and daughter Sarah Edmunds.
Sept. 12, 1777   R. Dec. 11, 1777
Wit. John Pope, Simon Revel.   Page 181

JONES, Nathan. Leg.- brother Thomas Jones; wife Mary with reversion to cousin Mary, daughter of Blyth Wiliams; if without heirs to Ann now the wife of Joshua Whitney
Ex., friend Lemuel Jones.
D. Sept. 20, 1777   R. Dec. 11, 1777
Wit. Martha Johnson, Ann Johnson, Mary and William Doyle
Lemuel Jones refused to act as Ex., Mary Jones qualified
Page 182

WESTBROOK, Thomas. Inventory. Signed by Hellen Westbrook and Henry Westbrook.   R. Dec. 11, 1777
Page 183

DRURY, Thomas. Estate appraised by John Gardner, James Vick and Lewis Joyner.   R. Dec. 11, 1777   Page 184
Signed, Elizabeth Drury.

FORT, Ann. Leg.- daughter Sarah Turner; son John; son Howell; son Littleton; son Turner Fort.
Exs., William Turner, Jeremiah Drew.
D. Oct. 20, 1777   R. Dec. 11, 1777
Wit. Solomon Cooper, Harris Johnson, Thomas Turner.

JOYNER, Israel. Parish of St. Luke. Leg.- wife Sarah, what was hers at our marriage and one third of my estate; son Charles tract adjoing Benjamin Worrell; son Amos, tract adjoining Nathan Barnes, Jesse Pope and Robert Newsom; remainder of my estate to my sons Joseph, Giles, Mathew and Jordan and daughter Martha; son John Joyner.
Exs., Wife Sarah and son Charles Joyner.
D. Nov. --, 1777   R. Dec. 11, 1777
Wit. Samuel Woodard, Temperance Woodward,
       Robert Washington.
Sarah Joyner acknowledged that she was satisfied with the estate left her by her husband

BOOTH, Robert. Leg.- son Beverley, tract bought of Benjamin Phillips; son Moses land given me by my father Robert Booth; daughter Elizabeth; grandson Robert Booth; daughter Lucy Sykes; granddaughter Maze Booth; grandson David Booth.
Exs., brother Moses Booth and son Beverley Booth
D. Aug. 27, 1777   R. Dec. 11, 1777
Wit. Moses Booth, Elizabeth Booth, William Salter, Jr.

FOWLER, James. Estate appraised by William Williams, Jonah Edwards, David Wright. R. Dec. 11, 1777

POND, Richard. Parish of Nottoway. Leg. - son Richard; son John Hawkins Pond the tract on which James Sedget formerly lived; daughter Elizabeth Moore; daughter Mary; daughter Sarah; daughter Martha; son Thomas; son James; wife Martha Pond.
Exs. wife and sons Richard and John Hawkins Pond.
D. Sept. 22, 1777   R. Jan. 11, 1778
Wit. Edwin Gray, Joshua Wood, Mary James

EDMUNDS, Mary. Inventory. Jan. 8, 1778

COBB, William. Estate appraised by Abraham Mitchell;
Thomas Lawrence and Henry Cobb. D. March --, 1777
Signed J. Denson. R. Jan 8, 1778   Page 191

KINNEBREW, Mrs. Ann. Account Current. Paid the ac-
counts of Shadrack and Jacob Kinnebrew. Paid legacies to
Shadrack, Edwin and Lot Kinnebrew. Signed, Benjamin Blunt.
  Audited by Charles Briggs and Arthur Foster.
R. Jan. 8, 1778   Page 192

LUNDY, Byrd. Leg.- wife Pheeba, land bought of Edward
Eppes decd. with reversion to the children I leave by her,
viz.- Christian, Elizabeth, Edwin, Byrd, Joshua, Claud and
James; son Edwin the land I purchased of Robert Wilkins;
daughter Molly Lundy.
  Exs., wife Pheeby, sons Edwin and Byrd Lundy and friend
       Lewis Thorpe.
  D. Dec. 29, 1777   R.
Wit. D. Fisher, William Claud, John Claud   Page 193

RIDLEY, James Day. Leg.- my three children, John Edwards
Ridley, Rebecca and Elizabeth Ridley; wife Mary Ridley
  Ex., wife Mary Ridley
  D. Aug. 10, 1776   R. Feb. 12, 1778
Wit. W. Edwards, Charles Portlock, Joseph Reece, Jr.
                                              Page 195

WRIGHT, James. Leg.- grandson John son of James Wright;
son Joseph Wright; dauughter Martha Connor; grandson James
Wright; wife Martha Wright.
  Ex., son Joseph Wright.
  D. Jan. 9, 1778   R. Feb. 12, 1778
Wit. John Pursell, Ledbetter Lowe, Saphera Fly   Page 194

WARREN, Joseph Parish of St. Luke. Leg.- wife Faith;
son Michael; the following children have already received
their part of my estate- Henry, Joseph, Sarah Smith; Faith
Duprey and Mary Day; daughter Elizabeth Duprey; grandson Hill
son of Thomas Day, Jr.
  Exs., wife and son Michael Warren.
  D. Aug. 15, 1775   R. Feb. 12, 1778
Wit. John Barrow, Richard Foster, Edith Kinnebrew.
                                              Page 196

JACKSON, Sarah.   Parish of St. Luke. Leg.- grandson
Nathan Jackson, estate in the hands of James Peden; daugh-
ter Mary Gurley.
Ex., friend William Edwards.
D. June 9, 1777   R. Feb. 12, 1778
Wit. William Edwards, Martha Gurley   Page 196

BEALL, John.   To son Drury land adjoining Dr. Browne
and Howell Whittington; son Burwell; son John; wife Liddia.
Ex., Joseph Johnson
D. Sept. 13, 1777   R. Feb. 12, 1778
Wit. George Gurley, Thomas Edwards, Jacob Braswell
                                                   Page 197

FOWLER, William. Leg.- wife Ann; son Benjamin; son
Charles; son William Fowler.
Ex., Burwell Barnes.
D. Oct. 8, 1777   R. Feb. 12, 1778
Wit. Edmund Barrett, Epaphroditus Williams,
      Jacob Williams.   Page 199

BUSKIN, John. Estate appraised by John Johnson, Lawrence
Joyner, Mathew Charles   R. Feb. 12, 1778   Page 199

KITCHEN, Benjamin. Leg.- son Benjamin; son Nathaniel;
son Frederick; son Etheldred; son Jesse articles bought of
Robert Bailey; daughters- Lucy, Sarah, Martha, Cela, Betsey
and Mary; wife Mary Kitchen
Ex., son Frederick Kitchen.
D. Jan. 14, 1778   R. Feb. 12, 1778
Wit. Anselm Jones, James Jones, Charles Briggs
                                                   Page 200

BOOTH, Robert.   Estate appraised by Barnaby Bailey,
Richard Bailey and Charles Bailey. R. March 12, 1778
                                                   Page 201

RIDLEY, Nathaniel. Inventory.   R. March 6, 1778
Signed, Sarah Ridley.   Page 20-

WRIGHT, James.   Estate appraised by Benjamin Crumpler,
Bennant Crumpler, Robbin Williamson.   R. March 12, 1778
                                                   Page 205

AUSTIN, William. Leg.- wife Ruth; son Charles, son
John; daughter Sarah Jackson; son Richard; daughter Molly.
D. Sept. 2, 1770   R. March 12, 1778
Wit. Samuel Bridger Collins, William Barden
Exs., wife Ruth and Edward Drew   Page 206

POND, Richard. Estate appraised by Joshua Woods, John
Cobb and Benjamin Exum.   R. March 12, 1778   Page 207

FOWLER, William. Estate appraised by Jacob Barnes,
James Barnes and Edmund Barrett   R. March 12, 1778
                                                Page 208

HOWELL, Hartwell. Estate appraised by William Millar,
Richard Blow and John Fort.   R. March 12, 1778   Page 209

SIMMONS, William. Of Nottoway Parish. Leg.- wife Sarah
land bought of Henry Browne, and another tract of Thomas
Langley; son John; son Thomas land purchased of Thomas
Clifton and another of John Meacum, adjoining Samuel Drewry
and one of James Ingraham; son Daniel Simmons.
Exs., friends Peter Butts, Edwin Gray, Benjamin Ruffin, Jr.
D. Nov. 12, 1775   R. April 9, 1778
Wit. Thomas Butts, Henry Adams, Benjamin Scarborough,
      William Butts.   Page 211

CARY, Miles. Inventory. Signed, Henry Taylor.
    D. March 6, 1767   R. April 9, 1778   Page 212

KITCHEN, Benjamin. Estate appraised by Joshua Wood,
Richard Wren and Moses Wood. R. May 14, 1778   Page 213

SPEED, Mary. Parish of Nottoway. Leg.- youngest daugh-
ter Rebecca; rest of my estate to my other two Children,
Isham Hill and Croker (Crocker ?) Cobb.
Exs.,-son Isham Hill and William Cobb
D. Feb. 15, 1773   R. May 14, 1778
Wit. William Gresswitt, Samuel Cobb, Lazarus Cobb.
                                                Page 215

COBB, Joseph. Inventory. Signed Henry Cobb.

D. Aug. 12, 1777   R. May 14, 1778.   Page 216

JONES, Nathan. Estate appraised by Moses Johnson, John
Summerell, Benjamin Crumpler.   R. March 11, 1778
                                              Page 216

LUNDY, Edward.   Of Parish of St. Luke.   Leg.- wife;
son Lunsford; daughter Frances, rest of estate between all
my children except Frances and son William.
     Exs. (omitted), but the will was presented by Elizabeth
          Lundy and William Lundy
     D. April 22, 1778   R. June 11, 1778
     Wit. Edward Harris, Charles Portlock, John Lundy,
          James Lundy   Page 217

HAILE, Joseph.   Account estate.   Signed Elizabeth Haile.
Audited by Edmund Tyler and Lewis Joyner   .
     R. June 11, 1778   Page 218

BYNUM, Michael.   Account current. Signed, John
Wilkinson. Legacies paid Benjamin Bynum; Nathan Bryant;
to Benja. Bryant guardian of Eliby Bynum, Turner Byrum
and Colen Whitehead Bynum, also for keeping Betsey Bynum.
and Michael Bynum.
     Audited by Benjamin Blunt and John Powell.   Page 218

THORPE, Aaron. Joshua Nicholson, Adm.   Refers to a
negro in dispute with Abram Johnson. Audited by J. Ridley,
Henry Taylor and Timothy Thorpe. R. June 11, 1778
                                              Page 220

BLUNT, Thomas.   Of Parish of Nottoway.   Leg.- wife
Ann, land bought of Henry Brownes' Exs.; son Henry; son
Joseph Gray; son Thomas; son Edmund; son William; son
James; daughters Sarah, Elizabeth and Ann Blunt.
     Exs., friends Edwin Gray and William Thomas
     D. Sept. 26, 1777   R. March 12, 1778
     Wit. Benjamin Williams, William Moore, John Bidgood
                                              Page 221

TATUM, John.   Signed, Elizabeth Tatum, Admtx. Paid
Richard Tatum, Joshua Tatum and Rebecca Tatum.

Audited by Lewis Joyner, Sr. and Lewis Joyner, Jr.
R. July 9, 1778   Page 222

JOYNER, Israel. Inventory. R. July 9, 1778   Page 223

BRADSHAW, Joseph. Leg.- son Joseph land adjoining Jethro
Joyner; wife Elizabeth; son Semor; son William; son Elias;
daughter Margaret Love; daughter Mary Boone; daughter Ann
Croker; at wife's death estate left her to Honour, Avey,
Semor, William and Elias Bradshaw.
Exs., wife Elizabeth and son Joseph Bradshaw.
D. July 11, 1778   R. Sept. 10, 1778
Wit. Lawrence Joyner, Thomas Bradshaw, Rebekah Joyner.
                                                Page 224

CALTHORP, Ellennere. Estate appraised by Barnaby
Bailey, Henry Coker and Jesse Harrell. R. Sept. 10, 1778
                                                Page 225.

BLUNT, Thomas. Inventory. Signed, Edwin Gray and
William Thomas. R. Oct. 8, 1778   Page 226

CLEMENTS, Benjamin. Of the Parish of Nottoway. Leg.-
son George my plantation in Prince George County, on which
he now lives, reversion to his children, Elizabeth, Thomas,
Lucy, George and Richard Clements; son Benjamin; son Thomas;
daughter Anna; grandson Jesse Butts the land bought of
Charles Gilliam; daughter Elizabeth Butts; daughter Sarah
Butts; to the nine children of Peter Butts, my grandchil-
dren, Thomas, John, Benjamin, William, James, Daniel, Lucy,
Mary and Elizabeth Butts; granddaughter Judith Gilliam;
grandson Thomas Clements Gilliam; to the five children of
Thomas Peete, my grandchildren, Elizabeth, Samuel, Benjamin,
Thomas and Alexander Peete; grandson Thomas Clement Butts.
Exs., Sons Benjamin and Thomas Clements.
D. July 9, 1778   R. Oct. 8, 1778
Wit. John Knight, John Brown, Thomas Peete   Page 228

DELOACH, William. Parish of Nottoway. Leg.- grandson
John Hudson Deloach, son of John Deloach; son Benjamin
D. April 11, 1772   R. Oct. 8, 1773
Wit. Eustace Windham, Jesse Windham, Ann Dunn. Page 229

WELLONS, John.   Parish of Nottoway. Leg.- son John;
son Henry; son Charles; daughter Mary; wife Annemeriah;
daughter Elizabeth the wife of Howell Branch; daughter
Barbary, wife of Benjamin Oney.
Exs., sons John and Charles Wellons.
D. Dec. 18, 1773   R. Oct. 8, 1778
Wit. Francis Rose, Johnson Barnes.   Page 230

VICK, William.   Leg.- wife Elizabeth; son Simon land
adjoining Epaphroditus Williams, also part of the tract
which I gave Simon Baret, adjoining my son William; son
Robert a tract adjoining Mathew Vick, Davis Bryant and
Thomas Vick; to granddaughter Rebecca Pope and her mother
Mary Pope land adjoining son William, William Fowler and
Simon Baret; son Isaac; daughter Elizabeth Pope and daugh-
ter Martha Baret.
Ex., sons Simon and Robert Vick
D. Feb. 15, 1777   R. June 9, 1778
Wit. Jacob Vick, Mathew Vick, Lewis Bryant   Page 231

WARREN, Joseph.   Inventory.   Signed Faith Warren
and Michael Warren.   R. May 14, 1778   Page 232

RAWLINGS, John. Of St Luke Parish.   Leg. daughter
Betty Sammons (?); son Isaac; daughter Mary Adams; wife
Mary Rawlings.
Exs, son Isaac and son-in-law Thomas Adams.
D. Sept. 17, 1777   R. Oct. 8, 1778
Wit. Richard Mason, George Bell (Beel ?) Henry Ivy
                                              Page 233

RAWLINGS, William.   Estate appraised by Joshua Thorp,
Henry Ivy and Joshua Nicholson.   D. Sept. 25, 1777
R. Oct. 8, 1778   Page 234

Lundy, Drury. Estate appraised by Joseph Reese,
Thomas Turner and John Myrick.   R. Oct. 8, 1778
                                              Page 234

MOORE, James. Leg.- wife; son James; son Jesse;
daughter Martha; daughter Elizabeth; daughter Sarah; son
Richard Moore.
Exs., Richard Pond, Richard Ricks, Edwin Gray

D. March 15, 1775   R. Oct. 8, 1778
Wit. Benjamin Stewart, James Bell, Eliplas Lewis
Isaac and Jesse Williams qualified as Exs.

Page 236

DAVIS,. Thomas. Of the Parish of Nottoway. Leg.-
wife Jeane; daughter-in-law Hannah Davis, relict of my son
Thomas; grandson Phillip Davis; son Henry land I bought of
my son Drury; daughter Hannah; granddaughter Sarah Long;
daughter Lucy Phillips; daughter Mary Tarver; to friend
Richard Renn a tract of land for value received adjoining
Charles Holt and John Thorpe; to sons of my son Drury,
Etheldred, Thomas and James Davis.
    Ex. son Henry Davis.
    D. June 4, 1778   R. Nov. 12, 1778
    Wit. Charles Briggs, Joel Davis John Mitchel   Page 236

TURNER, John. Account estate. Ex., Joshua Nicholson.
Legacies paid to son Jacob; son Joseph; son Amos; son
Jesse and paid to William Claud, guardian of son David.
Received his part of his father's estate from his Exs.
Audited by Henry Harris and Timothy Thorpe.
    R. Nov. 12, 1778   Page 237

TAYLOR, Harris. Leg.- son Bartin; daughter Mary
Sousberry; daughter Nancy Johnson; son Henry; daughter
Sarah Lisles; daughter Elizabeth Edwards; son Thomas;
wife Lucy Taylor.
    Ex., son Henry Taylor
    D. Nov. 18, 1777   R. Nov. 12, 1778
    Wit. James Maddra, Samuel Taylor, Elizabeth Ellis
                                              Page 238

LONGWORTH, John. Estate appraised by Ben -----,
John Cobb and Thomas Butts. R. Nov. 12, 1778   Page 239

FOGERSON, (?) John. Leg.- son William; son Josiah;
Ann thorpe; wife Ann.
    3 of 7 mo. 1778   R. Nov. 12, 1778
    Wit. Drury Beal, William Gwaltney, Michael Gwaltney
                                              Page 240

NEWSUM, Jacob. Parish of St. Luke. Leg.- wife; son
Gilliam at twenty one; to my four sons; to all my chil-

dren. Exs., wife, friends Anselm and Isham Gilliam.
D. Oct. 2, 1771
Codicil.- to my three sons, Littleberry, Isham and
Jacob Newsum   D. March 9, 1778   R. Nov. 12, 1778
Wit. Thomas Holt, Sr., Etheldred Taylor, Henry Taylor,
Temperance Taylor   Page 240

BEAL, John. Account estate. Legacies paid to
Liddia Beal, John Beal and Drury Beal. Auditors, Howell
Williamson, Samuel Story and John Crenshaw.
R. Nov. 12, 1778   Page 242

LONGWORTH, Joseph. Inventory. 1777. Signed
Benjamin Ruffin Adm.   R. Nov. 12, 1778   Page 243

WELLONS, John. Estate appraised by Charles Powers,
Sampson Pitman and Thomas Lane. R. Feb. 14, 1779
                                                Page 243

FORD, Ann. Estate appraised by Jesse Drew and
Thomas Turner   D. Dec. -- 1778   R. Feb. 14, 1779
                                                Page 243

SPEED, Mary. Inventory. Signed Isham Hill
R. Feb. 14, 1779   Page 244

VICK, William. Estate appraised by John Edwards,
James Bryant and Nathan Barnes.   R. Feb. 14, 1779
                                                Page 244

PHILLIPS, John. (Aged)   Leg.- son Joshua; grandson
Thomas Phillips; daughter Faithy Ellis; daughter Hannah
Davis; grandson Phillip Davis; son John reversion to his
daughter Lucy Phillips when she is eighteen; grandson
Edwin Ellis; grandson John Phillips at twenty one.
Ex., son Joseph Phillips.
D. Jan. 10, 1779   R. Feb. 14, 1779
Wit. Howel Jones, Edwin Kinnebrew, Milley Hix.
                                                Page 245

Bradshaw, Joseph. Estate appraised by Lawrence
Joyner and Arthur Bowing. R. Feb. 14, 1779 Page 246

TAYLOR, Harris. Estate Appraised by John Wilkins, John Pitman and Lazarus Cook. R. Feb. 14, 1779   Page 247

COOPER, John. Account estate. Signed Solomon Cooper. Audited by Hardy Harris, Joshua Nicolson.
R. Feb. 14, 1779   Page 247

TUCKER, Benjamin. Leg.- son William; son John; son Henry; son Benjamin; daughter Phebe; daughter Winifred; daughter Elizabeth Tucker. Exs. sons John and Henry Tucker
D. Jan. 13, 1778   R. Feb. 14, 1779
Wit. Henry Tucker, Priscilla Gurley, Sarah Edward.
     Page 248

REESE, Joseph. Of Parish of Nottoway. Leg.- son John; wife Mary; son Edward; grandson Joseph Reese, son of Edward; daughter Mary Thomas; son Joseph Reese. Exs., wife and son
D. Nov. 14, 1775   R. Feb. 14, 1779   Edward.
Wit. John Ivy, Moses Thorp, Robert Ivy, Joshua Nicholson.
     Page 248

BEALE, Hardy. Leg.-brother Burwell Beale, land on which Britain Jones lived; sister Sarah Beale with reversion to Thomas Joyner; to Thomas Taylor.
Exs. Absolom Joyner and Thomas Joyner
D. Dec. 21, 1778   R. Feb. 14, 1779
Wit. Jesse Joyner, Elizabeth Joyner, Daniel Massingaile
     Page 250

BEALE, William. Leg.- son William; son John; wife Priscilla; daughter Patty; son Burwell Beale. Exs. wife and
D. April 17, 1778   R. Feb. 14, 1779   son William.
Wit. Benjamin Beale, John Drake, Joseph Turner,
     William Bridger   Page 250

ONEY, Leonard. Of the Parish of Nottoway. Leg. daughters Lucy, Martha and Hannah; son Thomas; son John; son Benjamin; daughter Elizabeth, wife of John Atkinson; daughter Mary, wife of James Atkinson.
Ex., son Thomas Oney
D. Sept., 16, 1772   R. Feb. 14, 1779
Wit. Nathaniel Coker, Arthur Exum   Page 251

JOHNSON, Samuel. Of the Parish of Nottoway.
Leg.- son Giles; son John land bought of young John Bowen,
adjoining John Parr, Simon Johnson and Giles Johnson, son-
in-law William Gwi (Gwin); son Samuel; Son Simon; daughter
Mary Turner; wife Mary Johnson.
Exs., wife Mary and son Giles Johnson.
D. May 17, 1767   R. Feb. 14, 1779
Wit. Henry Pope, Simon Harris, Hardy Pope   Page 252

BRITT, John, Sr. Leg.- son John; son Jesse; son Henry;
son James; son William; wife Marthat Britt.
D. Feb. 15, 1777   R. Feb. 14, 1779
Exs., sons John and Jesse Britt.
Wit. Thomas Purner, John Rogers.   Page 253

JONES, Robert. Leg.- wife; daughter Frances; Daughter
Elizabeth; son Mathew; son Robey; son James; son Benjamin.
Exs. brother James Jones and brother-in-law John Simmons
D. June 23, 1778   R. Feb. 14, 1779
Wit. Benjamin Barram, Lucaucy Jones, David Jones
                                                   Page 254

JOHNSON, Jesse. Account Estate. Jesse Cooper, Adm.
Audited by Timothy Thorpe, John Blunt and Mark Nicolson
R. Feb. 14, 1779   Page 255

DELOACH, William. Inventory. Signed, Benjamin Deloach.
R. March 11, 1779   Page 255

ONEY, Leonard. Inventory. R. March 11, 1779
                                                   Page 256

LUTER, Thomas. Estate appraised by Simon Johnson,
Joshua Minard and Toomer Joyner   R. March 11, 1779
                                                   Page 256

RICKS, Richard. Of the Parish of Nottoway. Leg.-
wife Ann; nephew Richard Ricks; nephew Joseph Ricks; to
Samuel, son of my nephew Thomas Ricks; to Robert and John
sons of my nephew Thomas Ricks; nephew Robert Ricks; neice
Ann Jones; neice mary Ricks; to Thomas, Robert, Richard,

Joseph, Mary, Milisent and Ann children of my deceased
brother Robert Ricks.
  Exs., friends Thomas Blow and William Thomas and nep-
      hews, Robert, Richard and Joseph Ricks.
  D. Sept, 2, 1778   R. March 11, 1779
  Wit. Isaac Williams, Thomas Curney, Richard Johnson,
      John Bidgood.   Page 256

AUSTIN, William. Inventory. Signed, Ruth Austin.
R. March 11, 1779   Page 258

HINES, Joshua. Estate appraised by John Kirby, Jesse
Arrington and John Brown.   R. March 11, 1779   Page 259

WILLIAMS, Jacob. Estate appraised November 9, 1769,
by Nicholas Williams, George Washington, Job Wright.
R. March 11, 1779   Page 259

HATFIELD, Josiah. Leg.- father Philemon Hatfield and
mother Mary Hatfield; sisters Mary Daughtry, Charity, Selah,
Jemimy, Mildred, Tabitha and Elizabeth Hatfield.
  Exs., friends, Capt. Jesse Whitehead and James Maget.
  D. March 10, 1778   R. April 9, 1779
  Wit. Benjamin Blunt, John Thomas Blow, Thomas Edmunds
                                                   Page 260

WILSON, William. Leg.- sister Pheeby Wilson; brother
George Wilson.
  Ex. Capt. Jesse Whitehead
  D. March 10, 1778   R. April 9, 1779
  Wit. John Thomas Blow, Benjamin Blunt, Thomas Edmunds.
                                                   Page 261

BOOTH, Robert. Account current. Legacies paid to
Elizabeth Booth, Beverley Booth and to the guardian of
Moses Booth.
  Audited by Wil Salter, Jr, Richard Bailey, Barnaby Bailey
  R. May 13, 1779   Page 261

RIDLEY, James Day. Estate appraised by Joshua Thorpe,
John Myrick and John Blunt.   R. May 13, 1779
                                                   Page 262

NIBLETT, James. Inventory. Burwell Williamson Adm.
R. May 13, 1779   Page 263

POPE, Patience. Leg.- son-in-law Jonathan Pope; son-in-
Elijah Pope; son Nathan Pope; to my six other children -
Jehu, Phebe, Joel, Richard, Patience and Charity Pope.
Ex., Nathan Barnes.
D. Nov. 3, 1777   R. May 13, 1779
Wit. Joshua Johnson, Moses Johnson, Josiah Pope
                                                   Page 264

NEWSUM, Sampson. Leg.- wife Mary; son Hartwell; to my
three daughters and grandson, Agness Polly Newsum, Joice
Moseley, Mary Armstrong and Sampson, son of Jesse Newsum;
daughter Martha Johnson.
Exs., Robert Andrews and son Hartwell Newsum
D. Sept. 18, 1778   R. May 13, 1779
Wit. William Barham, John Fort, Nathaniel Tamer (?)
                                                   Page 264

EDMUNDS, Mary. Account Current. William and Samuel
Edmunds, Exs.   Legacies paid,- Howell Edmunds and daugh-
ters; to William , John, Samuel, Charles and Sarah Edmunds;
to Mary Nicolson; to Martha Mirick and child; to Lucy
Nicolson; to Elizabeth, Mary, Lucy and Martha, daughters of
Stephenson Williamson; to Etheldred son of Thomas Edmunds.
Audited by John Wilkinson, William Blunt, Arthur Foster
R. May 13, 1779   Page 26_

REESE, Joseph. Inventory. Signed, Edward Reese
R. May 13, 1779   Page 266

TURNER, William. Leg.- son Littleton, tract by my wife
near Meherrin River; son Arthur; son James; daughter Ann;
daughter Fanny Turner.
Exs., brother Benjamin Turner and son Littleton Turner
D. Feb. 20, 1779   R. May 13, 1779
Wit. Jacob Barnes, Sarah Barnes, Thomas Edmunds.
                                                   Page 266

RAMSEY, James. Account current. Signed, Catherine Ramsey
Audited by William Blunt and John Sturgeon
R. June 10, 1779   Page 267

DAVIS, Thomas.   Account current.   Paid Edwin Davis, or-
phan.   Signed, Henry Davis.
   Audited by Beverley Booth and John Powell
   R.   June 10, 1779   Page 268

   GRIZARD, William.   Parish of St. Luke.   Leg- wife Mary;
my land to be laid off by Joh Lewter, Sr., Cordal Norfleet,
John Blunt and John Crafford; son William; son Thomas land
bought of John Bird; son Hulin; daughter Milly Johnson;
daughter Ann Williams; daughter Priscilla Phillips; daugh-
ter Mary Munger; son Isum; son Jerry; daughters Dorcas,
Theba, Celia, Charlotte, Elizabeth and Tabitha Grizard.
   Exs., Moses Johnson and Henry Mounger.
   D.   April 7, 1779   R.   June 10, 1779
   Wit.   John Luter, John Blunt, Mary James   Page 268

   BARHAM, Benjamin.   Of the Parish of St. Luke.   Leg.-
wife Mary; son William land bought of Joseph Cornett; son
John land bought of Nathaniel Newsum; son Benjamin; daugh-
ter Lucy; daughter Fanny; daughter Elizabeth Barham.
   Exs., sons William and John Barham.
   D.   March 30, 1776   R.   June 10, 1779
   Wit.   Henry Taylor, James Ridley, Temperance Taylor
                                                  Page 269

   HARRISON, Samuel.   Estate appraised by James Lundy,
John Rogers and John Ivy.   Signed Joshua Nicolson, Ex.
   R.   June 10, 1779.   Page 270

   JOHNSON, Samuel.   Estate appraised by Micajah Griffin,
Hardy Pope, John Council.   R.   June 10, 1779   Page 271

   BEALE, William.   Estate appraised by William Williams,
David Wright and Jonah Edwards.   Signed William Beale, Ex.
   R.   June 10, 1779   Page 272

   LUTER, Thomas.   Account Current.   Audited by Elias
Herring and Hardy Pope   R.   June 1o, 1779 Page 272

   THORPE, Peterson.   Estate appraised by Benjamin Lewis,

Arthur Foster, Alexander Murry. Signed, Timothy Thorpe, Adm
R. June 10, 1779   Page 273

PHILLIPS, John. Inventory. Signed Joseph Phillips
R. June 10, 1779   Page 275

COBB, William. Estate appraised by Abraham Mitchell,
Thomas Lawrence and Henry Cobb. Signed J. Denson
R. July 8, 1779   Page 275

SCOTT, James Jordan. Estate appraised by Joseph
Mountfortt, Thomas Lankford and Shadrack Lewis.
R. July 8, 1779   Page 276

NEWSUM, Sampson. Estate appraised by Joshua Nicholson,
Owen Myrick, John Fort. Signed, Robert Andrews and
Hartwell Newsum. R. July -, 1779   Page 277

MOORE, James. Estate appraised by Samuel Drewry,
Thomas Butts and John Kirby   R. 7 -, 1779
                                                   Page 278

LUNDY, Bird. Estate appraised by Edward Harris, John
Mirick and Joseph Roose. Signed, Phebe Lundy and Lewis
Thorpe. R. July 8, 1779   Page 279

BEALE, William. Account estate - paid a legacy to
Martha Beale. Signed. William Beale, Ex.
Audited by Joseph Mountford and Thomas Lankford.
R. July 8, 1779   Page 281

ONEY, Leonard. Account estate. Signed Thomas Oney
Audited by Benjamin Deloach and Thomas Lane
R. Aug. 12, 1779   Page 281

RICKS, Richard. Estate appriased by Lewis Joyner, Jr.,
Isaac Williams, John Johnson   R. Aug. 12, 1779
                                                   Page 281

VASSER, Lydia. Current Account. Among items, paid
Jesse, Robert, Margaret and Mary Vasser; to legacy left
daughter Mary Vasser. Audited by William Thomas and
Jesse Whitehead. R. Aug. 12, 1779   Page 283

CLIFTON, Thomas. Estate appraised by Benjamin Clements,
John Simmons and William Foster. R. Aug. 12, 1779
                                          Page 283

BASS, Joshua. Leg.- Thomas son of Arthur Bass; Burges
son of Hardy Bass.
Ex. friend Lewis Thorpe.
D. Jan. 30, 1779   R. Sept. 9, 1779
Wit. Arthur Bass, Henry Bass, Selah Bass   Page 284

BARNES, Benjamin. Leg.- wife Mary; son John; son
William land purchased of Joshua Johnson and Richard Ricks
adjoining William Thomas and John Thomas Blow, from Robert,
Richard and Joseph Ricks , exs. of Richard Ricks, decd.;
son Jacob land bought of Richard Johnson, Arthur Allen,
and Mathew Johnson, also the plantation on which I live
after the death of my wife, adjjoining Albridgeton Jones,
Jordan Denson, Jacob Jenkins and Lewis Joyner; daughter
Mary, wife of Stephen Johnson; daughter Peninah Barnes;
daughter Milly Barnes.
Exs., wife Mary and friend George Washington (son of
        George) and son William Barnes
D. --- 20, 1779   R. Sept. 9, 1779
Wit. George Washington, Joseph Johnson, Benjamin
      Williams, Hardy Johnson.   Page 284

HARRIS, Joshua. Account Estate. Jesse Harris, Adm.
Audited by Joshua Nicholson, Hardy Harris.   1775
R. Sept. 9, 1779   Page 286

A ADAMS, Robert. Estate appraised. (Not signed)
R. Sept. 9, 1779   Page 286

COBB, William. Account estate. Jordan Denson, Adm.
R. Sept. 9, 1779   Page 287

POPE, William, Sr.   Inventory. Signed, William Pope
and Andrew Pope.   R. Sept. 9, 1779   Page 287

VAUGHAN, William.   Leg.- mother Sarah Vaughan; bro-
ther-in-law Nathan Turner.
Ex., Nathan Turner.
D. Oct. 28, 1776   R. Oct. 14, 1779
Wit. John ort, Thomas Turner.   Page 289

POPE, John.   Leg.- son Henson, land adjoining Samuel
Edmunds; son John; daughter Temperance; daughter Sally;
wife Ann Pope.
Exs., wife Ann and her brother Mathew Underwood.
D. July 11, 1779   R. Oct. 14, 1779
Wit. Nathan Barnes, Sarah Head. (?)   Page 289

BUFFKIN, John.   Account estate. Signed, Tuke Denson,
Adm. Audited by Lawrence Joyner, John Johnson.
R. Oct. 14, 1779   Page 290

WILLIAMS, Drury.   Estate appraised by Benjamin
Williams, George Washington and John Davis
R. Oct. 14, 1779   Page 290

CURL, Thomas.   Leg.- sister Martha Edwards.
Ex., Capt. Jesse Whitehead.
D. Oct. 2, 1777   R. Oct. 14, 1779
Wit. Howell Myrick, William Wilson, John Johnston
                                             Page 290

BURN, David. Of Parish of Nottoway. Leg.- son
David; daughter Martha Wheelis (Wheeler ?); daughter
Elizabeth Mason; daughter Rebecca Vaughan; daughter Mary
Council; son Sampson; son Hardy; wife Patience; daughter
Ann; daughter Sarah Council.
Ex., son-in-law Cutchins Council
D. Oct. 2, 1779   R. Nov. 11, 1779
Wit. Thomas Lankford, Theo Lewis, Joseph Mountfortt
Codicil: to Patience Burn and granddaughter Edith
Council. Nov. 5, 1779   R. Nov. 11, 1779
Wit. Joseph Mountfortt, Shadrack Lewis   Page 291

POPE, John. Estate appraised by Nathan Barnes, William
Whitehead abd Samuel Edmunds.   R. Dec. 9, 1779
                                             Page 292

POND, Richard. _ _ Account. _ Richard Pond and
Martha Pond. Audited by John Salter and John Pond.
R. Dec. 9, 1779 Page 292

GRIZARD, William. Estate appraised by John Suiter,
Cordall Norfleet, John Blunt. R. Jan 10, 1780 Page 293

BASS, Joshua. Estate appraised by John Reese, Edward
Reese, Henry Ivy. R. Jan. 10, 1780 Page 294

BARNES, Benjamin. Leg.- William Barnes; Jacob Barnes;
Pening Barnes; Milly Barnes. Proved by Benjamin Williams,
Abraham Mitchell, Isaack Williams and John Davis
D. Oct. 17, 1779 R. Jan. 10, 1780 Page 294

BREWER, John. Of Hertford County, Province of North
Carolina, Planter. Leg.- loving wife; son John; son Reace;
son Jacob; son Jesse; daughter Pacience; daughter Elizabeth;
daughter Ann; daughter Frances; son Hardy; son Henry Brewer.
Exs., wife and son Hardy Brewer.
D. R. Jan. 10, 1780
Wit. George Little, Abraham Poter, Rebecca.Morgan
Will presented by Ann and Hardy Brewer. Page 295

BURN, David. Estate appraised by Thomas Lankford, Henry
Joyner and Thad Lewis. R. 1780 Page 296

BURN, Patience. Appraisal ordered Nov. 11, 1779. Appraised by Joseph Mountfortt, Henry Joyner and Thad Lewis.
R. 1780 Page 296

FORT, Ann. Account current. Signed, William Turner, Ex.
Audited by Joshua Nicolson and Hardy Harris
R. May 11, 1780 Page 296

SMITH, John. Leg.-wife Martha, tract bought of Benjamin
Holleman. Exs.; wife and Joshua Bailey
D. Jan. 1, 1780 R. May 11, 1780
Wit. Benjamin Bailey, Micajah Holleman. Page 296

WOMBWELL, Jesse. Legacies paid Selah and Nancy Wombwell.

Audited by William Urquhart and Micajah Holleman.
R. May 11, 1780   Page 297

HINES, Joshua. Account estate. Audited by Joshua
Nicolson and Arthur Foster. R. May 11, 1780 Page 297

MACKEY, Joseph. Of the Parish of Nottoway. Leg.-
Joshua Miniard; Elizabeth Mackey.
Exs., Joshua Miniard and Elizabeth Mackey
D. Sept. 30, 1779   R. May 11, 1780
Wit. Toomer Joyner, Martha Joyner, Ann Joyner ,
     Elias Herring   Page 297

AVERY, Fortune. Leg.- daughter Elizabeth Grizard.
D. Feb. 18, 1778   R. May 11, 1780
Wit. Mary Coggan, Ann Coggan, David Edmunds Page 298

BUTTS, Peter. of the Parish of Nottoway. Leg.- sons
Thomas, Benjamin, John, William and James; daughter Lucy;
daughter Molly; daughter Betty; son Daniel at the death of
my wife my plantation on which I live; wife Elizabeth.
Exs., Benjamin Clements and sons Thomas and Benjamin Butts
D. March 24, 1780   R. June 8, 1780
Wit. Edwin Gray, Benjamin Kirby, Silas Kirby.
                                                Page 298

SCOTT, James Jordan. Signed Jordan Denson Ex. Account
estate. Among items, paid Miriam Scott as the will direct-
ed; paid Joseph Scott his specific legacy; paid Miriam
Scott guardian of James J. Scott his legacy.
Audited by Henry Briggs, Albridgton Jones, Lewis Joyner, Jr.
R. June 8, 1780   Page 299

MACKEY, Joseph. Estate appraised by Henry Jones, Giles
Johnson, John Johnson   R. June 8, 1780 Page 300

MILLAR, William. Estate appraised, Feb. 20, 1779 by
Arthur Foster, John Taylor, John Fort. R. July 13, 1780
                                                Page 300

BRITAIN, Elisha.   D. Jan.1, 1780   R. July 13, 1780
Page 300

FIGURES, Joseph. Leg.- Nephew Richard Mossom; son Thomas,
if he should return, reversion of bequest to neice Jane
Mossom; wife Elizabeth Lucy Figures; to sons Bartholomew and
Thomas if they return, reversion to Thomas and Rebecca Bage,
the children of Thomas Bage; Richard Figures, son of William
Figures; Richard and Jane Mossom, children of William Mossom.
Exs. Jesse Whitehead of Southampton County, Thomas Figures
     and John Maget of the County of Hertford in N. Car.
D. March 27, 1780   R. July 13, 1780
Wit. Nicholas Maget, John Boon, Reuben Hill, Rebeckah
     Stevenson   Page 301

STURGEON, John. Parish of St. Luke. Leg.- wife Saley;
son John Williams Sturgeon; son William Sturgeon.
Exs. Wife and friend William Blunt.
D. Oct. 28, 1779   R. Aug. 11, 1780
Wit. Simon Harris, Henry Harrison, Richard Harrison
                                                 Page 302

LUNDY, Drury.   Signed, James Lundy, Adm.   1778
Account estate. The same proportional part of the estate
paid the following: John Lundy; Elizabeth Lundy, Almtx of
Drury Lundy; Joseph Reose, Jr.; Lewis Thorpe Ex. of Byrd
Lundy; Edward Harris; Henry Holt's orphans and James Lundy.
R. Sept 14, 1780   Page 302

CLEMENTS, Benjamin. of Parish of Nottoway. Leg.- son
Thomas land on Angeliaa Swamp and land on Nottoway River
bought of Pleasant Cocke; son Francis land on which my fa-
ther lived and a sword loaned Thomas Butts; cattle on my
plantation in St. Luke's Parish to Samuel Clifton; son
John; daughters Sarah and Elizabeth my plantation in Bruns-
wick County; wife Elizabeth Clements.
Exs., brother Thomas Clements, Thomas Clements Butts and
     Dr. Thomas Peete
D. Dec. 11, 1778   R. Sept. 14, 1780
Wit. John Simmons, Benjamin Kirby, Thomas Butts, Richard
     Parker.   Page 303

JENKINS, Edmunds. Leg.- wife Sarah; son Valentine;
daughter Sally Bailey.
Ex., Son Valentine Jenkins

D. Oct. 6, 1779   R. Dec. 14, 1780
Wit. William Urquhart, Robert Eley   Page 304

EDMUNDS, David. Leg.- wife Ann, son Howell a tract
bought of Benjamin Clements, Cordall Norfleet and William
Bowers; daughter Mary Dawson; son William tract purchased
of Richard Taylor; land bought of Sterling Francis to be
sold; wife Ann Edmunds.
Exs., sons, Howell, John Dawson and William Edmunds.
D. July 29, 1780   R. Dec. 14, 1780
Wit. Samuel Nicolson, Molly Taylor, Barham Hines,
       Hardy Grizzard   Page 305

VICK, Arthur. Leg. -------- and his heirs; son
Shadrack; son Arthur; son Samuel.
Exs. sons Arthur and Samuel Vick
D. April 9, 1777   R. Dec. 14, 1780
Wit. George Gurley, Thomas Edmunds, John Beal.
                                                    Page 306

MORGAN, John. Leg.- son Jarret; son Foster; son
William the plantation bought of William Turner; daugh-
ters Patience, Elizabeth, Sarah and Ann Morgan.
D. March 24, 1775   R. Dec. 14, 1780
Exs. William Foster and son Jarret Morgan.
Wit. Lelas Kerby, William Foster, Lucy Hines.
                                                    Page 306

BASS, Charles. Leg.- son Henry; son Hardiman, land
adjoining Jeremiah Thorpe reversion to son's wife Ann
her widowhood and then to grandson Roger Bass; to my neighbor Moses Thorp; son Charles, reversion to said son's wife
her widowhood, then to grandson Edwin son of Charles, with
reversion to his brother Dixon and then to his brother
Howell Bass; remainder of estate to be sold and divided
between my sons Arthur and Newit Bass and daughter Mary
Matthews, grandson Jordan Bass, son of my daughter Tabitha
Bass.
Exs., sons Henry and Charles Bass and son-in-law
       Arthur Matthews
D. Sept. 11, 1780   R. Dec. 14, 1780
Wit. Joshua Nicolson, Jeremiah Thorp, John Ivy (son of
       John)   Page 307

CRENSHAW, Thomas. Leg.- son John land bought of William

West and recorded to belong to Josph West, also land adjoining James Daughtry; daughter Amey Bailey, land bought
of Ralph Carter; reversion to her son Samuel Maget Crenshaw;
daughter Ann Crenshaw.
Exs., John Crenshaw, Nicholas Maget, Jesse Whitehead.
D. Oct. 16, 1778   R. Dec. 14, 1780
Wit. Jacob Turner, Samuel Maget, John Thorp,
     William Gwaltney, Etheldred Holt   Page 308

HARRIS, John.   Leg.- brother Newit Harris; brother
Thomas; brother Nathan; neice Fanny Newsum; neice Lucy
Newsum; sister Martha Newsum.
Exs., Cordall Norfleet and brother Nathan Harris.
D. Sept. 15, 1780   R. Jan. 11, 1781
Wit. John Davis, Nathan Bryant, Jeremiah Grizzard
                                              Page 309

CLIFTON, Thomas.   Leg.- son Benjamin land in Northampton
County, N. Car.; son Cordey; son Claibourn; daughter Dorothy
Harrison; daughter Maria; daughters Sarah, Mary, Ann and
Eleanor Clifton.,(Sarah and Mary may be already married ?)
Exs., Wife Sarah and son Benjamin Clifton.
D. Oct. 9, 1779   R. Jan. 11, 1781
Wit. Thomas Turner, Benjamin Harrison, Simon Harris
                                              Page 309

PITMAN, John.   Leg.- daughter Sarah Boykin all the
land I possess in this state and in N. Car.; daughter Dorcas
Stevens; daughter Susanna Taylor; daughter Elizabeth
Williamson; daughter Mourning Pitman; refers to a note and
slaves due him from John Boykin.
Ex., son-in-law John Boykin
D. Dec. 12, 1780   R. Jan. 11, 1781
Wit. Micajah Edwards, William Newsum, John Wilkinson
                                              Page 311

LANKFORD, Thomas. Leg.- wife Elizabeth lands bought of
William Hobday and Albridgton Whitley; son Elisha land purchased of Wade Mountfortt and William Glover; son Jesse
tract bought of William Barrett, whereon James Wilson lives;
neice Mary Wakins (Watkins ?); friend Shadrack Lewis to
supervise slaves and extend fatherly care to my children;
whereas James Chapple did give to me his one third part of
a pair of mill stones, formerly belonging to my father, one
half the surplus to said Chapple, remainder to be divided
all my children, Elisha, Jesse, Margaret, Rebecca and Ann
Lankford; -if my Exs. disagree in interpreting my will to

be left to the judgment of Joseph Mountfortt, Benjamin
Ruffin, William Urquhart and J. m Hines (son of Thomas)
    Exs., wife Elizabeth, friend Shadrack Lewis and bro-
        ther Jesse Lankford.
    D. Nov. 20, 1780   R. Jan. 11, 1781
    Wit. Joseph Mountfortt, Thomas Mountfortt, James Wilson
        W. Denson   Page 312

STEPHENSON, Simon. Estate appraised by John Summerell,
James Summerell and William Boykin, Jr.
    R. Jan. 19, 1781   Page 314

SMITH, John. Inventory. R. Feb. 8, 1781
                                       Page 315

HARRIS, John. Inventory. Signed, Nathan Harris
R. Jan. 8, 1781   Page 315

REVIL, Sampson. Leg.- brother Holliday Revil **if he**
ever returns from the Northward, reversion to my sister's
son Jesse Holt; sister Joannah Holt; sister Mourning
Revil; siter Charlotte Revil.
    Ex., friend Samuel Edmunds.
    D. April 12, 1779   R. Feb. 8, 1781
    Wit. Nathan Barnes, Samuel Woodard, Robert Carr.
                                       Page 316

KIRBY, Richard. Of the Parish of Nottoway. Leg.-
son Benjamin; daughter Susannah Clifton; son Silas;
daughter Patty Pond; son Richard; son Thomas; son Miles
    Ex., son Richard Kirby.
    D. Feb. 24, 1780   R. Feb. 8, 1781
    Wit. Benjamin Stewart, John Kirby, Henry Adams
                                       Page 316

PITMAN, John. Estate appraised by Lazarus Cooke,
Charles Joiner, Micajah Edwards. R. March 8, 1781
                                       Page 317

KENNEBREW, Edwin. Of the Parish of St. Luke. Leg.-
to Henry KEnnebrew, land on which my father lived; to
Priscilla Kennebrew; Shadrack Kennebrew.
    Exs., friend John Barrow and brother Shadrack Kennebrew

D. Nov. 4, 1780   R. Feb. 8, 1781
Wit. Phoeby H. Barrow, John Denson   Page 319

LUNDY, James. Leg.- neice Mary, daughter of Byrd Lundy,
the plantation on which my father lived, also the part of
the land given by my father to Drury Lundy and the land he
bought of Isham Lundy; cousin James son of Robert Lundy,
said James to allow Solomon Harrison to occupy the house as
long as he desires; cousin Sarah, daughter of Robert Lundy;
Suckey Morris, sister to Chislin Morris; Creasy daughter of
Arthur Bass; to Darling, Edwin and Collen, sons of Mary
Adams; my slaves to be divided by my friends, Daniel Fisher,
Lewis Thorpe, William Baunt, John Rogers and John Myrick;
reversion of the bequests to the Adams boys to James, Molly
and Sarah Lundy; Chislin Morris
  Exs., James Lundy and Chislin Morris.
  D. March 14, 1780   R. March 8, 1781
  Wit. Daniel Fisher, James Harris, Drury Harris
                                              Page 319

ATKINSON, Mial. Leg.- wife Mary; son Joseph; son
William at twenty one; son John at twenty one; daughter Lucy.
  Ex., son Joseph Atkinson.
  D. Dec. -- 1780   R. April 12, 1781
  Wit. James Chanel (Channell), Benjamin Kindred.
                                              Page 320

JONES, Martha. Of the Parish of St. Luke. Leg.- son
Timothy Thorp; granddaughter Mary Cook Simmons; grandaughter
Peggy Ridley; granddaughters Rebecca Simmons, Martha Ridley,
Ann Thorp, Martha Thorp, Temperance Atherton; Polly Person,
and Martha Person; grandson John Thorp Ricgardson.
  Ex., son Timothy Thorp.
  D. Dec. 11, 1780   R. April 12, 1781
  Wit. Hardy Harris, Sally Jarrell, Sarah Hasty   Page 321

BYRD, John. Leg.- son Arthur; Joshua Hunt; Susanneh,
daughter of Arthur Byrd; son John; son James; son Charles;
son Philip; son Moses; son Natah Byrd.
  Ex., son Arthur Byrd.
  D   R. April 12, 1781
  Wit. John Wood, Elizabeth Williams, William Brooks
                                              Page 322

LANKFORD, Thomas. Estate appraised by John Oberry, Joseph
Mountfortt, Thomas Mountfortt. R. June 14, 1781   Page 323

32

MYRICK, Mary. Of the Parish of St. Luke. Leg.- son
Edward Harris; son Lewis Harris; son Amos Harris; daughter
Mary Lewis; daughter Anne Applewhite; **granddaughter** Olive
Harris wife of Joseph Harris; granddaughter Priscilla
Harris; son Hardy Harris.
    Exs., sons Amos and Hardy Harris .
    D. June 16, 1775   R. April 12, 1781
    William Moore, Mary Nicholson, Joshua Nicolson
                                                    Page 324

BRIGGS, Henry. Of Nottoway Parish. Leg. son Charles
land in Sussex County at twenty one; son Henry land in
Southampton County on the Nottoway River; daughter Ann.
Trustees, Charles Briggs and John Thomas Blow
    D. March 23, 1781   R. June 14, 1781
    Wit. Samuel Scarbrough, Robert Barredell, Joseph Johnson,
        Mathew Wills.   Page 325

TAYLOR, Henry. Of the Parish of St. Luke. Leg- **wife**
my plantation adjoining Benjamin Lewis, the riding chair
and harness now being made by Randolph Newsum and Josiah
Jordan; son Etheldred the plantation called "Ridleys" daughter Elizabeth; son John; son Henry (not of age); daughters
Charlotte, Mary and Martha Taylor. My Executors to be
guardians to my sons, my wife guardian to my daughters.
Son Henry to be sent to college
    Exs. son Etheldred Taylor and friend Daniel Fisher
    D. March 8, 1781   R. June 14, 1781
    Wit. Mary Mason Taylor, Robert Taylor, D. Fisher
        Kinchen Peterson.   Page 326

WOODWARD, Charles. Leg.- son William; wife Elizabeth;
son Jesse Woodard; refers to money which he owes Jo. Vick.
    Exs., brothers Josiah Vick and Samuel Woodard.
    D. Oct. 28, 1780   R. June 14, 1781
    Wit. John Pledger, Henry Vaugan, Robert Speed
                                                    Page 328

EDWARDS, Micajah. Of the Parish of St. Luke. Leg.-
brother Richard; brother Benjamin; sisters, Elizabeth and
Ann Edwards.
    Exs., brothers William and Richard Edwards
    D. April 15, 1781   R. June 14, 1781
    Wit. Mary Blow, Susannah Edwards, William Edwards.
                                                    Page 329

THORPE, John. Leg.- wife Martha; to wife's daughter

Nancy Atkinson (whom I own to be my daughter); provision
for unborn child; reversion to my brothers and sisters,
Midda Spence, Sarah Harris, Mary Reese, Jeremiah Thorpe,
to four of my brother Aaron Thorpe's children- Thomas,
Edith, Phebe and Henry Thorpe.
Exs., wife Martha and friend Hardy Harris
D. May 15, 1779   R. July 12, 1781
Wit. John Nicholson, Thomas Adams, Jr., Mary Nicholson.
     Sally Kirby, Howell Adams   Page 329

NICHOLSON, Joshua.   Leg.-son Charles Briggs Nicholson;
wife Mary during my Mother's life; to all my children.
Exs.,   brothers-in-law Howell Edmunds, John Kirby and
        friend Hardy Harris.
D. Jan. 12, 1781   R. July 12, 1781
Wit. Sarah Moore, Betsey Moore, Rebecca Moore ,
      Edwin Seward.   Page 330

EDWARDS, Thomas. Of the Parish of St. Luke. Leg.- son
Jordan hunting gun and brandy, which he had of Joseph
Washington as his substitute in the service; son Newit,
long gun, brandy and 200 L in the hands of Thomas Taylor,
being what he was to receive from him as his substitute in
the service; son Benjamin; daughter Mary; daughter Ann; wife
Ann; daughter Lucy; daughter Elizabeth Edwards.
Exs.,   Wife Ann and son Benjamin Edwards.   Trustees,
        friends William Thomas and George Gurley
D. March 26, 1781   R. July 12, 1781
Wit. Thomas Newsum, James Atkinson, Martha Gurley
                                                   Page 331

REVILL, Sampson.   Inventory. Signed Samuel Edmunds,
R. July 12, 1781   Page 333

TURNER, Benjamin. Leg.- son Benjamin my tract of land
bought of David Edmunds, adjoining Thomas Porter; son Henry;
son Nathan; daughter Ann; grandsons Turner and James Newsum;
daughter Phebe Newsum.
Exs., sons Nathan and Henry Turner.
D. May 26, 1771   R. Aug. 9, 1781
Wit. Cordall Norfleet, Elizabeth Crocker, Edith Kinnebrew.
                                                   Page 333

MORGAN, John. (alias John Martin)   Leg.- sister Celia,
alias Celia Martin my land in Sussex and Southampton Counties

devised to me by my father John Morgan; to brother-in-law
Mathew Morgan.
Ex., friend, Littleberry Mason.
D. May 8, 1781   R. Aug. 9, 1781
Wit. James Sammons, John Sledge, Sally Sledge
Salia Morgan qualified. Security, John Ivy.   Page 334

BROWN, John. Leg. mother Olive Brown.
Extx., mother Olive Brown.
D. Oct. 23, 1780   R. Aug. 9, 1781
Wit. William Foster, Jane Clements, Lucy Hines.
Thomas Lane qualified.   Page 535

RIGHT, Mary. Leg.- James Right, son of Joseph Right;
John Right, son of Joseph Right.
Exs., son Joseph Right and John Pursell.
D. Dec. 22, 1780   R. Sept. 13, 1781
Wit. West Tines, Mathew Smith.   Page 335

WARREN, Faith. Parish of St. Luke. Leg.- daughter
Elizabeth Dupree; grandson Henry, son of Michael Warren.
Exs., friend Henry Bittle and son Michael Warren.
D. Jan. 13, 1781 R. Sept. 13, 1781
Wit. Joel Harris, John Barrow, Sarah Barrow.
                                                Page 336

RIDLEY, James. Leg.- daughter Mary Blunt; daughter
Jane Parker; daughter Sarah; son Bromfield; Frances Ridley,
wife of son Bromfield; son William the tract on which I live
granddaughter Rebecca, daughter of my son Arhur Ridley, re-
version to Rebecca Ridley, daughter of James Day Ridley;
Elizabeth Ridley, daughter of James Day Ridley, reversion
to Rebecca, daughter of Arthur Ridley; grandson John Edwards
Ridley, son of James D. Ridley, a tract on the Meherrin
River bought of John Johnson and the land on which the said
J. D. Ridley died, purchased of Joseph Thorp; Elizabeth
Ridley, widow of Arthur Ridley, deceased, bond of Sterling
Capel; bond of John Francis and balance due from Miles Cary
and Sterling Francis to support the said Elizabeth and her
daughter Rebecca Ridley;
Exs., sons Bromfield and William Ridley.
D. Aug. 20, 1781 ' Sept. 13, 1781
Wit. Hardy Harris, John Blunt, Benjamin Blunt Jr.
                                                Page 337

RIDLEY, James. Inventory. Sept. 13, 1781. John

Blunt released and forever quit claimed all benefits and advantages to any estate devised me by the last will of James Ridley   R. Sept. 13, 1781
     Wit. Hardy Harris, James Jones.   Page 339

DREWRY, William. Leg.- wife Rachel; to my seven children, William, Mary Morgan; Richard; James; Rachel; Nicholas and granddaughter Sarah Drewry. Sons, Richard, James and Nicholas to be bound out until twenty one.
     Exs., Son William and friend John Blunt.
     D. Oct. 3, 1780   R. Sept. 13, 1781
     Wit. Jesse Cooper, Chrles Ross, Hardy Harris.   Page 340

FRANCIS, Thomas. Leg.- daughter Sally; daughter Elizabeth; daughter Milly Colliar Francis; son Wilie, a tract bought of Benjamin Clements and David Edmunds; daughter Charlotte; daughter Molley; daughter Jane Briggs Francis; wife Elizabeth Francis.
     Exs., wife and friend Howell Edmunds.
     D. May 14, 1779   R. Aug. 9, 1781
     Wit. Jesse Cooper, John Francis.   Page 341

CLAUD, Philip. Account Current. 1773. Signed, Jeremiah Drew and John Claud, Exs.
     Audited by Jesse Drew and Thomas Turner.
     R. Sept. 13, 1781   Page 342

BROWNE, Jesse. Leg.- daughter Sally; son Henry land adjoining Simon Stevenson at twenty one; son Thomas; wife Esther Browne.
     Exs., wife and Bailey Branch
     D. Sept. 24, 1777   R. Nov. 8, 1781
     Wit. William Stephenson, Patience Stephenson,
          James Summerell   Page 343

FORT, Joshua. Of the Parish of St. Luke. Leg.- son Joshua land adjoining Moses Foster; son Joseph land in Brunswick County; son John; son Edwin; wife and all my children.
     Exs., son Joshua, wife and brothers-in-law Joshua and
          Lewis Thorpe.
     D. March 15, 1781   R. Nov. 8, 1781
     Wit. John Simmons, Benjamin Lewis, Spratley Simmons.
                                                       Page 344

WARREN, Faith.   Inventory.   Signed Michael Warren.
R. Nov. 8, 1781   Page 345

GRIFFIN, Benjamin.   Leg.- son James land adjoining
Hary Doyle and John Carstaphney; son Wiley land bought of
William Doyle; wife Olive; son Jack; son Benjamin Griffin.
Ex., Micajah Griffin. D. March 23, 1781   R. Nov. 8, 1781
W. R. Kello, John Worrell, Hartwell Crocker.
                                                  Page 345

BRANCH, Howell.   Leg. wife Elizabeth; son Drewry; son
Peter; son Jesse at sixteen; daughter Martha Branch
Exs., Bailey Branch and John Wellons, Sr.
D. Oct. 12, 1781   R. Nov. 8, 1781
Wit. Benjamin Branch, Henry Branch, John Summerell.
                                                  Page 346

JOHNSTON, Joseph.   Leg.- son Henry; wife Charity;
       son Benjamin; daughter Patty; daughter Molly;
daughter Olive Johnston.
Exs., Henry Briggs and Drury Beal.
D. Feb. 23, 1781   R. Nov. 8, 1781
Wit. Shad Lewis, Thomas Butts, Joshua Beal   Page 347

CROCKER, Sarah.   Leg.- daughter Ann Kindred; daughter
Sarah Miller; daughter Phoebe Vaughan. Ex., grandson John
   D. Nov. 19, 1779   R. Nov. 8, 1781   Kindred
Wit. Benjamin Blunt, Benjamin Kindred, Elisha Kindred
                                                  Page 348

DEMMERY, Frederick.   Leg.- Richard, Tempy, Micajah,
Day and Collin Demmery.
Ex. David Demmery.
D. Aug. 28, 1780   R. Nov. 8, 1781
Wit. John Bittle, Richard Griffin, Thomas Holladay
                                                  Page 348

HOLT, Charles.   Estate appraised, Oct. 1781, by John
Simmons and Benjamin Lewis.   R. Dec. 13, 1781
                                                  Page 349

PITMAN, John.   Account current. Signed John Boykin, Ex
Audited by John Wilkinson and Lazarus Cook.
R. Dec. 13, 1781   Page 349

WRIGHT, Mary. Estate appraised by John Summerell, John
Britt and Lightborn Low.
D. Oct. 1781   R. Dec. 13, 1781   Page 350

CROCKER, Sarah. Inventory. Signed J. Kindred.
R. Dec. 13, 1781   Page 350

.FORT, Joshua. Estate appraised by Benjamin Lewis, John
Simmons and Mark Nicholson. Signed, Lewis Thorp, Ex.
D. Dec. 13, 1781   Page 351

COKER, Nathaniel. Inventory. Signed, R. Kello, Adm.
Slaves appraised by Sampson Pitman amd Moses Phillips.
R. Dec. 13, 1781   Page 352

EDWARDS, William. Leg.- wife Sally, children Charlotte
and George; provision for child in esse.
Ex., my uncle George Gurley.
D. March 5, 1681   R. Dec. 13, 1781
Wit. George Edwards, George Gurley, Thomas Edwards.
                                               Page 352

MOORE, James.   Account current.   Jesse and Isaac
Williams, Adms. 1778. refers to sale of land in N. Car.;
paid Elizabeth Moore her specific legacy; Audited by
Solomon Shepherd, Richard Ricks and J. Denson
R. Dec. 13, 1781   Page 353

BARNES, Benjamin. Account Current. Exs., Mary Barnes
and William Barnes.   Among items,- paid William Barnes his
legacy; paid for hiring a substitute for the 44th Division;
paid John Powel as guardian to Milly Barnes; paid Mary
Barnes; paid William Barnes as guardian of Peninah Barnes;
paid Stephen Johnson as guardian to Jacob Barnes.
  Audited by Solomon Shepherd, Richard Ricks and J. Denson
R. Dec. 13, 1781   Page 354

WILLIAMS, Michael. Inventory. R. Dec. 13, 1781
                                               Page 354

EVERITT, Thomas, Sr.   Leg.- son Keton; son Thomas
land adjoining Robert Gilliam; son Exum; daughter Ann;
daughter Elizabeth; daughter Mary; daughter Femby and
wife Elizabeth Everitt.
D. Oct. 26, 1780   R. Dec. 13, 1781
Wit. John Chitty, John Gilliam, Jacob Barrett.
                                          Page 355

BARKER, William. Of the Parish of St. Luke. Leg.-
wife Mary and my six children.
Exs., wife, Richard Marks, Joseph Marks.
D.   R. Dec. 13, 1781
Wit. Richard Marks, Lucy Barker, Nancy Barker
The widow being deceased, Richard and Joseph Marks, qual-
ified.   Page 355

HALL, George. Leg.- son James; daughter Ann Woodard;
son George; to wife all the estate, which formerly belonged
to Joseph Hail, now in her possession, reversion to her son
Obadiah Hail; wife Elizabeth Hall.
Exs., sons James and George Hall.
D. Feb. 6, 1781   R. Dec. 13, 1781
Wit. Lawrence Joyner, Benjamin Haisty, John Haisty
                                          Page 356

TAYLOR, James. Of the Parish of St. Luke. Leg.- all
debts to be paid, but the bond Silas Kirby is security to
and Jeremiah Tyler has paid and had a receipt for, but lost
it; to Charles Taylor, son of John Taylor; to beloved wife.
Extx. wife.
D. Nov. 13, 1781   R. Jan. 10, 1782.
Wit. Mary Murray, Mark Nicholson, John Simmons.
Elizabeth Taylor qualified.   Page 357

LUNDY, James.   Estate appraised by Thomas Turner, John
Freeman and Thomas Porch   R. Jan. 10, 1782   Page 357

PORTER, John.   Estate appraised by Edward Day, John
Powel and Nathan Harris.   R. Jan. 10, 1782   Page 358

CRAWFORD, John. Estate appraised by John Wilkinson,
Lazarus Cook and John Lutar.
R. Jan. 10, 1782.   Page 359

JONES, Richard. Leg.- beloved wife; Willis Joyner, son of
Amos Joyner. Ex. friend Jacob Burn-
 D. Sept. 27, 1781   R. Jan. 10, 1782
 Wit. Will Ridley, Lucy Bittle, Mary Barnes.
 Jacob Barnes, qualified.   Page 359

GEORGE, William. Leg.- daughter Sarah Savage; son John;
wife Ann; between all my children.
 Exs., wife Ann and Benjamin Spratley.
 D. Sept. 21, 1779   R. Jan. 10, 1782
 Wit. William Lane, William Riggan, Burwel Sharp.
                                                 Page 360

HATFIELD, Charles. Jemima Hatfield refused to accept
the bequest made her in the will of Charles Hatfield and delivered management to David Barrow, who qualified as Ex.
 R. Jan. 10, 1782.   Page 360

GRESSWIT, William. Of the Parish of Nottoway; Leg.-
beloved wife; son Mathew; to wife all I have due me for
schoolkeeping; daughter Sarah Gresswit.
 Exs., wife and Mathew Wills.
 D. Aug. 13, 1781   R. Jan. 10, 1782
 Wit. John Edwards, Thomas Lawrence.   Page 360

EVERITT, Thomas. Inventory. Signed Thomas Everitt, Ex.
 R. Jan. 10, 1782   Page 361

GILLIAM, Jesse. Leg.- wife Penelopy and her children.
 Exs., wife and John Gilliam.
 D. Oct. 23, 1781   R. Jan. 10, 1782
 Wit. Edward Britt, Samuel Mathews.   Page 361

POWERS, Charles. Estate appraised by Edward Tyler, Carr
Doyle and Sampson Pitman. Signed Moses Johnson, Adm.
 R. Jan. 10, 1782   Page 362

GRESWITT, William. Estate appraised by Abram Mitchel,
Thomas Lawrence and John Rochell
 R. Feb. 14, 1782.   Page 362

GARDNER, John. Of the Parish of Nottoway. Leg.- son
Jesse; daughter Lydia Joyner; wife Ann; daughter Mitty; son
John land bought of William Worrel; daughter Ann; son James;
daughter Mary; daughter Pheby; son Amos Gardner.
Exs., sons Jesse and John Gardner.
D. Oct. 21, 1778   R. Feb. 14, 1782
Wit. Henry Love, Silas Love, William Gray   Page 363

GILLIAM, Joseph.   Inventory.   Signed John Gillaim.
R. Feb. 14, 1782   Page 364

SCARBOROUGH, John.   Leg.- son Benjamin; heirs of Robert
Scarborough; to Ann wife of John Hines; Lydia wife of
Benjamin Stewart; wife Mary; to Brittain Scarborough; son
John, at death of my wife my estate to be divided among my
five youngest childre, viz.- John, Sukey, Patty, Betsey and
Sarah Scarborough.   Extx. wife Mary Scarborough.
D. Jan. 13, 1778   R. Feb. 14, 1782
Wit. Lewis Joiner, Drury Cotton, Richard Tatem
                                                Page 364

BROWNE, Jesse.   Estate appraised by Joseph Washington,
Newsom Branch and William Stephenson.   R. Feb. 14, 1782.
                                                Page 365

KINNEBREW, Edwin.   Inventory.   Signed John Barrow, Ex.
R. Feb. 14, 1782   Page 366

BRANCH, Howell.   Estate appraised by James Summerell,
Robert Shield and Arthur Doles.   R. Feb. 14, 1782
                                                Page 366

WILLIAMSON, Francis. Of the Parish of Nottoway. Leg.-
brother Turner Williamsburg land in Greensville County;
sister Polly Williamson; Micajah Holliman; brother John
Williamson.   Ex., **Micajah Holliman**.
D. Nov. 16, 1781.   R. Feb. 13, 1782
Wit. John Woodward, Arthur Williamson, Person Williamson
                                                Page 367

BARRETT, William, Sr.   Of Nottoway Parish.   Leg.- son
Pressley when he is eighteen; son Hancock; daughter Lucresly
Toney (?); son William; son Charles; son Rolley; daughter

Suzanna Peircy; daughter Lucy Hancock; rest of my estate to
my two daughter and four sons.
    Exs., sons William and Rolley Barrett. I impower them
        to make a right to the land I sold Giles Joyner.
    D. Jan. 15, 1782   R. Feb. 14, 1782
    Wit. Henry Jones, Toomer Joyner, Joshua Miniard.
                                      Page 368

    BAILEY, Robert. Account Current. 1775. Audited by
Arthur Foster and Arthur Boykin. R. Feb. 14, 1782
                                      Page 369

    COBB, Hardy. Estate appraised by Abraham Mitchell,
Mathew Wills, David Edwards and William Westra
    D. Dec. 6, 1781   R. March 14, 1782   Page 370

    WOODARD, Charles. Estate appraised by Joseph Pope,
John Benjamin Waller, John Pleger. R. March 14, 1782
                                      Page 371

    CLEMENTS, Benjamin. Appraisal in Southampton not sign-
ed, but filed. Appr. in Brunswick County made by Henry
Nicholson, Federic Lucas, William Clack, Jr.
    R. March 14, 1782.   Page 372

  CLEMENTS, Benjamin, Jr. Of Nottoway Parish. Estate
appraised by Charles Briggs and John Simmons.
    R. May 9, 1782.   Page 374

    WILLIAMS, Michael. Estate appraised by William Thomas,
John Thomas Blow, James Martin. R. March 14, 1782
                                      Page 377

    GARDNER, John. Estate appraised by Lewis Joyner, Jr.,
James Vick and Joseph Vick. R. March 14, 1782.
                                      Page 377

    CLEVELAND, William. Leg.- mother; sister Patsey; bro-
ther John Cleveland.
    Exs. friends John Andrews and Stephen Summerell
    D. Dec. 16, 1775   R. Feb. 14, 1782.   Page 379
    Wit. Armstead Vellins, Lucy Andrews, Silvy Jackson

JONES, Richard. Estate appraised by Thomas Fitzhugh, Jeremiah Drew and Thomas Ridley. R. March 14, 1782
Page 379

FRANCIS, Thomas. Estate appraised by Hardy Harris, Michael Warren and John Kirby. R. March 14, 1782
Page 380

HATFIELD, Charles. Estate appraised by Henry Jones, Simon Johnson and John Johnson. R. March 14, 1782
Page 381

TURNER, William. Inventory. Signed, Thomas Turner. R. March 14, 1782
Page 382

TURNER, Arthur. Estate appraised by James Wilson, Dempsey Johnson and Henry Joyner. R. March 14, 1782
Page 383

EDWARDS, Elizabeth. Leg.- son William; son Richard; son Benjamin a tract bought of Richard Ricks; daughter Elizabeth; daughter Ann Edwards.
Exs., son William Edwards and brother Benjamin Blunt.
D. Feb. 24, 1782   R. March 14, 1782
Wit. John Thomas Blow, Benjamin Spivey.   Page 384

AVERY, Joell. D. July 12, 1779. Estate appraised by Howell Edmunds, Henry Turner and John Powell
R. May 9, 1782   Page 385

POPE, Patience. Estate appraised by Arhthur Foster and Thomas Edmunds. R. May 9, 1782.   Page 386

BARNES, Burwell. Inventory 1781 R. May 9, 1782
Page 386

THORPE, John. Inventory. Signed Hardy Harris and Martha Thorpe. R. May 9, 1782.   Page 387

BUTTS, Peter. Estate appraised by (not signed).

Thomas Butts and Benjamin Butts, Exs. R. May 9, 1782
Page 389

ATKINS, Mial. Inventory. D. April 24, 1781
R. May 9, 1782   Page 389

MORGAN, John. Estate appraised by Joshua Thorpe, Henry
Ivy and H'y Applewhaite.   R. May 9, 1782   Page 390

NEWSOM, Jacob.   Estate appraised by James Battle and
Howell Harris.   Signed, Isham Gilliam and Tabitha
Newsom, Exs.   R. May 9, 1782   Page 390

BARKER, William. Estate appraised by James Battle,
James Barham and Howell Harris   R. May 9, 1782
Page 392

WILSON, William.   Inventory. Signed Jesse Whitehead
R. May 9, 1782   Page 392

CURL, Thomas. Inventory. Signed, Jesse Whitehead
R. May 9, 1782   Page 392

JOHNSON, Joseph. Estate appraised by Mathew Wills,
David Wright and James Wright   R. May 9, 1782
Page 393

HARRIS, Mary. Leg.- daughter Winney Cheaves (?)
Exs., son James Harris and Drewry Harris.
D. Aug. 24, 1781   R. March 14, 1782
Wit. Thomas Turner, Priscilla Womack, Rebecca Johnson
Page 394

PERSON, Philip. Of the Parish of St. Luke. Leg.- bro-
ther Turner Person; son Timothy when twenty one; wife
Temperance; daughter Patsey and to all my children.
Exs., Wife and friend William Andrews.
D. Aug. 25, 1781   R. May 9, 1782   Page 395
Wit. John Turner, Richard Clifton, John Westbrook

PERSON, Collier. Leg.- wife Elizabeth; daughter Nancy
at fifteen; to wife Elizabeth and all her children legally
begotten by me.
Exs., wife and brother Philip Person.
D. Nov. 18, 1780   R. May 9, 1782
Wit. Thomas Turner, Dorcas Clifton, John Main.
Page 396

NICHOLSON, Joshua. Estate appraised by William Moore,
Timothy Thorpe and Amos Harris.
Signed, Howell Edmunds and John Kirby, Exs.
R. May 9, 1782   Page 397

BRACY, Francis. Estate appraised by Abraham Mitchell,
Mathew Wills and William Williams. R. May 9, 1782
Page 398

DREWRY, William.. Inventory. Signed, William Drewry, Jr.
R. May 9, 1782   Page 399

VICK, Arthur. Inventory. Signed, Samuel Vick, Sr. Ex.
R. May 9, 1782   Page 400

VAUGHAN, William. Inventory. Signed Nathaniel Turner,
Ex. R. May 9, 1782   Page 400

EDWARDS, William. Inventory. R. May 9, 1782
Page 401

JONES, Mrs. Martha. Inventory. Signed, Timothy Thorpe,
Ex. R. May 9, 1782   Page 401

BRIGGS, Henry. Inventory. Signed, John Thomas Blow
and Charles Briggs   R. May 9, 1782
Page 402

JOHNSON, Elibey. Inventory. Signed, William Johnson
R. May 9, 1782   Page 403

BIRCHETT, James.   June 20, 1772. Estate appraised by
Henry Holt, Edward Lundy, Jr. and James Lundy.
Signed, John Rogers, Adm. R. May 9, 1782.   Page 403

CROCKER, Hartwell. Inventory. Signed, Joseph Bradshaw
R. May 9, 1782.   Page 403

REESE, Edward. Estate Appraised by -------   Signed,
Olive Bunn, Admtx.   D. Dec. 19, 1781
R. May 9, 1782   Page 404

JOHNSON, Robert. Estate appraised by Hardy Doyle,
Carr Doyle and John Carstaphen. Signed Benjamin Beal, Ex.
R. May 9, 1782   Page 405

ATKINSON, TIMOTHY.   Estate appraised by John Andrews,
Benjamin Britt and Philip Moody
R. May 9, 1782   Page 406

SIMMONS, Joseph. Leg.- wife Oluf; son **John; son**
William; daughter Katherine Barnes; daughter Silviah;
daughter Milly Taylor Simmons and daughter Lucy Simmons
Exs., wife, son John Simmons and John Chitty, Sr.
D. May 6, 1781   R. Jan. 10, 1782
Wit. Newit Edwards, Joseph Pope, Elizabeth Jackson,
       Anne Edwards.   Page 407

FERGUSON, John. May 1, 1779 Inventory.
Signed, Jesse Whitehead, Adm. R. May 9, 1782
                                            Page 407

CRENSHAW. Thomas. Inventory. Signed Nicholas Maget
and Jesse Whitehead.   R. May 9, 1782   Page 408

BRADSHAW, Arthur. Inventory. Signed Thomas Bradshaw,
Adm. R. May 9, 1782   Page 408

FREEMAN, James.   Inventory. Signed, Olive Freeman.

46

D. 1781   R. May 9, 1782   Page 408

JENKINS, Edmund.   Estate appraised by John Pursell,
William Judlins and Benjamin Crumpler.   Signed by
Valentine Jenkins.   R. May 9, 1782
                                            Page 409

HANDCOCK, Henry.   D. Dec. 30, 1777.   Appraised by
Edward Harris, Joseph Reese, Jr. and John Lundy
R. May 9, 1782   Page 410

PILES, Vincent.   D. Nov. 26, 1774.   Estate appraised
by Edward Lundy, Edward Harris, Sr., John Lundy.
R. May 9, 1782   -   Page 411

TAYLOR, Henry.   Inventory.   R.   June 13, 1782
                                            Page 411

HALL, George. Inventory. Signed, James Hall and
George Hall, Exs.   R. June 13, 1782   Page 413

GRIFFIN, Benjamin.   Inventory.   Signed, Micajah
Griffin, Ex.   R. June 13, 1782   Page 413

MURPHEE, James.   Leg.- wife Susannah; neice Elizabeth
Poole; reversion to James Poole and William Murphee Poole.
Extx. wife Susannah Poole
D. April 21, 1782   R. June 13, 1782
Wit. Edward Archer, John Archer, William Urquhart.
                                            Page 414

BARRETT, William, Sr. Inventory.   Signed, William
Barrett and Rawleigh Barrett, Exs.   R. June 13, 1782
                                            Page 415

SIMPSON, Samuel. Estate appraised by Howell Edmunds,
William Edmunds and William Vaughan.   R. June 13, 1782
                                            Page 416

EDWARDS, Micajah. Inventory. Signed, Richard Edwards
R. May 13, 1782   Page 416

MORGAN, **John.** Estate appraised by Thomas Turner, Drury
Harris and Colin Person.   R. June 13, 1782   Page 416

JONES, Thomas. Leg.- daughter Sarah land on which my
father Thomas Lones lived; son Mathew Jones.
Ex. son Mathew Jones.
D. Dec. 9, 1781   R. June 13, 1782
Wit. Thomas Bradshaw, Mary Williams, Edmund Johnson.
                                                    Page 417

BITTLE, Drury. D. Feb. 25, 1777. Estate appraised by
Samuel Kindred, William Vaughan and John Powell. Signed,
Robert Bittle, Adm.   R. June 13, 1782   Page 418

JOHNSON, Richard, Sr. D. March 28, 1782. Estate appraised by A. Jones, Jr. and George Edwards.
R. June 13, 1782.   Page 419

TURNER, Thomas. Account current. Paid Robert Gilliam
for schooling Mathew and Thomas Turner; paid John Edwards
for boarding Mathew Turner in 1771; paid board and schooling
ing Lewis Turner; paid Richard Harris for keeping Jesse
and Simon Turner; paid Simon Harris for keeping Harris
Turner; paid Elias Fort for keeping William Turner; paid
Edward Drew for keeping T. Turner; paid Joshua Nicholson
for John Turner. Audited by Jesse Whitehead and John
Whitehead. R. June 13, 1782   Page 419

WADE, Christopher. Of the Parish of Nottoway. Leg.-
son Wilson, land on which he and his family now dwell;
friend Sarah Turner the use of the plantation on which I
now live bought of Samuel Eley; reversion to grandson John
Wade and Samuel Wade; wife Ann; daughter Sarah Wade; daughter Martha Wade. Ex., friend Joshua Brantley.
D. Oct. 3, 1781   R. June 13, 1782
Wit. Joseph Mountford, Samuel Turner, Joyner Joyner (?)
                                                    Page 422

SUETER, Thomas. Estate appraised by William Andrews,
Henry Smith and Michael Harris.   R. July 11, 1782
                                                    Page 422

DAVIS, David. Estate appraised by Samuel Bristol,

William Holleman and Harmon Harris.   Samuel Bailey, Adm.
R. July 11, 1782   Page 423

WINDHAM, Benjamin. D. June 27, 1782. Estate appraised
by Richard Bailey, Benjamin Deloach and Thomas Oney.
R. July 11, 1782   Page 424

GEORGE, William. Estate appraised by Joshua Wood,
Brittain Travis and Thomas Wood. Signed by Benjamin
Spratley and Anne George, Exs. R. July 11, 1782
                                               Page 424

GRESSWITT, William. Account current. Signed Mathew
Wills, Ex. Audited by Benjamin Ruffin, Jr. and John Blunt
R. July 11, 1782   Page 424

HUTCHINGS, Capt. Daniel. Estate appraised by Jacob
Barnes, John Fort, Mark Nicholson. R. Aug. 8, 1782
                                               Page 425

TAYLOR, James. Inventory. Signed by the Extx.
R. Aug. 8, 1782   Page 427

JONES, Thomas. Estate appraised by Leighbourn Lowe
and James Johnson. Signed, Mathew Jones, Ex.
R. Aug. 8, 1782   Page 428

WILLIAMSON, Hannah. Inventory. R. Aug. 8, 1782
                                               Page 429

WESTBROOKE, Samuel. Of the Parish of St. Luke. Leg.-
wife Hannah; son Turner at twenty one, also my land that
formerly belonged to William Westbrook; my children- David,
Joel, Samuel H. and Phebe Westbrook.
Exs., wife and friend John Barrow.
April 14, 1781   R. Sept. 12, 1782
Wit. Henry Butler, Samuel Blake, William Claud, John
      Ivey, George Stephenson   Page 429

TURNER, William. Inventory. Signed Benjamin Turner,
Ex. R. Sept. 12, 1782   Page 430

MURFEE, Richard, Jr.   D. Feb. 27, 1782. Estate appraised by A. Jones, jr., Brittain Joyner, William Williams
R. Sept. 12, 1782   Page 431

JARRELL, Benjamin. Account current. Signed Albridghton
Jones. Audited by Timothy Thorpe, Hardy Harris, Thomas
Fitzhugh and Benjamin Lewis.   R. Sept. 12, 1782
                                        Page 432

WILLIAMS, Henry.   D. July 22, 1782. estate appraised
by Stephen Summerell, John Summerell and Arthur Boykin.
R. Aug. 12, 1782   Page 434

DREW, Jesse.   Leg. Estate to be divided between
Jeremiah Drew and Thomas Fitzhugh.
Exs., brother Jeremiah Drew and Thomas Fitzhugh.
D. Sept. 27, 1776   R. June 13, 1782
Wit. Richard Blow, Timothy Thorpe   Page 434

BLUNT, Priscilla. Of the Parish of St. Luke. Leg.-
son John, the tract bought of Alexander Watson; grandson
James Turner, son of Jacob Turner; reversion of bequest to
grandson John Blunt, son of John Blunt; son William Blunt;
daughter Priscilla Turner; grandson Edmund Turner; granddaughters, Martha, Temperance and Elizabeth Turner.
Ex., son John Blunt.
D. Feb. 25, 1778   R. Sept. 12, 1782
Wit. Savory Atkins, Nathan Bryant, Celia Bryant.
                                        Page 435

DAY, Thomas.   Signed Elizabeth Day and George Gurley.
Account current, audited by John T. Blow, Thomas Edmunds
and Howell Edmunds.   R. Sept. 12, 1782   Page 436

ADAMS, Thomas.   Of the Parish of Nottoway. Leg.-
daughter Betty Sammons; daughter Olive Hubbard; son Thomas.
Ex. son Thomas Adams
D. March 23, 1782   R. Sept. 12, 1782   Page 436
Wit. Charles Sledge, Tamer Adams, Richard Mason.

50

LUNDY, Edward. Estate appraised by Moses Thorpe,
Moses Harris and Thomas Turner.   R. Sept. 12, 1782
Page 437

WESTBROOK, Samuel. Inventory. Signed Hannah Westbrook
R. Oct. 9, 1782   Page 437

MOSS, Henry. Estate appraised by Thomas Gilliam, Jr.
and Henry Westbrrok.   D. Oct. 28, 1778
R. Oct. 10, 1782   Page 438

SIMMONS, Sarah. Inventory. Signed John Simmons.
R. Oct. 10, 1782.   Page 439

BARNES, Benjamin.   Account estate. To cash paid Philip
Moody for a balance due his late wife;- the late Mary Barnes
deceased, as per former accounts returned by Mary and William
Barnes.   Signed William Barnes, Ex. R. Oct. 10, 1782
Audited by Joseph Vick and J. Denson.   Page 439

BROWNE, John. Inventory.   D. Oct. 12, 1781
Signed Thomas Lane, Adm.   R. Oct, 10, 1782   Page 440

KINNEBREW, Edwin. Account current. Signed John Barrow.
Audited by Jesse Cooper, Jeremiah Drew.   R. Nov. 14, 1782
Page 440

SALTER, John. Estate appraised by Rice B. Peirce,
Richard Pond and William Spivey   R. Nov. 14, 1782
Page 440

WILLIAMSON, Arthur, Sr.   Account estate. Paid T.
Phillips for schooling F. Williamson; cash paid Exum
Williamson's orphans.   Ex., Jesse Williamson.
Audited by Beverley Booth and Arthur Foster
R. Nov. 14, 1782   Page 441

HARRISON, William.   Estate appraised by John Sturgeon,

Thomas Turner and Simon Harris.   R. Nov. 14, 1782
                                            Page 442

HARRIS, Mary. Inventory. Signed Drewry Harris.
R. Dec. 12, 1782   Page 443

BEEL, Sarah. Leg.- unbaptised daughter, whom I desire to
be called Sallie; with reversion of bequest to Henry Doles
and brother Burwell Beel.
Ex., friend Henry Doles.
D. Nov. 27, 1782   R. Dec. 12, 1782
Wit. Robert Washington, Elizabeth Williams,
        Annais Randolph   Page 443

BRACEY, Francis. Signed Frances Bracey.   March 1782
Paid Mary Bracy her part; paid Patience Bracy; paid James
Wright for his wife Mary; paid Elizabeth Cobb; Paid Ann
Bracy; paid Meriam Bracy; paid my own proportion; to balance
in my hands, belonging to Sarah Bracy.
Audited by Lewis Joyner and Joseph Mountfort.
R. Dec. 12, 1782   Page 444

IVY, John. Leg.- wife Elizabeth; daughter Priscilla
Bullock; son James land on the Great Ploughman's Swamp, mark-
ed by my neighbors, Thomas and Edward Pate, on the line which
divides my land from John Reese and Ambrose Grizzard; son
John; son Davy; daughter Anne Morgan; daughter Rebecca Ivy
Ex. friend, Joshua Nicholson.
D. March 4, 1780   R. April 12, 1781
Wit. Thomas Pate, Edward Pate, William Pate   Page 445

TURNER, William. Account estate.   Signed, Ben. Turner
Paid John Simmons for schooling James and Nancy Turner.
Audited by John Taylor, Thomas Ridley and Mark Nicholson
R. Sept. 12, 1782   Page 446

--------- 0 ---------

WILL BOOK FOUR

MURPHREE, James. Inventory. Signed Susanna Murphree
R. Feb. 13, 1783   Page 1

WILLIAMS, William.   Leg.- wife Sarah; son Jacob land on
Blunt's Swamp, Barrow's Road and Thomas' Swamp; son Kinchen,
land adjoining Isaac Pope; son Elisha; daughter Rhoda
Exs., friends Samuel Edmunds and Thomas Vaughan.
D. Dec. 1, 1782   R. Feb. 13, 1783
Wit. Richard Deloach, Mathew Underwood, Thomas Edmunds.
                                                   Page 1

DAY, Edmund. Of the Parish of St. Luke. Leg.- wife;
son Abner, land at his grandfather's decease, and I wish him
bound to a house carpenter; son John the land bought of
Faircloth and he is, to be kept at an Academy until he is
twenty one; sister Susanna Day.
Exs., friends Thomas Edmunds and William Whitehead.
D. Dec. 12, 1782   R. Feb. 13, 1783
Wit. William Vester, Christopher Bromadge, Asa Street
                                                   Page 3

DAY, Edmund. Estate appraised by Nathan Harris, Samuel
Edmunds and Nathan Barnes.   R. April 10, 1783
                                                   Page 4

DRAKE, Thomas. A deed is to be made to Jordan Denson for
fifty acres, which he has paid for, adjoining Absalom and
Lewis Joyner and the said Denson's land on which Timothy
Drake now lives and I direct that Absalom Joyner is to run
the dividing line; wife Sarah; daughter Mary; daughter Celia
Joyner; grandson Joseph Joyner is to have an education suit-
able to his station in life.
Exs., wife Sarah and son-in-law Absalom Joyner.
D. March 6, 1783   R. April 10, 1783   Jr.
Wit. Lewis Joyner, Sr., Lewis Joyner, Jr., Joseph Denson,
                                                   Page 9

MOODY, Philip. Leg.- son Samuel land purchased of
William Barnes; son West; daughter Elizabeth; among all my
children.
Exs., friends John Andrews, Josiah Vick; Stephen Johnson,
     Jordan Denson.

D. Feb. 24, 1783   R. April 10, 1783
Wit. John Barnes, William Barnes, Jerry Williams.
Page 11

FOSTER, John. Leg.- son Haley.
Exs., son Haley and Richard Foster.
D. July 24, 1776   R. April 10, 1783
Wit. John Mundell, John Mundell Jr., James Black.
Page 11

CRENSHAW, Anne. Leg.- sister Amey Bailey all my
estate. Ex., Jacob Bailey.
D. April 11, 1781   R. Feb. 14, 1783
Wit. Nicholas Maget, Samuel Maget, Jesse Vick.
Page 12

FIGURES, Joseph. Inventory. Signed, Jesse Whitehead,
Thomas Figures, Edmund Barrett and John Edwards, Exs.
D. Aug. 24, 1780   R. April 11, 1783   Page 13

MILLAR, William. Account current, signed Sarah Millar.
Audited by John Taylor, Thomas Ridley, Mark Nicholson.
R. May 8, 1783   Page 13

McLEMORE, John. Leg.- sons John and Joel, with rever-
sion to daughters, Elizabeth, Olive and McKerina; son James
to pay my indebtedness to George Ivy; daughter Martha
Morgan; daughter Mary Norvill; daughter Priscilla, with re-
version to her daughter Elizabeth McLemore; wife Elizabeth.
Exs., John Rogers and Thomas Turner.
D. Dec. 27, 1782   R. May 8, 1783
Wit. John Gray, Frederick Emmory, Thomas Blake,
      Thomas Turner.   Page 15

FOSTER, John. Estate appraised by Howell Edmunds, John
A. Rogers, Samuel Blake.   R. May 8, 1783   Page 16

SIMPSON, Samuel. Estate appraised by Howell Edmunds,
William Edmunds and William Vaughan.
R. May 8, 1782   Page 16

DRAKE, Thomas. Estate appraised by Lewis Joyner, Jr.,

John Davis and John Beaton.   R. May 8, 1783
Page 17

WILLIAMS. William.   Estate appraised by Arthur Foster,
William Francis and William Pope   R. May 8, 1783
Page 18

JOHNSON, John.   Leg.- wife Peninah, land descended to
me from my father and tract bought of John Denson; son
James; son John land purchased of Benjamin and William
Kitchen; son Jacob land bought of Mathew Wills; son Josiah
land purchased of Robert Tyler; son Jesse, land bought of
David Chalmers; daughters, Rebecca, Ann, Lydia and Alice;
to youngest son not yet named.
Exs., son James and neighbor Jordan Denson.
D. Jan. 30, 1783   R. May 8, 1783
Wit. William Kitchen, Joshua Councill, Dempsey Johnson.
Page 19

POPE, Henry.   Accouunt estate.   May   1782   Signed,
Sarah Lewis, Adm.   Audited by Hardy Pope and Mathew
Charles (or Clarke)   R. May 8, 1783   Page 20

TURNER, Littleton.   May 1, 1783.   Estate appraised
by John Blunt, Michael Harris and William Drury.
D. May 1, 1783   R. June 12, 1783   Page 21

WOOD, Joshua.   Of the Parish of Nottoway.   Leg.- **wife**
Sarah land bought of Richardson Riggin, also Hardin's place;
son Benjamin the bond due me from John Butts' estate; son
Joel, land purchased of Isham Davis; son Edmund; daughter
Rebecca; daughter Mary; daughter Anna Wood
D. Dec. 26, 1782   R. June 12, 1783
Wit. Edwin Gray, John Pond, John Cobb.   Page 21

JOHNSON, Joseph.   Account Estate. Signed Drewry Beale.
Audited by George Curley and William Thomas.
R. June 12, 1783   Page 23

APPLEWHITE, Henry.   Of the Parish of St. Luke.   Leg.-
wife Ann , with reversion to sons Henry and Thomas; son
Arthur land bought of Hardy Harris; daughter Salley; son

Hardy; son John; son Benjamin; son William; daughters,
Priscilla, Janey, Beckey and Nancy Applewhite; daughter
Mary Barham, wife of John Barham; son John to make a deed
to William Maley for the land I have sold him.
Exs., wife and sons John and Arthur Applewhite.
D. May 11, 1783.   R. July 10, 1783
Wit. Richard Mason, Selah Reese, John Reese.   Page 23

BEAL, Priscilla   D. May 1, 1783   Signed William
Beal. Estate appraised by Jonas Edwards, William Williams,
David Wright.   R. July 10, 1783   Page 25

SIMMONS, Joseph.   D. July 2, 1783   Estate appraised
by Micajah Edwards, Jacob Williams, Henry Taylor
R. Oct. 10, 1783   Page 26

BARKER, William.   D. Aug. 6, 1783.   Signed, Richard
Marks and Joseph Marks. Account estate audited by John
Simmons, Sr., Benjamin Lewis and Etheldred Taylor.
R. Aug. 14, 1783   Page 26

WILLIFORD, William. Leg.- wife Mary; son Belah the
plantation bought of my brother, Thomas Williford; son
Jordan the tract purchased of Jordan Thomas; son Jeremiah;
son Johnson, the land my father purchased of Lawrence
Lancaster, which I possess by virtue of my father's will;
son James; daughter Sarah; daughter Mary Williford.
Exs., sons Belah and Jordan Williford.
D. Jan. 6, 1782   R. Aug. 14, 1783
Wit. M. Holliman, Mrs. Boykin, William Holliman.
    Page 27

POPE, William. Estate appraised by Mathew Wills, John
Johnson and Simon Murfree.   R. Aug. 14, 1783   Page 29

CLARK, John. Of the Parish of Nottoway. Leg.- my chil-
dren; William, James, Mary, Anne Warren, Rebecca, Milly
Richardson, Sally and Judith Clarke; son James the land I
bought of Alexander Murray in July 11, 1768; wife Rebecca.
Exs., Arthur Williamson and Micajah Holloman.
D. Nov. 11, 1778   R. Aug. 14, 1783
Wit. John Woodard, Benjamin Harris, Micajah Holloman
    Page 29

COBB, Hardy. Account estate. Signed, Elizabeth Cobb, Admtx. Audited by Josiah Vick and Mathew Wills.
D. Feb. 1783   R. Aug. 14, 1783   Page 30

MORGAN, William. Inventory. Signed, William Andrews.
D. April 15, 1782   R. Sept. 11, 1783   Page 31

JONES, Robert. D. Feb. 25, 1779. Appraisal, not signed. Ex., John Simmons. R. Sept. 11, 1783
Page 31

SMITH, Martha. Leg.- Exum Bailey, son of Joshua Bailey; Edmund Bailey; Rhoda Sadler, with reversion to her son John Smith Sadler; Tryal Bailey; Martha Bailey, daughter of Absalom Bailey; Burwell Brock, son of Sarah Brock: remainder of my estate to be divided between six of my brothers and William Bailey, son of Elijah Bailey and my four sisters, namely; - Tryal, Joseph, Absalom, Edmund, Abidan and Joshua; Miriam Hargrave, Sarah Brock, Mourning Russell and Rhoda Sadler.
Exs.. Abidan and Joshua Bailey
L. Aug. 18, 1783   R. Sept. 11, 1783
Wit. M. Holleman, B. White, Sarah Kitchen
Page 33

EDWARDS, Elizabeth. Estate appraised by Thomas Vaughan, Thomas Edmunds and William Francis. R. Sept. 11, 1783
Page 33

VICK, William. Account current. Audited by Lewis Vick and Nathan Barnes. R. Sept. 11, 1783   Page 35

CROCKER, Hartwell. Signed Joseph Bradshaw, Adm. Appraised by Edmund Tyler, Arthur Bowin and Lawrence Joiner. R. Sept. 11, 1783   Page 35

DREW, Newit. Inventory. Signed, Jeremiah Drew and Jesse Drew. R. Oct. 9, 1783   Page 36
Account estate audited by John Barrow and Timothy Thorpe
R. Oct. 9, 1783   Page 37

DOYELL, William. Inventory. R. Oct. 9, 1783
Page 37

WASHINGTON. George. Of Nottoway Parish. Leg.- wife
Sarah; daughter Martha; son David, land adjoining Joseph
Washington; provision for unborn child.
  Exs., wife Sarah Washington and Henry Briggs
D. Nov. 5, 1730   R. Oct. 9, 1783
  Wit. Joseph Charity, Mary Johnston.
Mary Johnston qualified as Admtr. of will

Page 38

EDWARDS, Captain Micajah. Account estate. Signed
Benjamin Blunt and John Thomas Blow, Exs. 1771. To paid
the following their legacies, - Elizabeth Edwards, Micajah
Edwards, Richard Edwards, Benjamin Edwards, Mary Butts,
Lucy Edwards, Elizabeth Edwards; Ann Edwards, Martha
Edwards and William Edwards.
  Audited by Thomas Holladay and J. Denson.
R. Oct. 9, 1783   Page 39

TURNER, Benjamin. Of Buckhorn. Leg.- son Joel a tract
bought of Mary Person and another purchased of Richard
Avery; son William; daughter Rebecca Turner.
  Exs., brother and brother-in-law Thomas Turner and
Nathan Harris and John Barrow.
D. Aug. 3, 1783   R. Oct. 9, 1783
  Wit. John Simmons, Mark Nicholson, Arthur Turner.
                                            Page 41

BAILEY, Barnaby. Leg.- wife Mary; son James; daugh-
ter Celia Barlow; daughter Martha Booth; daughter Elizabeth
Hayes; son Richard my land in Sussex County; daughter Lucy
Calthorpe; with reversion Mary Bailey Calthorpe; granddaugh-
ter Lucy Bailey; to my grandchildren, the children of my
daughter Ann Coker.
  Exs., wife Mary and son Richard Bailey
D. Sept. 1, 1783   R. Nov. 13, 1783
  Wit. Jordan Judkins, James Gray, Halcott Briggs Pride.
                                            Page 42

WHITLEY, Giles. April 1783 Inventory
R. Nov. 13, 1783   Page 43

WADE, Christopher. Signed, Joshua Brantley. Estate
appraised by Joseph Mountfortt, Thomas Mountfortt, William
Joyner. R. Nov. 13, 1783   Page 44

KIRBY, Turner. D. Sept. 18, 1783. Estate appraised by William Edmunds, Thomas Holladay and John Barrow.
R. Nov. 13, 1783   Page 44

NICHOLSON, Samuel. Leg.- wife Sarah; son Howell (not 21); son John; daughter Rebecca.
Exs., wife Sarah Nicholson and Thomas Mason.
D. April 20, 1783   R. Nov. 13, 1783
Wit. Howell Myrick, William Prince, John Barham.
                                                        Page 45

LUNDY, Robert. Leg.- daughter Elizabeth; son William my land in Halifax County, N. Car.; son James; Drury Harris; grandson Isham, son of my son Isham Lundy; grandson Lunsford Lundy; grandson James, son of William Lundy; grandson Thomas with reversion to my son William; grandson William: son of James Lundy; granddaughters, Mary, Sarah and Winifred, daughters of Isham Lundy; to my four grndchildren, offsprings of said son Isham, decd.; sister Elizabeth Hoof; residue of estate to my three children, William, James and Elizabeth Lundy. Exs., sons William and James Lundy
D. May 1, 1783   R. Oct. 9, 1783
Wit. John Rogers, Solomon Harrison, Thomas Porch,
       Thomas Morris, Jr.   Page 46

CRENSHAW, Ann. Inventory. D. Feb. 15, 1783
Signed, Jacob Bailey. R. Nov. 13, 1783
                                                        Page 48

EDWARDS, Elizabeth. Account current. Signed, William Edwards. D. 1782. Paid Richard Edwards, his proportion of his father's; to same as an Ex. of Micajah Edwards, decd. to Benjamin Edwards his proportion of his father's estate; to Ann Edwards, sundries given her; to William Edwards his legacy. R. Nov. 13, 1783.
Audited by David Barrow and Mark Nicholson.   Page 48

EDWARDS, Micajah. Account Estate. Nov. 22, 1780. Paid Elizabeth and Ann Edwards, the proportional part of their father's estate paid William Edwards and Benjamin Edwards. Audited by David Barrow and Mark Nicholson.
R. Nov. 13, 1783   Page 49

BASS, Charles. Account Current   D. Dec. 13, 1783

Signed, Arthur Matthews, Ex.   Paid Charles Bass, Jr.;
paid Hardy Bass for a proportion of hire in the service
Audited by James Lundy and Benjamin Clifton.
R. Dec. 13, 1783   Page 50

APPLEWHITE, Henry.   D. Dec. 10, 1783.   Inventory
R. March 11, 1784   Page 51

DREW, Jesse.   Estate appraised by William Ridley.
Thomas Turner, Timothy Thorpe.   R. March 11, 1784.
                                                      Page 51

VAUGHAN, Henry.   Leg.- son Thomas; son Howell Vaughan.
Exs., sons Thomas and Howell Vaughan.
D. Jan. 20, 1784.   R. March 11, 1784
Wit. Samuel Haisty, Moses Johnson, Thomas Edmunds.
                                                      Page 52

MURRAY, Alexander. Of the Parish of St. Luke.   Leg.-
daughter Mary Harwood; daughter Elizabeth Smith; daughter
Sarah Murray.
   Exs., wife and John Simmons.
   D. Aug. 15, 1783   R. March 11, 1784
   Wit. Jacob Barnes, Mark Nicholson, Jesse Fort.
   Will presented by Mary Murray.   Page 53

BEAL, Sarah.   Estate appraised by Lazarus Cook, Moses
Johnson and Elijah Crocker.
D. March 22, 1783   R. March 11, 1784   Page 54

STEPHENSON, Simon.   Account Current.   Jan. 1781
Audited by James Summerell, Arthur Boykin and William
Boykin.   R. March 11, 1784   Page 55

RAY, William.   Account current.   Audited by Charles
Birdsong and Micajah Edwards.   R. May 13, 1784 Page 55

DAY, Patty.   Estate appraised by John Wilkinson and
Jonas Bryant. D. Nov. 12, 1783   R. May 13, 1784
                                                      Page 55

WASHINGTON, George. Estate appraisal. Oct. 1783. Signed, Sarah Washington, Ex. Appraised by Joshua Beal. Shad.
Lewis and Benjamin Boal R. May 13, 1784   Page 56

BEALE, Priscilla. Account current. Signed, William
Beale, Adm. Paid to John and Burwell Beale, orphans of
William Beale, decd.   R. May 13, 1784. Audited by
Joseph Mountford, Shad Lewis.   Page 58

WELLONS, Henry. Leg.- Wife Elenor and all my children.
Extx. wife Elenor Wellons.
D. June 10, 1779   R. May 13, 1784   Page 58
Wit. Thomas Lane, Henry Powers.

MOORE, William. Of the Parish of St. Luke. Leg.-
mother Sarah Moore; sisters, Sarah Jarrell, Elizabeth and
Rebakah Moore and brother John Moore.
D.   R. May 13, 1784
Wit. James Jones, Nancy Jones, Thomas Scott.
                                             Page 59

WILKINSON, John. Leg.- son John; son James, land pur-
chased of Henry, Joshua and David Dawson, Benjamin, John
and Henry Crafford Tucker; wife Elizabeth; daughter Sarah.
Exs., sons John and James Wilkinson.
D. Feb. 24, 1784   R. May 13, 1784
Wit. Simon Everett, Susannah Raley, Thomas Edmunds.
                                             Page 59

WADE, Christopher. Account current. D. 1783.
Signed, Joshua Brantley.   Paid legacies.- Sarah Turner,
John Wade, Ann Wade, Wilson Wade, Sarah Wade and Martha
Wade. Audited by Joseph Mountford and Shad. Lewis.
R. May 13, 1784   Page 61

MURFREE, Richard. Account current. Signed, Simon
Murfee. D. 1782 Audited by J. Denson and Shad. Lewis.
R. May 13, 1784   Page 62

MURRAY, Alexander. Inventory. Signed, Mary Murray
and John Simmons. R. May 13, 1784   Page 63

BAILEY, Barnaby.   Inventory.   Signed, Mary Bailey
D. Oct. 10, 1783   R. June 10, 1784   Page 63

WALLER,   John. Estate appraised by George Edwards,
James Butts and Charles Speed.
D. Dec. 19, 1783   R. July 8, 1784   Page 64

COOPER, John.   Estate appraised by Abraham Mitchell,
Thomas Lawrence and Henry Cobb.
D. April 24, 1734   R. July 8, 1784   Page 65

RAWLINGS, John.   Estate appraised by Joshua Thorp,
Henry Ivy and Mathew M. Kenny.   Page 65
D. Dec. 21, 1778   R. July 8, 1784

WELLONS, Henry.   Estate appraised by Samuel Pitman,
William Wellons and Thomas Lain.   Signed, Elender
Wellons.   R. July 8, 1784   Page 67

VAUGHAN, Henry.   Estate appraised by Samuel Edmunds,
Thomas Turner and Henry Bittle.
D. March 27, 1784   R. Aug. 12, 1784   Page 67

SMITH, Martha.   Estate appraised by Benjamin Harris,
Burwell Williamson and Thomas Brock.   Signed, -----
Bailey and Joshua Bailey.   R. Aug. 12, 1784
                                                  Page 68

JOHNSON, John.   Estate appraised by Lewis Joyner and
William Kitching. R. Aug. 12, 1784   Page 70

TURNER, Benjamin.   Estate appraised by John Barrow,
Nathan Harris and Thomas Turner.   R. Aug. 12, 1784
                                                  Page 71

LUNDY, Robert.   Inventory.   Signed, William and
James Lundy.   R. Oct. 14, 1784   Page 72

SPENCER, Edmund. Of the Parish of St. Luke. Leg.-
son David; son William; son Ezekiel; son-in-law Nathan
Jackson and his wife Sarah, land bought of Arthur Vick;
son Jesse; wife Mary; son-in-law Drewry Beal; daughter
Elizabeth Spencer.
Exs., friend George Curley and son-in-law Drewry Beal.
D. Sept. 1, 1784   R. Oct. 14, 1784
Wit. Howell Whittington, John Beal.   Page 73

TURNER, Arthur. Account Current.   Received of
Parrot Turner's guardian, her proportional part of George
Washington's estate account versus the estate of Benjamin
Turner; due from Cordial Row his wife's part of same.
Signed Lewis Joiner and J. Denson.   R. Nov. 14, 1784
                                            Page 74

WILLIFORD, William. D. Sept. 15, 1783. Estate appraised by Burwell Williamson and Harmon Harris.
Signed Belah and Jordan Williford   R. Oct. 14, 1783
                                            Page 75

JOHNSON, Robert. Account estate. 1783. Signed,
Benjamin Beale.   Audited by J. Denson and Shad. Lewis.
R. Oct. 14, 1784   Page 76

MOORE, William. Estate appraised by Howell Myrick,
John Applewhite and John Reese.
D. Sept. 30, 1784   R. Oct. 14, 1784
                                            Page 77

NICHOLSON, Sarah. Leg.- granddaughter Sarah Myrick;
daughter Elizabeth Rivers; daughter Fanny Myrick; grand-
daughters Fanny, Lucy and Matilda, daughters of Joshua
Nicholson, decd; grandson Edwin Seward; granddaughter Sarah
Briggs Thorp; granddaughters Sarah and Lucy Edmunds, daugh-
ters of my daughter Lucy Edmunds, decd.
Exs., sons-in-law Col. Howell Edmunds and Owen Myrick.
D. April 7, 1783   R. Nov. 11, 1784
Wit. Henry Thorp, Amos Harris, Hardy Harris.
                                            Page 77

ONEY, John. Leg.- wife Sarah; daughter Mary Gay;
daughter Martha King; daughter Sarah Denson; daughter Lucy
Martin; daughter Elizabeth and daughter Rebecca Oney
Extx, Wife Sarah Oney.

D. March 17, 1784   R. Nov. 11, 1784
Wit. John H. Pond, Arthur Exum.   **Page** 78

ATKINSON, Hardy.   D. April 13, 1784. Estate appraised by Nathan Harris, John Kindred and John Powell.
R. Nov. 11, 1784   Page 79

VICK, William.   Leg.- son Lewis, land adjoining Robert
Newsum, Jr.; son Pilgrim, land adjoining Council Vick and
William Newsum; son Joshua, land adjoining Lewis Vick and
William Thomas; son Richard, land adjoining Jacob Vick; son
Giles, land adjoining John Everett; son Silas, land adjoin-
ing Jacob and Mathew Vick; wife Anne; daughter Mildred
Newsum; daughter Sally Vick; daughter Piety Vick.
Exs., sons Lewis and Pilgrim Vick and John Chitty, Sr.
D. May 15, 1782   R. Nov. 11, 1784
Wit. W. Burwell Vick, Patience Vick, Dorcas Vick, John
      Jackson.   Page 80

TURNER, Jacob, Sr. Leg.- wife; son James (not of age);
son John; rest of estate to all my children.
D. Oct. 22, 1784   R. Oct. 25, 1784
Wit. John Pursell, Holland Turner, Jacob Turner, Jr.
                                                   Page 82

SUMMERELL, John. Leg.- son John; wife Sarah; son
George; son Samuel; to my eight children, viz.- Nancy,
Stephen, Elizabeth Doles, John, George, Janey, Sarah,
Samuel and Lucy Summerell; provision for unborn child.
Exs., sons Stephen and John Summerell.
D. Jan. 8, 1783   R. Nov. 11, 1784
Wit. James Summerell, Thomas Summerell, Jeremiah
      Summerell   Page 82

STORY, James. Leg.- son Daniel, land adjoining Samuel
Story and George Gurley; son James; son Lewis; to John,
Salah, Nanny, Sally, Elizabeth and Samuel Story; provi-
sion for wife.
Ex.. son Daniel Story
D. Sept. 26, 1784   R. Dec. 9, 1784
Wit. Drewry Beal, John Willson.   Page 84

RUFFIN, Benjamin.   Leg.- beloved wife; son Benjamin.
Exs., wife and son Benjamin Ruffin.
D. Jan 29, 1777   R. Dec. 9, 1784   Page 85
Wit. Francis Newsum, John Ruffin, Joseph Longworth.

ONEY, John. Estate appraised by Thomas Lain, Richard Pond and William Spivy. Signed, Sarah Oney.
R. Dec. 9, 1784   Page 86

MOORE, Sarah. Of the Parish of St. Luke. Leg.- daughter Sarah Jarrell; daughter Elizabeth; daughter Rebecca; son John Moore.
Ex., friend, John Simmons.
D. May 15, 1784   R. Jan 13, 1785
Wit. Mary Nicolson, Mary Nicholson, Jr., Sally Applewhite
                                                   Page 87

PORTER, John. Account Current. Signed, William Hines, Sheriff and William Blunt. Paid Etheldred Brantley for keeping the children; paid said Brantley his wife's part of the estate. R. Jan. 14, 1785   Page 88

BAILEY, Benjamin. Leg.- son Trial; son Absalom; son Joseph land in Sussex County on which he lives, according to a patent granted Henry Sharp; son Edmund, land in Sussex on which he lives; son Abiaan, land in Sussex; to Josiah Davis the plantation, whereon his father died; wife Sarah, with reversion at her death to Edmund and Abidian Bailey and daughter Miriam Hargrave; to Elijah Bailey; to son Joshua Bailey; daughter Mourning Russell; daughter Rhoda Sadler; daughter Sarah Brock.
Exs., sons Abidian and Joshua Bailey
D. April 18, 1784   R. Feb. 10, 1785
Wit. Thomas Brock, Benjamin Brock, Martha Bailey
                                                   Page 89

RICKS, Mary. Leg.- son Thomas; son Robert; son Richard; son Joseph and daughters, Mary, Milisent and Ann Ricks.
D.   R. Feb. 10, 1785
Wit. Lemuel Hart, Josiah West Cathen.   Page 90

CHANNELL, James. D. Jan. 25, 1785. Estate appraised by Henry Smith, John Blunt and John Suter.
R. Feb. 10, 1785   Page 91

DELOACH, Benjamin. Leg.- wife Ann; to Mary, Allen, Martha and Thomas Deloach, born before my marriage with said Ann; to Averilla, Ann and Elizabeth the children of Ann Deloach.

Exs., Richard Kello the Elder and Samuel Kello
D. Jan. 6, 1785   R. Feb. 10, 1785
Wit. Richard Bailey, Richard Kello, Jr.   Page 91

WOOD, Joshua.   Inventory. Signed Benjamin Wood
R. Feb. 10, 1785   Page 93

WILKINSON, John. Inventory.   R. Feb. 8, 1785   Page 93

BRADSHAW, Elizabeth.   Inventory.   Signed, Martha
Bradshaw.   R. March 10, 1785.   Page 94

REESE, Joseph. Inventory. Signed, John Reese.
R. March 10, 1785   Page 94

BRITT, Benjamin.   Leg.- son Britain, land on Tarropin
Swamp; son Mathew; son Benjamin; to Jordan Britt;
daughter Sally, wife of Edmund Stephenson; daughter Anne,
wife of John Coging; daughter Holland; son Joseph; refers to
wife, but does not name her.
Ex. son Joseph Britt.
D. April 14, 1783   R. March 10, 1785
Wit. Arthur Allen, James Allen, Anne Allen   Page 95

STORY, James.   Estate appraised by Howell Whittington,
Drewry Beale, Jeremiah Drake.   R. March 10, 1785
Signed, Daniel Story.   Page 97

VICK, William. (son of Richard Vick).   D. Dec. 11, 1784
Estate appraised by Thomas Newsum, Edmund Barrett, Amos
Joyner.   R. March 10, 1785   Page 98

KINDRED, Samuel.   Leg.- son Benjamin land adjoining
Henry Vaughan; son Elisha (not of age); son Henry (not of
age); wife Anne; the interest he is entitled to at the
death of Sarah Crocker, to my four children, Mary, Elizabeth,
Henry and Sarah Kindred.
Ex., friend Benjamin Blunt.

D. Aug. 1, 1780   R. March 10, 1785
Wit. Henry Bittle, Howell Vaughan, Joseph Atkinson.
Page 99

SMITH, William.   Estate appraised by Mark Nicholson,
Miles Cary and Arthur Foster.   D.   July 24, 1784
Estate appraised in Surry, by William Maget, William
Hamlin and John Lane.   R.   March 10, 1785   Page 102

MOORE, Sarah.   Inventory.   Signed, John Simmons.
R.   March 10, 1785
Page 102

DELOACH, Benjamin.   Estate appraised by Richard Bailey,
Franklin Clark, Boaz Gwin Summerell.   R.   March 11, 1785
Page 103

JOHNSON, Charity.   Leg.- daughter Betty; son Elias
Ex., friend, Josiah Vick
D   Jan. 3, 1785   R.   March 11, 1785
Wit. William Barnes, Sarah Johnson, Joseph Vick
Page 104

SPENCER, Edmund.   Estate appraised by Howell Whittington,
Jeremiah Drake, William Thomas. Signed, George Gurley and
Drewry Beal.   R.   April 15, 1785   Page 105

GAY, Edmund.   D.   July 1776.   Signed, William Scott.
Account current.- paid Elizabeth Scott's legacy; paid legacy
left Thomas Gay's four children; paid legacy left Edmund
Blunt of Thomas
Audited by John T. Blow and Thomas Vaughan.
R.   April 15, 1785   Page 107

JOHNSON, Abraham.   Of the Parish of St. Luke.   Leg.-
wife Sarah; son Harris; son Jacob; son Josiah; son Micajah;
Exs., sons Harris and Josiah Johnson.
D.   March 19, 1785   R.   April 15, 1785
Wit. Joel Harris, John Blake, George Stephenson
Page 109

JENKINS, Jacob.   Account Current. 1775   Signed,
Richard Edwards.   R.   April 15, 1785   Page 110

BRYANT, Lewis.   Leg.- son Lewis; son James; son Jonas;
wife Sarah Bryant.
Exs., sons Lewis and Jonas Bryant.
D. Aug. 29, 1776   R. April 15, 1785
Wit. Nathan Bryant, Jonas Bryant, Seley Bryant
Page 111

BRANCH, Ogborne. Of Nottoway Parish.   Leg.- wife Sarah;
son Arthur; son Moses; son William Branch.
Ex., friend Joshua Wood.
D. Nov. 23, 1776   R. April 15, 1785
Wit. Charles Briggs, John Cobb.
Moses Branch qualified as Ex., Joseph Wood being deceased.
Page 112

LANCASTER, Joseph.   Leg.- wife Mary; son Etheldred; son
James Lancaster.
Exs., sons Etheldred and James Lancaster.
Wit. Richard Edwards, William White, B. Bailey
D. Sept. 8, 1783   R. May 12, 1785   Page 112

HOLDEN, Benjamin.   Leg.- son Benjamin, land adjoining
Howell Branch; son William; wife Janey Holden.
Extx., wife Janey Holden.
D. March 24, 1781   R. May 12, 1785
Wit. James Summerell, George Summerell, Arthur Doles.
Page 113

EXUM, Benjamin.   Of Nottoway Parish.   Leg.- wife Mary;
grandson William Salter; daughter Ann Salter; daughter Mary
Cobb; granddaughter, Ann Salter.
Exs. son-in-law John Cobb and grandson Exum Cobb.
D. March 19, 1785   R. May 12, 1795
Wit. Benjamin Ruffin, Michael Cobb, Silve M ----
Page 115

ATKINSON, Samuel.   Leg.- daughter -----; son Samuel;
son Isham; son Jesse, land adjoining William Whitehead; to
Martha Newsum; son-in-law Jesse Johnson; daughter Mary
Johnson; wife Martha; daughter Phebe Atkinson.
Ex., son Isham Atkinson
D. March 12, 1782   R. May 12, 1785
Wit. Thomas Edmunds, Samuel Edmunds, William Tucker.
Page 115

JONES, Captain James. Inventory. Signed, John Simmons
R. May 12, 1785   Page 116

LUNDY, James. Account current. Signed, James Lundy
and Chislon Morris, Exs. Audited by William Blunt,
Thomas Turner and John Myrick.
D. March --, 1781   R. May 12, 1785   Page 117

BRYANT, Lewis. Estate appraised by Samuel Maget, James
Maget and James Wilkinson. R. June 9, 1785   Page 119

HATFIELD, Josiah. Account Current. Audited by
Nicholas Maget and Samuel Maget. R. June 9, 1785
                                                Page 120

FIGURES, Joseph. Account Current. Audited by
Nicholas Maget and Samuel Maget. R. May 9, 1785
                                                Page 120

CURLE, Thomas. Account current. D. April 11, 1783
Audited by Nicholas Maget and Samuel Maget
R. June 9, 1785   Page 120

VICK, Samuel. Leg.- wife Elizabeth; daughter Peggy;
brother Shadrack Vick; brother Arthur Vick
Exs., brother Shadrack and Nathan English
D. Feb. 11, 1785   R. June 9, 1785
Wit. Drewry Beal, Edmund Ashley   Page 121

HOLDEN, Benjamin. Estate appraised by Boaz G. Summerell,
Robert Sheild, Benjamin Branch   R. July 14, 1785
                                                Page 122

JOYNER, William. Estate appraised by Shadrack Lewis,
Joseph Mountfort, Hardy Pope and Micajah Griffin
R. July 14, 1785   Page 123

HATFIELD, Charles. Account current. 1782. Legacy
paid Mills Hatfield. Audited by Henry Jones and Simmons
Johnson. R. July 14, 1785   Page 123

DREW, Jeremiah. Leg.- wife Mary land adjoining

Dolphin Drew on Angelica Swamp; son James (not of age);
son Newit; son James; daughters, Susanna, Mary, Sarah and
Priscilla Drew.
    Exs., wife Mary and friends William Myrick and Randolph
        Newsum
    D. Nov. 24, 1784   R. July 14, 1785
    Wit. Thomas Ridley, Henry Thorp, Anne Drew

Page 124

RICKS, Richard.   Account current. D. 1779. Paid
Joseph Ricks his legacy; paid Thomas Ricks the legacies
left his sons.   Audited by Joseph Vick and Isaac Williams
    R. July 15, 1785   Page 126

BRIOUNT, John. (Probated as Bryant) Of Nottoway
Parish.   Leg.- son John; wife Mary; daughter Sarah; daughter Mary Bryant.
    Ex., son John Bryant.
    D. July 29, 1783   R. Aug. 11, 1785
    Wit. Benjamin Beal, William Fowler   Page 129

SMITH, Mathew.   Leg.- wife Mourning; my brothers,
Joseph, Arthur, Benjamin and Virgus Smith; father Arthur
Smith.
    Exs., wife and friends Hardy Pope and Lemuel Jones.
    D. Sept. 19, 1783   R. July 4, 1785
    Wit. John Pope, Joseph Wright, William Worrell

Page 130

SHARPE, Richard.   Estate appraised by Micajah Griffin,
Henry Jones, Giles Joyner.   Signed, D. Barron (Barrow ?)
    R. Aug. 11, 1785   Page 130

JOHNSON, Abraham.   Estate appraised by John Barron (?),
Thomas Turner and Thomas Fitzhugh. R. Aug. 11, 1785
                                            Page 131

DREWRY, William Sr.   Account current. Signed,
William Drewry Jr., Ex. Audited by John Blunt and Henry
Smith.   R. Aug. 11, 1785   Page 133

EXUM, Benjamin.   Inventory R. Sept. 8, 1785
                                            Page 134

JOHNSON, Simon Jr.   Estate appraised by Giles Johnson,
John Johnson and John Luter.
  D. June 21, 1785   R. Sept. 8, 1785   Page 135

SALTER, John.   Account current.   Signed, Ann Salter,
Admtx.   Audited by Robert Bailey and Howell Edmunds.
  D. May 1780   R. Sept. 8, 1785   Page 136

JOHNSON, Jacob.   Leg.- wife Anne; son Benjamin Johnson.
Extx. wife Anne Johnson.
  D.   1784   R. Aug. 11, 1785
  Wit. Thomas Edmunds, Sarah Johnson, Mary Johnson
                                              Page 137

REESE, Joseph.   Account current.   Signed John Reese.
Audited by Jesse Cooper and Arthur Applewhite
  R. Sept. 8, 1785   Page 137

SPENCER, Edmund.   Account current.   Audited by John
Whitehead, Samuel Maget and Jesse Vick.   R. Sept. 8, 1785
                                              Page 139

SUMMERELL, John.   Estate appraised by William Stephenson,
Arthur Doles and William Boykin.   R. Sept. 9, 1785
                                              Page 139

CLEMENTS, Thomas, Jr.   Of the Parish of Nottoway. Leg.-
wife Martha; daughter Sally Williamson Clements.
  Exs., Col. Thomas Williamson, Mr. William Urquhart, Col.
       John Hartwell Cocke and Mr. Hartwell Cocke.
  D. July 19, 1784   R. Dec. 9, 1785
  Wit. Jacob Faulcon, Richard Cocke, Arthur Sinclair,
       William Edwards, Hartwell Cocke.   Page 141

THORPE, John.   Estate appraised by John Cobb, Joel
Davis and Phillip Davis.
  D. Oct. 10, 1785   R. Dec. 8, 1785   Page 142

BRANCH, Ogborne.   Inventory. Signed, Moses Branch
  R. Dec. 8, 1785   Page 143

WESTBROOK, Samuel.   Leg.- son Burwell, land adjoining
Jacob Westbrook; wife Mary; son John; daughter Patty
Newsum; grandchildren, the orphans of son Samuel, decd.-
namely, Turner, David, Joel, Samuel and Phebe Westbrook;
children of my daughter Lucy Andrews, decd.; children of
daughter Mary Wommack, decd.
   Exs., sons John and Burwell Westbrook
   D. Nov. 13, 1784   R. Dec. 8, 1785
   Wit. Arthur Foster, Henry Collier Foster, James Foster
                                             Page 143

WESTBROOK, John.   Leg.- wife Lucy; daughter Dorcas at
eighteen; son John Person Westbrook at twenty one; brother
Burwell Westbrook.
   Exs., wife Lucy, Sterling Foster and Thomas Turner
   D. Oct. 31, 1785   R. Dec. 8, 1785
   Wit. Daniel Porter, Ananias Randall, Elizabeth Moore
                                             Page 145

LANCASTER, Joseph.   Inventory.   Signed, Etheldred
and James Lancaster.   R. Dec. 8, 1785   Page 146

HARRIS, Nathan.   Leg.- wife Mary; son Newit at twenty-
one; son John; son Edwin; son Richard; provision for unborn child; daughter Charlotte; daughter Nancy; refers to
brother John's estate.
   Exs., friends Thomas Turner, son of Simon and John
           Barrow
   D. Sept. 15, 1785   R. Dec. 8, 1785
   Wit. John Kindred, Nathan Bryant, Cordall Bynum
                                             Page 148

REESE, Edward.   Account estate.   Signed, Olive Reese,
Admtx.   Audited by Jesse Cooper, John Williamson,
Arthur Applewhite.   R Dec. 8, 1785   Page 149

LANKFORD, Thomas.   Account current.   Signed, Shadrack
Lewis, Ex.   Among items- paid James Chapple his legacy;
paid Elisha Langford ditto; paid Jesse Lankford ditto; paid
Elizabeth Lankford, widow her part of estate; paid Mary
Watkins her legacy; paid Shad. Lewid ditto.
   Audited by Ja. Denson and Joshua Beal.
   R. Dec. 8, 1785   Page 150

BARRETT, William.   Account current.   Audited by

E. Herring and Joseph Mountfort.　R. Dec. 9, 1785

Page 152

SMITH, Mathew.　Estate appraised by Benjamin Crumpler, James Johnson, John Worrell
D. Oct. 12, 1785　　R. Dec. 9, 1785　　Page 153

HARRISON, Amy.　Leg.- daughter Mary Harrison.
Ex., Daniel Harrison.
D. Jan. 10, 1783　　R. Jan. 12, 1786
Wit. James Lundy, Drewry Harris　　Page 155

ATKINSON, Samuel.　Estate appraised by John Powell, John Kindred and Jacam Newsum　R. Jan. 12, 1786
Signed, Isam Atkinson, Ex.　　Page 156

JOYNER, Ann.　Leg.- daughter Elizabeth Drake; son Jethro; son Lawrence; son Eley Eley; grandson William Eley; daughter-in-law Mary Joyner; grandson Josiah Joyner; granddaughter Catie Joyner; granddaughter Nanne Joyner; to Ann, daughter of Lewis Joyner; granddaughter Peggy, daughter of Gethro Joyner; grandsons Gethro and William, sons of William Joyner, decd.
Exs., son Gethro Joyner and Arthur Bowen.
D. May 26, 1785　　R. Jan. 12, 1786
Wit. William Barrett, Giles Joyner, Joshua Miniard, Mary Joyner　　Page 157

JONES, James.　Of St. Luke's Parish.　Leg.- son Nathan land purchased of my brother Abraham P. Jones; son Howell, and wife Ann Jones.
Exs., wife and brother-in-law Jesse Vasser.
D. Jan. 11, 1784　　R. Jan. 12, 1786
Wit. Marget Newsum, John Simmons, Sr., Marget Vasser
Page 159

KINDRED, Samuel.　Estate appraised by Samuel Edmunds, Henry Bittle and John Powell.　R. Jan. 12, 1786

Page 160

JONES, James.　Inventory.　Signed, Ann Jones.
R. Jan. 12, 1786　　Page 161

BARHAM, Thomas. Inventory. Signed, Elizabeth Barham
D. July --, 1784   R. Jan. 12, 1786

Page 162

BRYANT, John. Estate appraised by William Williams,
William Edwards and Richard Beal. Signed, John Bryant, Ex.
D. Aug. --, 1785   R. Jan. 12, 1786   Page 162

WESTBROOK, Samuel, Sr. Estate appraised by John
Claud, Joshua Harris, James Womack
R. Jan. 12, 1786   Page 164

BLUNT, Thomas. Inventory. Signed Edwin Gray and
William Thomas. R. Feb. 19, 1786   Page 166

JOYNER, Ann. Estate appraised by David Denson,
Charles Council and William Denson.
Signed, Arthur Bowing, Ex.   R. Feb. 9, 1786

Page 168

POND, Daniel. Of the Parish of Nottoway. Leg.- wife
Mary; son John; son Richard; daughter Elizabeth Morris;
daughter Mary Wood; son Daniel Pond's surviving children;
son Samuel Pond's surviving children.
Exs., sons John and Richard Pond.
D. Dec. 10, 1785   R. Feb. 9, 1786
Wit. Richard Pond, Elizabeth Pond, Sarah Pond.

Page 170

DOLES, Joseph. Leg.- daughter Olif, wife of Bailey
Branch; daughter Sarah, wife of John Summerell; daughter
Mary, wife of Stephen Andrews; wife Sarah; son Benjamin;
son Arthur, son Jesse.
Exs., wife and son Benjamin Doles.
D. June 8, 1774   R. Feb. 9, 1786
Wit. Arthur Allen, Richard Manning, Thomas Carrel

Page 171

VICK, Samuel. Estate appraised by Drewry Beal, John
Rochelle and Jeremiah Drake. Signed, Shadrack Vick and
Nathan English, Exs.   R. Feb. 5, 1786   Page 172

TURNER, Littleton. Account current. R. Feb. 9, 1786
                                              Page 173

RICKS, Mary. Inventory. Signed, Richard and Robert
Ricks. R. Feb. 9, 1736   Page 174

HARRIS, Carter. Leg.- mother Elizabeth Harris; friend
Anselm Harrison; all my brothers and sisters.
Exs., brothers John and James Harris
D. Nov. 20, 1785   R. March 9, 1786
Wit. William Owins, John Pillar   Page 175

MYRICK, Owen. Leg.- son Henry at twenty one; son Owen
land adjoining Richard Jelks, Hartwell Newsum, John Barham
and my mother's land; wife Fanny; son John; daughter Sarah;
daughter Nancy; daughter Fanny; daughter Lucy Myrick.
Exs., brothers William and Howell Myrick.
D. Jan 6, 1786   R. March 9, 1786
Wit. Thomas Peete, Arthur Applewhite, William Newsum
                              Page 176

THORPE, John. Of the Parish of Nottoway. Leg.-
daughter Susannah; granddaughter Lucy Thorpe; daughter
Hannah Barly (Bailey ?); daughter Sarah Seward; daughter
Mary Holt; son Joseph; daughter Olive Thorpe
Exs., daughter Susannah and friend Richard Renn.
D. Dec. 30, 1784   R. Sept. 8, 1785 (1786 ?)
Wit. William Wrenn, Charles Briggs, Faithy ------
(Richard Wrenn was a Quaker)   Page 177

CHANNEL, James. Account estate. Audited by John Luter
and Henry Smith. Signed, Mary Channel, Admtx.
D. Sept. 14, 1785   R. March 9, 1786   Page 178

BLOW, Richard. Of St Lukes Parish. Leg.- wife Ann
the negroes left in Thomas Blunt's will; son Thomas; son
Benjamin; son James; son Peter; daughter Ann Blow.
Exs., friends John Thomas Blow, Sr, William Thomas and
       Thomas Vaughan
D. Dec. 19, 1785   R. March 9, 1786
Wit. Thomas Scott, William Vaughan, James Millar
                                Page 179

WASHINGTON, George. Account current. Signed, Sarah
Washington, Extx. Among items- paid Joshua Beal, David
Washington's legacy; paid John Darden his wife Martha's

legacy; paid Zebediah Washington's legacy. Audited by
Joseph Scott, Jr. and A. Jones. R. July 12, 1786
Page 180

JOHNSON, John. 1783. Account current. Signed,
Peninah Johnson Admtx. Paid Rebeckah, Ann, Lidia, Alice
and Jordan Johnson. Audited by Joseph Scott, Jr and
A. Jones. R. May 11, 1786   Page 182

JONES, Albridgton. Leg.- son Mathew, land bought of
Charles Binns and that bought of Robert Care, called
Cedar Island in Nansemond County; son William when of age
land purchased of Thomas Holt and Ann his wife and John
Holt; also a tract bought of Richard Williams, adjoining
Josse Johnston, also a tract bought of Farecloth Revell
and negroes purchased of Richard Kirby; son Albridgton
when of age; refers to married children, who have re-
ceived their proportion of his estate.
Ex., son Albridgton Jones.
D. Sept. 22, 1784
Codicil: bequest to Ann Simmons, daughter of Mason
Simmons. D. Dec. 12, 1785
Wit. Mathew Calvert, Arthur Williams, Thomas Wainwright
Wit. (to will) Samuel Calvert, Simon Murfee, Benjamin
     Boal   R. July 19, 1786   Page 183

BLUNT, Thomas. Account current. Signed, Edwin Gray
and William Thomas, Exs. Among items- paid Ann his late
widow; division between four sons, remainder of estate
divided between the seven children.
Audited by Richard Kello and Benjamin Ruffin.
R. July 12, 1786   Page 186

POND, Daniel. Inventory. Signed, John and Richard
Pond, Exs. R. Sept. 14, 1786   Page 187

CARR, John. Leg.- wife Abigail; son Lawrence when of
age; son Dickinson; son Robert; son John Carr.
Exs., wife and friends Elisha Dardon and Lemuel Lawrence
D. May 30, 1786   R. Sept. 14, 1786
Wit. David Edwards, Josse Carr, Charles Hodgpeth
Page 188

POND, Daniel. Account current. Signed John and
Richard Pond, Exs. Audited by Benjamin Ruffin and

Charles Briggs.   R. Oct. 12, 1786   Page 190

MYRICK, Owen.   Estate appraised by Randolph Newsum,
Richard Johnson and Thomas Peete.   R. Oct. 12, 1786
                                                     Page 191

WESTBROOK, William. 1768. Signed, Samuel Westbrook, Adm.
Audited by Thomas Edmunds, Samuel Edmunds and Arthur Foster.
R. Oct. 12, 1786   Page 194

MUNDELL, John.   Of St. Luke's Parish. Leg.- son John;
son Joseph at twenty one; to Hannah, wife of Samuel Ellis;
daughter Lidia; daughter Mary; son William; wife Elizabeth;
daughter Elizabeth, slaves at death of Sarah Harrison,
which she holds by jointure, made her by John Scott, which
descend to me; rest of estate among all my children.
Exs., wife and Mr. John Rogers
D. March 29, 1785   R. Oct. 12, 1786
Wit. John Claud, William Claud, Basill Pain.   Page 195

WILLIAMSON, Francis.   Cash being his proportional part
of his grandmother's estate. Signed, Ned Holleman, Ex.
Audited by Burwell Williamson and Absalom Williamson
D. Jan. 2, 1782   R. Oct. 12, 1786   Page 197

BRYANT, John.   Account current. Paid legacies to
John Bryant, Mary Bryant, Jacob Wheeler and John Joyner.
Signed, John Bryant, Wx.
Audited by Joseph Scott, Jr. and A. Jones.
R. Oct. 12, 1786   Page 198

DREW, Jeremiah.   Account estate. Audited by
Thomas Turner and John Barrow.   R. Oct. 12, 1786
                                              Page 199

WILLIAMS, John.   Appraisel of estate, by Etheldred
Everett, John Bishop and William Hart.
D. July 27, 1786   R. Feb. 8, 1787   Page 200

BAILEY, Benjamin. Estate appraised by Thomas Brock,
Joseph Hart and John Hart. R. Feb. 8, 1787   Page 203

BEAL, Benjamin, Sr.   Leg.- son Benjamin; son John;
wife Rachel; daughter Isbel Beal.
Exs., David Wright and John Beal.
D. March 26, 1786   R. Feb. 8, 1787
Wit. William Williams, Anne Williams.   Page 204

BYNUM, William.   Account current.   Signed, William
Blunt and John Blunt.   Audited by Thomas Turner, James
Lundy and John Rogers.
D. March -, 1786   R. April 12, 1787   Page 205

MOUNTFORT, Thomas.   Of the Parish of Nottoway.   Leg.-
wife Sarah; son Thomas; son Wade, land bought of Jacob
Turner; daughter Francis; daughter Susannah Mountfort.
Exs., wife, brother Wade Mountford and friend David
        Barrow.
D. March 10, 1787   R. April 12, 1787
Wit. Lemuel Lewis, Thomas Camps, Presley Barrett.
(Error in recording ? for this will is signed,
  Joseph Mountfortt)   Page 206

PRETLOW, Thomas. Leg.- wife Mary; nephew Thomas, son
of Joshua Pretlow, decd.; nephew Benjamin, son of Samuel
Pretlow, decd; land purchased of Jordan Thomas in Isle of
Wight County to Joseph the grandson of Joseph Pretlow,
decd.; rest of estate to be divided, one-fifth each to
children of brother Joseph decd; children of brother
Joshua decd.; children of brother Samuel decd.; children
of sister Mary decd.; and brother John Pretlow.
Exs., Thomas Pretlow, Jr. and Robert Ricks.
D. March 14, 1786   R. June 14, 1787
Wit. Jenney Pretlow, Mary Sebrell, Samuel Bailey
                            Page 207

CARY, Ann.   Estate appraised by Jeb. Darden, William
Hart and John Bishop.
D. Dec. 16, 1786   R. June 14, 1787   Page 208

WASHINGTON, Arthur.   Leg. son James, land adjoining
Benjamin Blayley (? Bailey), brother Jesse Washington and
Joseph Phillips; son Arthur land given me by my father;
son Amos land descended to me from my brother Thomas
Washington decd.; daughter Olive Washington.
Exs., friends Joseph Washington and James Gray

D. Sept. 6, 1770   R. June 14, 1787
Wit. J. Gray, Jesse Carrel
Micajah Holleman, qualified as Executor.   Page 209

CRENSHAW, John.   Leg.-wife Elizabeth; children Elijah
and Polly; son Elijah the land adjoining Dr. Browne with
reversion of bequest to Elemuel Darden, son of Benjamin
Darden, decd.
Exs.,   William Thomas, Samuel Maget (of Nich[s]), Jacob
    Turner, William Maget (of Nich[s])
D Dec. 3, 1784   R. Dec. 14, 1786
Wit. Nicholas Maget, Robert Daughtrey   Page 210

DOYEL, Kinchen.   Estate appraised by Jacob
Bradshaw, John Drewry and Charles Powers.
D. March 2, 1787   R. June 14, 1787   Page 211

BRIGGS, Henry.   Account current.   Signed, Charles Briggs
and John T. Blow, Exs.   Paid Peter Fagon for teaching
Charles and Henry Briggs to dance.   Audited by Thomas
Edmunds and William Thomas   R. June 14, 1787
                                          Page 212

WILLIAMS, William.   1784   Signed Samuel Edmunds and
Thomas Vaughan, Exs.   Audited by John T. Blow and William
Thomas.   R. June 14, 1787   Page 217

IVEY, John.   Account estate.   Signed, Joshua Nicholson,
Ex.   Audited by Thomas Edmunds and Michael Warren.
R. July 12, 1787   Page 218

NICHOLSON, Sarah.   Account Current.   1784.   Signed,
Howell Edmunds and Owen Myrick, Exs.   Among items, paid
Fanny Mirick, her proportional part of her mother's estate;
paid the guardian of Fanny, Lucy and Matilda Nicholson,
their proportional part; paid Edwin Seward and Sarah Briggs
their part; paid Sarah and Lucy Edwards their part; paid
Elizabeth Rivers her proportional part of estate.   Audited,
by Thomas Edmunds and Michael Warren.   R. July 12, 1787
                                          Page 219

CARR, John.   Estate appraised by Jordan Williams and

Jacob Darden.   Signed Elisha Darden, Ex.
   R. July 12, 1787   Page 220

   BOWDEN, Robert. Leg.- wife Mary; son Bille; daughter
Elizabeth; daughter Salley; daughter Milley Bowden.
Exs., Thomas Bowdin and John Pursell.
D. Nov. 5, 1783   R. July 12, 1787
Wit. Elias Bowden, John Powell, Rady Bowden   Page 222

   POPE, John. Estate appraised by Stephen Johnson,
John Pledger and John Rawl (Rawls ?) Signed, Joseph
Vick, Adm. D. Dec. 13, 1784   R. July 12, 1787
                                                Page 223

   WILLIAMSON, Thomas. Of the Parish of Nottoway. Leg.-
daughter Elizabeth Clements; grandson John Clements;
grandchildren, Sarah Cocke, Elizabeth Clements, Francis
Clements; daughter Sarah Taylor, land in Northampton
County, N. C., purchased of Anthony Armistead;- her hus-
band, John Taylor Esq.; to Thomas Turner of Nottoway
Parish the land on which he lives.
Exs.,   son-in-law John Taylor, Esq. and friend William
     Urquhart and grandson John Clements.
D. June 24, 1787   R. July 12, 1787
Wit. John Andrews, Mary Urquhart, Samuel Kello
                                                Page 225

   MOUNTFORT, Thomas.   Estate appraised by Thad Lewis,
Micajah Griffin and Joseph Scott, Jr.
   R. July 12, 1787   Page 227

   BEAL, Benjamin. Estate appraised by David Wright,
James Wright and Richard Beal. R. July 12, 1787
                                                Page 228

   JOHNSON, Jacob. Estate appraised by Arthur Foster,
Arthur Turner and Jacob Barnes. R. July 12, 1787
                                                Page 229

   WOMACK, James. Estate appraised by John Claud,
William Claud and Basel Payne.
   D. April 4, 1787   R. Sept. 13, 1787   Page 230

BLUNT, William, Sr. Leg.- wife Mary my land adjoining
John Myrick and James Lundy; refers to David Johnson (?);
son William all my land in Virginia and N. C., reserving
the plantation left wife, also land I have paid Thomas
Person for, which was purchased by John Person; grandson
Jesse Drew when twenty one, reversion to children of my
daughter Ann Wright; daughter Mary; daughter Rebekah Mason.
Daughter Ann the wife of William Wright and Rebekah the
wife of Littleberry Mason. Friends Benjamin Blunt, Thomas
Turner, John Turner and brother John Blunt to divide my
estate.
   Exs., son William Blunt and son-in-law Littleberry Mason
   D. June 3, 1787   R. Sept. 13, 1787
   Wit. John Blunt, Henry Wright, Susannah Cooper
                                                 Page 231

WESTBROOK Helen. Of the Parish of St. Luke. Leg.-
daughter Lucy Linear; daughter Martha Judkins; son Henry.
   Ex., son Henry Westbrook.
   D. March 16, 1786   R. Sept. 13, 1787
   Wit. John Simmons Sr., Samuel Drewry, William Rose
                                                 Page 233

ATKINSON, Hardy. Leg.- wife Ann; son Elias; son Elisha.
   Ex. friend Benjamin Blunt.
   D. Oct. 25, 1783   R. Dec. 13, 1783
   Wit. William Whitehead, Richard Deloach, Samuel Atkinson
                                                 Page 234

WILLIAMS, Benjamin. Leg.- son Ethelbert Carr Williams
at eighteen; wife Mary; son Richard Egbert Williams; daugh-
ter Marian when sixteen.
   EXS., Josiah Tick and wife Mary Williams
   D. June 9, 1787   R. Sept. 13, 1787
   Wit. James Moore, Hardy Johnson, Rebecca Johnson
                                               Page 234

ELLIS, Jeremiah. Leg.- wife Ann; son Jeremiah; son
Henry Ellis
   Exs., wife and sons Jeremiah and Henry Ellis
   D. April 7, 1786   R. Sept. 13, 1787
   Wit. William Thomas, Joel Newsum, Sally Newsum
                                               Page 236

BARNES, Burwell. Account current. Signed, Nathan
Barnes, Adm. Audited by Thomas Edmunds, Samuel Edmunds,
James Wilkinson. R. Sept. 13, 1787   Page 237

WESTBROOK, Miday.   Leg.- sister Ann Westbrook; sister
Rebecca Westbrook
   D. July 23, 1786   R. Oct. 11, 1787
   Wit. John Blake, Hannah Westbrook   Page 237

   MORGAN, Foster. Leg.- brother Jarrett Morgan; refers to
land sold Thomas Turner; James R. Morgan, son of brother
Jarrett Morgan
   Ex. brother Jarrett Morgan.
   D. Feb. 4, 1736   R. Oct. 11, 1787
   Wit. Thomas Turner, Simon Harris, Richard Harrison
                                              Page 238

   JACKSON, Kindred.   Leg.- brother William; Jean Brewer;
brother Isham Jackson
   Exs., uncle John Jackson and friend Newit Edwards
   D. Feb. 23, 1787   R. Oct. 11, 1787
   Wit. Patience Jackson, Mathew Williamson, Charles Joyner
                                              Page 239

   UNDERWOOD, John.   Leg.- son Mathew land patented in
Feb. 14, 1761; son John; daughter Sarah Williams; daughter
Elizabeth Pope; to all my grandchildren.
   Exs., friends Thomas Edmunds and Thomas Vaughan
   D. June 29, 1787   R. Oct. 11, 1787
   Wit. Robert Carr, Patience Pedin, James Pedin
                                              Page 240

   TURNER, Sampson.   Account current. Signed, Clear
Turner.   Audited by Benjamin Ruffin and Thomas Edmunds
   R. Oct. 11, 1787   Page 241

   GEORGE, William.   Signed, Benjamin Spratley, Ex.
Audited by Thomas Holliday and Edmund Pyler
   R. Oct. 11, 1787   Page 242

   JACKSON, Kindred.   Estate appraised by Micajah Edwards,
Charles Birdsong, Bartur (?) Taylor
   R. Dec. 13, 1787   Page 243

   JOHNSON, Simon Jr.   Signed, Simon Johnson, Adm.
Account current.   Balance due widow and orphans.

Audited by James Clark and Henry Jones.   D. 1785
R. Dec. 13, 1787   Page 243

CRUMPLER, Benjamin   Leg.- son John land adjoining John
Mercer and West Tynes; son Benjamin land adjoining
Benjamin Cocke, Mathew Boykin and Valentine Jenkins; son
William; son Arthur land adjoining Thomas Turner; wife
Elizabeth.   Ex., son John Crumpler
   D. March 23, 1785   R. Dec. 13, 1787
   Wit. John Pursell, Joseph Wright, John Wright
                                                  Page 244

APPLEWHITE, Thomas.   Leg.- Arthur Applewhite, son of
Arthur Applewhite; Henry Wills Applewhite, son of John
Applewhite; Mary Jean Carr, daughter of Joshua Carr; George
Thomas Williams, son of Absalom Williams.
   Ex. Absalom Williams
   D. June 26, 1787   R. Dec. 13, 1787   Page 245
   Wit. James Williams

POPE, Joseph.   Account estate.   Signed, William Pope,
Ex.   Audited by Thomas Edmunds, Nathan Barnes and Samuel
Edmunds.   R. Dec. 13, 1787   Page 246

WESTBROOK, Mrs. Helen.   Inventory.   Signed, Henry
Westbrook.   R. Jan. 10, 1788   Page 247

PORCH, James.   Leg.- wife Ann and my six children,
Peggy, Thomas, Peterson, James, Pennington
   Exs., Jesse Cooper, Jesse Wrenn and wife Anna
   D. May 3, 1787   R. Jan. 10, 1788
   Wit. Patience Bass, Lucy Johnson, John Smith, Arthur
        Matthews.
   Exs., refused to qualify, administration granted
        Moses McKenny   Page 248

VASSER, Joseph. Of Parish of Nottoway.   Leg.- son
Etheldred, land adjoining James Calthorpe and Thomas Lane;
son Benjamin; son Joseph; daughter Mary Underwood; son
William Vasser.   Ex., son Etheldred Vasser.
   D. Oct. 30, 1786   R. Jan. 10, 1788
   Wit. John Pond, John H. Pond, Stephenson Pond
                                                  Page 249

JOYNER, Jonas. Inventory. Signed Elisha Darden.
Adm. D. Jan. 8, 1788   R. Feb. 14, 1788
Page 250

POWERS, Charles. Signed, Moses Johnson, Adm. Audited
by Arthur Bowin and Lemuel Jones   R. Feb. 14, 1788
Page 250

WILLIAMS, Henry. Moses Johnson, Adm. D. Jan 21, 1788
Balance due the orphans. Audited by E. Herring, Lemuel
Jones, Sampson Pitman.   R.   April --, 1788   Page 251

BARRETT, William.   Leg.- son William; son Willis my
plantation in Nansemond; rest of my estate among all my
children.   Exs., wife and friend Jordan Denson
   D. Dec. --, 1787   R. Feb. 14, 1788
Wit. Giles Joyner, William Joyner, Henry Jones.
Page 252

VASSER, Joseph. Inventory.   R. Feb., 14, 1788
Page 253

HOLT, Thomas.   Leg.- son Charles; son Thomas; daughter
Amy Martin; daughter Sarah Land; granddaughters Rebecca and
Ann Rawlings; granddaughter Nancy Rawlings; to Polly
Rawlings's daughter Nancy Rawlings at eighteen; granddaugh-
ter Mason Kirby Holt; son Frederick Holt; my security on a
bond to Burrel Bell to be takrn out of son Thomas' portion.
Exs., son Thomas Holt
   D. Dec. 29, 1786   R. April 11, 1738
Wit. Thomas Gilliam, Jr., William Barnes, Joseph Fort.
Thomas Holt, refused extx., and Nathan Holt qualified.
Page 253

UNDERWOOD, John. Estate appraised by John T. Blow,
William Thomas and Samuel Francis.   R. April 11, 1788
Page 254

RUFFIN, Benajmin. Inventory   R. May 8, 1788
Page 256

SUTER, John, Sr. Leg.- son John; son Henry; daughter
Elizabeth; son William (not twenty one) son Arthur)not
twenty one); daughter Rebecca at eighteen; if either should

die without issue, estate given them to be divided between the two brothers or brother and sister, that I had by the same woman.
Exs., son John Suter and Henry Smith.
D. March 31, 1786   R. June 12, 1788
Wit. James Vaughan, Phobe Vaughan, John Holloome (?)
Page 257

DAUGHTRY, Elizabeth. Leg.- friend James Gardner, Jr., all my part of John Daughtry's estate due from David Wright and bonds from David Edwards and William Tallaugh; friend Peter Hines, if he continues at the place called Littletown; friend Elizabeth Boyt; sister Mary Wright.
Ex., friend James Gardner, Jr.
D. May 25, 1785   R. June 12, 1788
Wit. James Gardner, Sr., Mathew Garner, Elisha Darden
Page 259

BAILEY, Mary. Inventory. Signed, Jordan Judkins.
R. July 10, 1788   Page 260

APPLEWHITE, Thomas. Estate appraised by John Whitehead, John Bishop and Thomas Oberry   R. July 10, 1788
Page 261

WILLIAMSON, William. D. Dec. 30, 1785. Estate appraised by William Stephenson, Sr., Arthur Boykin, Solomon Holmes
R. July 10, 1788   Page 260

STEPHENSON, Thomas. Leg.- wife Mary; son Robert; son Willis, son John; daughter Charlotte; son Charles; son Stephen; provision for unborn child; daughter Elizabeth; son Edmund; son Thomas Stephenson.
D. Feb. 15, 1788   R. July 10, 1788
Wit. Samuel Brister, Stephen Summerell, James Summerell
Exs., sons Edmund and Thomas Stephenson   Page 262

DAUGHTRY, Elizabeth. Estate appraised by William Fowler, Holland Darden, Joshua Gardner.
R. Sept. 11, 1788   Page 263

WESTBROOK, Mary. Leg.- granddaughter Beck Westbrook, daughter of Patty Newsum; daughter Patty Newsum
Ex., brother Arthur Foster

D. April 22, 1788   R. Sept. 11, 1788
Wit. William Claud, John Claud, Jr.   Page 265

DREW, Newit. Account current. Ex., Jeremiah Drew.
1775. Signed, William Myrick and Randolph Newsum, Exs. of
Jeremiah Drew. Audited by John Wright, John Simmons, Sr.
Mark Nicholson.   R. May 11, 1788   Page 265

TURNER, Thomas. Leg.- wife Ann; son Thomas; son Amies;
to all my children, Thomas, Amos, Chacy, Holland, Nanny and
Charlotte.
D. Oct. 20, 1785   R. Sept. 11, 1788
Exs., wife and son Thomas Turner.
Wit. Benjamin Crumpler, Arthur Turner, Arthur Crumpler
    Page 267

WILLIAMSON, Robert   Of the Parish of Nottoway. Leg.-
wife Selah; John, son of Jacob Williamson;
Joshua, son of Jacob Williamson; rest of estate to John and
Joshua Williamson and Valentine Jenkins
D. Feb. 27, 1787   R. Sept. 11, 1791
Wit. John Crumpler, Benjamin Crumpler, Arthur Crumpler
Exs. wife Selah and friend John Crumpler.   Page 268

BOYKIN, Simon. Leg.- son Arthur land bought of James
Baisden; son Simon, land bought of Rand's Exs.; daughter
Martha Bridger; grandchildren James, William, Patsy and John
children of Martha Bridger; granddaughters, Sally Williams
Boykin and Charlotte,- daughters of Simon Boykin.
Exs., sons, Arthur and Simon Boykin
D. June 16, 1787   R. Sept. 11, 1788
Wit. Elizabeth Williams, John Summerell, Daniel Herring.
    Page 268

JENKINS, Spencer. Leg.- wife Ann; son Jesse; son
William; daughter Sally Britt; daughter Molly Williford;
daughter Betsey Jenkins.
Exs., wife and sons Jesse and William Jenkins.
D. March 29, 1788   R. Sept. 11, 1788
Wit. Hartwell Cocke, John Andrews   Page 270

CRUMPLER, Benjamin. Inventory. Signed, John Crumpler.
R. Nov. --, 1788   Page 272

BARNES, Burwell. Account current. Signed Nathan Barnes

Adm.   Audited by J. Wilkinson, Samuel Edmunds, Thomas
Edmunds.   R. Sept. 11, 1788   Page 272

SCOTT, James Jordan.   Account current.   Signed, Jordan
Denson, Ex.   1780   Among items, Joseph Scott, paid in full
his share of the estate; paid Miriam Scott her share and as
guardian of the orphans.   Audited by Shadrack Lewis,
A. Jones and Jos (or Jas. ?) Vick
     R. Sept. 11, 1788   Page 273

BROOKS, William.   Of the Parish of St luke.   Leg.-
daughter Ann Dunkin; to Hannah Swett, wife reversion to my
son William Swett; Etheldred Brantley.
Exs., friends, Etheldred Brantley, Henry Bittle, Michael
Warren.
D. May 9, 1788   R. Oct. 9, 1788
Wit. John Powell, William Bittle, Joseph Gurley
                                                         Page 276

PORTER, Thomas, Sr.   Leg.- wife Julan (written later
Julia); son Thomas; son Henry the plantation on which
Britton Porter now lives; son Newit, land on which Richard
Demory now lives; grandson Drury Porter when twenty one the
land on which my son Solomon Porter formerly lived.
Exs., wife and son Thomas Porter
D. Aug. 7, 1785   R. Oct. 9, 1788
Wit. Nathan Bryant, Etheldred Brantley   Page 276

JOYNER, Jethro.   Leg.- wife Martha; to all my children.
Exs., wife and friend Arthur Bowing.
   D. July 6, 1788   R. Oct. 9, 1788
   Wit. Joseph Bradshaw, Mathew Charles, Jethro Charles
                                                         Page 278

WORRELL, Richard.   Leg.- son Shadrack land bought of
Henry Pope; son Richard; son William; son Mathew; son-in-
law Charles Council; daughter Molly; sons-in-law John
Lankford and Joseph Brewer or their heirs are to have no
part of my estate; granddaughter Cherry Worrell; friend
Jethro Charles.
Exs., son-in-law Charles Council and son Shadrack.
D. Sept. 19, 1788   R. Oct. 9, 1788
   Wit. Benjamin Bradshaw, Richard Pope, Mathew Charles
                                                         Page 279

BARNETT, William, Jr.   D. May 1788.   Estate appraised

by Henry Jones, John Bowers and Tamer Joyner.
R. Oct. 9, 1788   Page 280

WILLIAMSON, Thomas. Estate appraised by John Andrews,
John Clayton and Timothy Atkinson.
Signed, John Taylor, Ex.   R. Oct. 9, 1788   Page 282

EDWARDS, William. Account current. 1783. Signed,
Thomas Holladay and John Taylor. R. Oct. 9, 1788
                                                   Page 284

VICK, Mathew, Sr. Leg.- son Simmons; son Kirby; wife
Sarah; daughters Milly Porter, Winny Porter, Lydia Vaughan
and Isabell Vick; son Council; son Mathew; son Joseph; son
Knowell, land bought of Hardy Johnson; son Joel Vick.
Exs., friends Jesse Vick and Shad Lewis.
D. Sept. 26, 1788   R. Oct. 9, 1788
Wit. Joseph Vick, Hardy Johnson, Martha Doyel
Exs., refused and Josiah Vick, qualified   Page 284

WORRELL, Richard. Estate appraised by William Joyner,
Jethro Charles and Martha Charles.
D. Dec. 11, 1788   Page 286

NORFLEET, Cordall. Leg.- Cordall N. Bynum a tract,
formerly belonging to James Fason in Northampton County,
N. C.; reversion to my children, Elizabeth, John (not of
age) and Sarah Norfleet; wife Mary Norfleet
Exs., wife and friends John and James Wilkinson.
D. March 21, 1788   R. Dec. 11, 1788
Wit. Moses Johnson, John Williford, James Wilkinson
                                                   Page 288

MERCER, Robert. Account Current. 1775. Paid
Robert Mercer a portion of his legacy. Signed, Joseph
Holliman, Ex. of Joseph Holleman, who was ex. of Robert
Mercer. Audited by M. Holleman, William Urquhart and
Burwell Williamson. R. Dec. 11, 1788   Page 290

BLUNT, Colonel William. Estate appraised by Chs Ross,
Jos. (or Jas. ?), Turner, Henry Smith. R. Feb. 1788
                                                   Page 291

JOYNER, Jethro. Estate appraised by Hardy Pope, John
Carstarphen, Joseph Bradshaw, Charles Council
R. Feb. 12, 1789   Page 293

POPE, William. Of the Parish of St. Luke; Leg.- sister
Mourning Pope; wife Prudence Pope.
Exs., wife and friend Simon Harris.
D.   1772   R. Feb. 12, 1789
Wit. Henry Pope, Rebecah Harris, William Mackey
                                                Page 294

LUTER, John (Listed in Torrence as Suter)   Estate appraised by John Blunt, Lazarus Cook and James Turner.
R. Feb. 12, 1789   .   Page 294

BLAKE, Thomas. Leg.- son Samuel; son John; son Etheldred;
son James; son Benjamin; son Thomas Blake.
Exs., sons, Samuel, John and Benjamin Blake.
D. Oct. 5, 1784   R. Feb. 12, 1789
Wit. Howell Edmunds, William Vaughan, John Claud, Burwell
      Westbrook.   Page 296

CLEMENTS, Thomas, Jr.   Inventory. Signed by William
Urquhart and Hartwell Cock.
D. Feb. 2, 1785   R. Feb. 14, 1788   Page 298

POPE, Patience. Account current.   Signed Nathan Barnes
Ex.   Audited by Samuel Edmunds and Jesse Cooper.
D. 1779   R. Feb. 12, 1789   Page 298

PARKER, Drury. Of the Parish of St. Luke. Leg.- wife
Milly and her child begotten by me; son Howell; son Richard;
son William; son Thomas land I bought of Benjamin Cooper;
son Edwin; son Frederick; daughter Lewcy; daughter Patty;
daughter Nanny; daughter Luky (or Suky); daughter Tempy;
daughter Judith; daughter Betsey; daughter Polly; son Mathew
    Exs., brother Richard Parker, Jeremiah Drew and Randolph
      Newsum
D. June 13, 1783   R. Feb. 12, 1789
Will signed Drewry Parker.   Page 299

COBB, Samuel. Leg.- son Mathew; son Kinchen, land ad-

joining Demsey Cowper, Will Creswitt's orphans and Dr.
Samuel Browne; son Samuel; son Burgwin, land adjoining
Simon Murfee and Henry Cobb; my brother Henry Cobb and
Simon Vaughan to divide my land; wife Mary Cobb.
D. April 4, 1785   R. Feb. 12, 1789
Exs., sons Mathew and Kinchen Cobb.
Wit. Demsey Cooper, Thomas Pope, Nicholas Cobb.

Page 301

HINES, David.   Leg.- to James Bowing, natural son of
Lucy Bowing; to my sister Mary Hines' child.
D. Dec. 14, 1788   R. Feb. 12, 1789
Wit. Richard Hallcome, John Arrington, Lemuel Stewart,
      Mary Bowing.
John Simmons, qualified as Ex.   Page 303

BOYKIN, William, Sr.   Leg.- daughter Patience Whitehead;
daughter Catherine Harris; son William, residue of estate
to my following children, Brittain, William, Shadrack, Sarah
Williamson , widow and Martha Hough.
Exs., sons William and Shadrack Boykin.
D. Oct. 26, 1786   R. Feb. 12, 1789
Wit. Edward Neal, Stephen Summerell, James Hough.

Page 304

SUMMERELL, John.   Account current.   Signed, Jacob
Turner and Henry B---- , trustees.   Audited by William
Urquhart and H. Holleman.   R. Feb. 12, 1789   Page 305

TUNNELL, Mary.   Estate appraised by James Lundy,
Richard Harrison and Benjamin Harrison.
D. Feb. 1, 1737   R. April 9, 1789   Page 307

STANTON, James.   Leg.- wife Christian; son Sampson; to
my three sons and five daughters, Silvanus, James, Sampson,
Elizabeth, Sarah, Lucy, Mary and Faith Stanton.
Ex., son Sampson Stanton.
D. July 29 , 1762   R. April 9, 1789
Wit. Benjamin Bayley, Joseph Watkins, Nathaniel Briggs,
      Stephen Hamlin, William Hamlin.   Page 307

GRAY, Ann.   Leg.- Lyda Ramsey, with reversion of bequest to brother John Gray; sisters Honour Sharp, Lyda
Ramsey and Mary Blake; Catron Ramsey; Mary Morgan; Thomas

Turner and Mary Smith.
Exs., Henry Ramsey and brother John Gray.
D. Feb.21, 1784   R.   April 9, 1789
Wit. Martha Morgan, Mary Morrell, Priscilla McLemore
         Susanna Turner   Page 308

BROWNE, Benjamin. Estate at "Round Hill" appraised by
Arthur Exum, John H. Pond and Thomas Wood.
   D. April 5, 1788   R. April 10, 1789   Page 309

THORPE, Timothy.   Of St Luke's Parish. Leg.- nephew
John T. Richardson; nephew John, son of William Person,
land on Angelica Swamp; neice Peggy Ridley; neice Patsey
Thorpe; nephew John, son of Phillip Person; mother and the
bequest at her death to be equally divided between John T.
Richardson; John son of Phillip Person; Dorothy Atherton;
Peggy Ridley and Patsey Thorpe.
   Exs., Peterson Thorpe and Phillip Person
   D. Jan. 27, 1776   R.   April 9, 1789
Wit. William Moore, Sarah Atkinson.
Jordan Richardson, qualified as Executor.   Page 310

EVERITT, John.   At a Court held for Nansemond County,
John Lawrence and Etheldred Everitt gave bond for adminis-
tration on his estate, Jan. 14, 1782.   Appraised by Elisha
Dardon, Etheldred Warren and William Hart.   Examined by
Richard Baker, Etheldred Warren and William Hart
   D. Sept. 9, 1782   R. April 9, 1789
Copy produced by Ethel and John Everitt of Nansemond
County to be put on the records of Southampton County
                                                Page 311

JOHNSON, Giles. Of Nottoway Parish.   Leg.- son Stephen;
daughters, Sarah, Mary and Penelope, when twenty one; wife
Mary Johnson.
Exs., friends David Barrow and John Johnson
D. Feb. 19, 1789   R.   June 11, 1789
Wit. James Clark, Simon Johnson, Pottaway Johnson,
         Elizabeth Johnson   Page 313

HOLLEMAN, Josiah John.   Account current. Signed, John
Clayton, Ex.   Paid Solomon Holmes estate, proportion for
clothing for soldiers; paid for Mrs. Holleman's funeral ser-
mon; paid for hiring a soldier.   Audited by William
Urquhart, Solomon Holmes.   R. June 11, 1789   Page 314

JOHNSON, Charity. Estate appraised by Isaac Williams, William Crichlow and James Butts. Signed, Joseph Vick, Ex. R. June 11, 1789   Page 316

HINES, Richard. Estate appraised by Benjamin Stewart, Micajah Ellis and John Kirby. R. July 9, 1789
                                                          Page 317

STANTON, James. Account estate. Signed, Sampson Stanton. Audited by Thomas Edmunds and Jacob Randolph R. July 11, 1789   Page 318

DARDEN, Elisha. Leg.- wife Pheribe; son Jacob; son Jonas (not fourteen), lots in Murfreesborough on the Meherrin River; daughter Salley Barnes, with reversion to her children; daughter Esther; daughter Betsey; daughter Clotilda; daughter Milley Darden.
Exs., son Jacob and friends John Bowers and David Barrow
D. Dec. 3, 1788   R. July 9, 1789
Wit. James Scoggins, Charles Hedgpeth, Polly Glover
                                                          Page 319

HINES, David. Estate appraised by Jesse Arrington, John Simmons, Jr., and Micaj Ellis. Signed, John Simmons R. July 9, 1789   Page 321

VICK, Richard. Of Nottoway Parish. Leg.- wife Elizabeth; brothers Joshua, Giles and Silas; sister Sarah; sister Piety Vick.
Exs., brothers, Joshua and Giles Vick
D. May 1, 1789   R. July 9, 1789
Wit. Jesse Arrington, Martha Arrington, Lucy Arrington
                                                          Page 321

JOYNER, Henry. Estate appraised by Thad Lewis, Benjamin Beale and Joshua Beale. R. July 9, 1789   Page 322

BULLS, Jesse. Estate appraised by Edmond Johnson, Etheldred Pitman and Benjamin Bradshaw.
D. Sept. 25, 1788   R. July 9, 1789   Page 324

JOYNER, Ann. Account current. Signed, Arthur Bowin.

Audited by Daniel Simmons and David Barrow.
R. July 9, 1789   Page 324

WORRELL Richard. Account current. Paid Mary Worrell.
paid Shadrack Worrell, paid Charles Council, paid William
Worrell's guardian, paid Mathew Charles, guardian of Richard
paid John Carstarphan, guardian of Mathew Worrell.
Audited by James Clark, John Johnson, Arthur Bowing.
R. July 9, 1789   Page 325

HARRIS, Amos. Of the Parish of St Luke. Leg.- son
William; son West,- friends Joshua Thorpe, John Applewhite
and Arthur Applewhite to divide the land between them; young-
er sons Amos and Henry, the land on which I and James
Wentworth now live; four daughters, Mary McKenny, Salley,
Rebecca and Patience Harris; my three youngest children,
Amos, Patience and Henry; daughter Ann Horn.
Exs., friend Joshua Thorp, son William Harris and nephew
    Arthur Applewhite.
D. July, 15, 1785   R. Sept. 10, 1789
Wit. Thomas Peete, Joshua Thorpe, William Johnson
                                                   Page 325

VICK, Shadrack. Estate appraised by John Rochelle,
Jeremiah Drake and Drewry Beal
D. Nov. 28, 1788   R. Sept. 11, 1789   Page 327

TURNER, Benjamin. Signed, John Barrow, Thomas Turner
and Nathan Harris. Audited by Thomas Edmunds and Richard
Blow. R. Sept. 11, 1789   Page 328

VICK, Jacob. Leg.- daughter Mourning Jordan, land grant-
ed me by patent in Nov. 3, 1750; wife Patience; son Jacob;
daughter Lydda Vick
Exs., wife and son Jesse Vick
D. Oct. 20, 1784   R. Nov. 11, 1789
Wit. Benjamin Whitfield, Trial Bailey, Martha Bailey
                                                   Page 329

NICHOLSON, Joshua. Account current of Howell Edmunds,
one of his Ex. Cash paid Mary Nicolson, one third part of
the estate. Audited by Ben. Blunt, Mich. Warren and Thomas
Edmunds   R. Oct. 8, 1789
    Account current with John Kirby, one of his Ex. Audited
by Thomas Edmunds and Michael Warren   Page 332

HARRIS, James. Leg.- nephew Joel, son of brother Drewry
Harris, reversion to nephew James, son of brother Moses
Harris; then to Nancy, daughter of brother Drewry Harris
Exs., friends John Rogers and James Lundy
D. June 16, 1789   R. Oct. 8, 1789
Wit. John Rogers, John Tunnell, Martha Britt,
     Priscilla McMore   Page 333

JOHNSON, Abraham. Account current. Signed, Josiah
Johnson, Ex.   Audited by Thomas Turner and John Barrow
R. Oct. 8, 1789   Page 334

GRAY, John. Estate appraised by James Lundy, Samuel
Francis and Benjamin Blunt, Jr.
D. March 14, 1789   R. Oct. 8, 1789   Page 334

NEGRO Tom. (formerly the property of Lemuel Jones).
Leg.- wife Fanney.   Ex., Edmund Johnson
D. Oct. 26, 1787   R. Oct. 8, 1789
Wit. Lemuel Jones   Page 336

MERCER, John. Estate apprised by John Crumpler and
Arthur Boykin. D. Dec. 1788.   R. Oct. 8, 1789
                                             Page 336

BOWDEN, Robert. Estate appraised by John Britt, Joseph
Wright and Lighborn Lowe   R. Oct. 8, 1789   Page 339

COKER, Jonathan. Estate appraised by John Hart, Joseph
Hart and Jesse Washington. Signed, Thomas Clary
D. Feb. 23, 1787   R. Oct. 8, 1789   Page 339

BROOKS, William. Estate appraised by Benj[a] Kindred,
John Powell and William Bittle. Signed, Henry Bittle and
Michael Warren. R. Oct. 8, 1789   Page 341

VICK, Robert. Leg.- son Jordan; to all my children.
Ex., son Jordan Vick
D. Aug. 21, 1788   R. Oct. 8, 1789
Wit. James Bryant, Jesse Vick, John Vick.   Page 342

IVY, John, Sr. Leg.- wife Mary; son Benjamin; son
Phillips; daughter Becky Bass
Exs., sons Benjamin and Phillips Ivy.
D. Jan. 16, 1787   R. Dec. 10, 1789
Wit. John Williamson, Richard Gilliam, John Reese Jr.
Page 343

LUNDY, John. Leg.- son Peyton; son John; wife Edith;
daughter Nancy Rivers; daughter Elizabeth; daughter Pattey;
daughter Clarimon Holt Lundy.
Exs., friends Buckner Wittemore, John Rogers and wife
    Edith Lundy
D. July 28, 1789   R. Dec. 10, 1789
Wit. John Rogers, John Berryman, Jr., David Johnson
Page 344

TYLER, Jeremiah. Of St. Luke's Parish. Leg.- (refers
to land bought of William Jarrell, which he is to give him
a title to at twenty one); wife Elizabeth; son William
Jarrell Tyler, when of age; daughter Martha Kinchen Tyler;
provision for unborn child.
Exs., wife and father Edmund Tyler
D. Feb. 4, 1789   R. Dec. 10, 1789
Wit. John T. Blow, Sr., Robert Wellons, William Blow
Page 345

EDWARDS, John. Leg.- son Micajah; son Newit, land adjoining William Simmons, Emslus Derring, William Jackson
and Mathew Williamson; son Joel land adjoining John Wood,
Benjamin Whitfield, Robert Furgunson, Apaphroditus Williams
and Ephraim Williams; son James, land adjoining James Barnes
and Jordan Vick; son West, land adjoining Newit Edwards;
daughter Mary Whitfield; grandson George Whitfield; daughter
Elizabeth Everit; daughter Sally Birdsong; wife Anne Edwards
Exs. sons Micajah and Newit Edwards.
D. June 30, 1789   R. Dec. 10, 1789
Wit. James Foster, William Simmons, John Cook
Page 346

HINES, Howell. Leg.- wife Ann; children Dolly C.; Sarah
Elizabeth C. Hines.
Exs., Captain Josiah Vick and Mr. James Chappell
D. Nov. 4, 1789   R. Dec. 10, 1789
Wit. Nath Davis, Bolding Hines, Ann Derby   Page 349

JENKINS, Spencer. Estate appraised by Timothy Atkinson,
Jacob Turner and John Andrews   R. Dec. 10, 1789
Page 350

BRITT, Thomas. D. July 1789. Estate appraised by
John Andrews, Simon Boykin and John Pursell.
D. Dec. 10, 1789   Page 352

VICK, Robert D. 1789   Estate appraised by Nathan
Barnes, Jacob Williams and Charles Birdsong.
R. Dec. 11, 1789   Page 352

WILLIAMS, Elias. Leg.- nephew Mathew Peirce; nephew
Nicholas Williams; nephew Elias Williams; brother John
Williams, rest of estate to all my brothers and sisters.
Ex., friend Rice B. Peirce
D. Jan. 10, 1781   R.
Wit. Nicholas Williams, Benjamin Williams   Page 353

MURFEE, Richard, Sr. Leg.- wife Lucy; son Simon; son
William; daughter Molly; daughter Lucy Daughtrey; daughters
Celia, Sally and Nancy; grandson Francis Murfee; daughter
Elizabeth Williams
Exs., sons Simon and William Murfee
D. Nov. 21, 1738   R. Dec. 11, 1789
Wit. Josiah Vick, Wilson Davis   Page 354

KELLO, Richard. Leg.- daughter Mary Cocke; son Samuel;
son Richard Kello
Ex., son Samuel Kello
D. May 25, 1789   R. Jan. 14, 1790
Wit. Benjamin Parker, Richard Cocke, Jr.   Page 355

BROWN, Jean. Leg.- sister Elizabeth Day; Benjamin son
of Joshua Hines and his wife Lucy; Henry Hines son of afore-
said; to William Foster the grandfather of Benjamin and
Henry Hines; Lucy Hines, daughter of William Foster
Ex., Col. Samuel Kello
D. Sept. 5, 1789   R. Jan. 14, 1790
Wit. Thomas Lain, Micah Ellis   Page 356

DREWRY, Samuel. Leg.- son Samuel, land adjoining Joel
Woods and William Crichlow; daughter Mary Salter; grand-
daughter Katherine Johnson when eighteen; daughter Ann
Simmons; wife Elizabeth; son James; son Humphrey; son
Joseph when twenty one.

Exs., son Samuel and son-in-law Spratley Simmons.
D. Feb. 4, 1789   R. Jan. 10, 1790
Wit. Edwin Gray, Joel Wood, Humphrey Drewry   Page 357

POPE, Henry. Estate appraised by John T. Blow, Richard
Blow and Benjamin Edwards.   R. Feb. 11, 1790
                                                Page 359

DARDEN, Elisha. Inventory. Signed, Jacob Darden, Jr.
R. April 8, 1790   Page 360

CARR. John. Account current. D. 1786   Signed, Elisha
Darden, Ex.   Audited by Jacob Darden, Sr., Holland Darden
and Henry Gardner.   R. Feb. 8, 1790   Page 362

JOYNER, Jonas.   Account current. Signed, Elisha Darden
Adm.   D. 1788 Audited by Jacob Darden, Sr., Holland
Darden and Henry Gardner.   R. Feb. 8, 1790   Page 364

COBB, Samuel. Estate appraised by Abraham Mitchel,
Mathew Wills and Thomas Lawrence.   Signed, Mathew Cobb
and Kinchen Cobb, Exs.   R. April 8, 1790   Page 365

THORPE, Moses. Leg.- wife; son John, with reversion to
his son Aaron; daughter Elizabeth Harris; daughter Sarah
Briggs Thorpe, with reversion of bequest to Moses Harris'
two sons; son John my land in N. C. and a negro bought of
Benjamin Barham; to Jordin son of Tabitha Bass
Exs.,   son John, Lewis Thorpe and John Williamson
D. Dec. 1, 1786   R. June 10, 1790
Wit. Wike Ivey, John Williamson
Codicil witnessed by John Williamson and Charles Southward
                                              Page 366

JOHNSON, Ralls.   D. Feb. 16, 1789   Estate appraised
by James Johnson, Arthur Bowing, Joseph Bradshaw
R. June 10, 1789   Page 369

BRADSHAW, Arthur. Account current. Signed, Thomas
Bradshaw.   Among items- paid his quota for clothing for a
soldier. Audited by Dc Barrow, Hardy Pope
D. April 14, 1790   R. June 10, 1790
                                              Page 370

DREWRY, Samuel, Sr.   Inventory.   R. July 8, 1790
Page 371

BRITT, Edward, Sr.   Leg.- son Edward; son Johnson;
daughter Patience Williams; son-in-law Arthur Holleman;
daughter Mary Allen; wife Sarah; daughter Sarah Summerell;
daughter Caty; daughter Betsey Britt.
Exs., sons Edward and Johnson Britt
D. July 26, 1789   R. July 8, 1790
Wit. A. Holleman, John Williamson, John Clayton
Page 372

JOHNSON, Giles.   Estate appraised by James Clark, Henry
Jones and Hardy Pope.   R. July 8, 1790   Page 373

WILLIAMS, Benjamin. Inventory.   Signed, J^O. Vick and
Mary Williams, Exs.   R. July 9, 1790   Page 375

CALVERT, Christopher. Estate appraised by Joseph Scott,Jr.
William Edwards and Joshua Beal.
D. July 11, 1789   R. Sept. 9, 1790   Page 377

COKER, Henry. Leg.- daughter-in-law Mary, now the widow
of my son Jonathan, with reversion to my grandson Jonathan;
grandson James, son of Jonathan; wife Sarah; grandson Wilson
Coker; daughter Holland; daughter Mary Coker
Exs., Jordan Judkins and Joshua Bailey
D. Aug. 14, 1789   R. Oct. 14, 1790
Wit. Thomas Phillips, Absolum Bailey, Thomas Hart
Page 379

GRAY, Edwin. Leg. son Joseph, land adjoining Charles
Briggs and John Cobb; son Thomas the land I bought of
Anthony Calthorpe; son Edwin; son Henry land adjoining
Benjamin Ruffin; daughter Mary; brother James Gray the land
we purchased together of Wills Cowper in Nansemond Co.; wife.
Exs., brother James; sons Joseph, Thomas and Edwin and
        friend Daniel Simmons.
Provision for education of young son Henry
D. Sept. 3, 1788   R. June 1790
Wit. Benjamin Ruffin, Benjamin Ruffin, Jr. Samuel Kello
Page 380

LEWIS, Benjamin.   Parish of St. Luke.   Leg.- wife Mary

son Zebulon land adjoining Joshua Thorp; son Benjamin land bought of Mial Harris; daughter Elizabeth Butts; daughter Fanny Butts; daughter Nanny Turner with reversion to her children Elizabeth and Edwin Turner; daughter Sally Rochell with reversion to her children; daughter Becky; daughter Jenny Lewis.

Exs., wife, son Zebulon and son-in-law Benjamin Butts.
D. Aug. 13, 1788   R. Oct. 14, 1790
Wit. Etheldred Taylor, James McNiel, Henry Westbooke, John Simmons, Sr.   Page 383

MOORE, Thomas. Account current. Signed Sarah and James Moore and Richard Blow.   D. Jan. 1773   Audited by Joseph Vick, John T. Blow and George Gurley.   R. Oct. 14, 1790
                                                        Page 385

SLADE, Samuel. Leg.- wife Mary; son William; son Jethro; son Joshua; rest of my estate to my seven youngest children.
Ex., Samuel Slade
D. Nov. 21, 1789   R. Oct. 14, 1790
Wit. Henry Lane, William Slade, Jethro Slade.   Page 389

WILLIAMSON, Robert. Estate appraised by Leighborn Lowe, (Love ?); Joseph Wright and Jacob Turner.
R. Oct. 14, 1790   Page 391

COUNCIL, James. Leg.- wife Elizabeth; daughter Elizabeth Turner, land adjoining Richard Worrel, Joshua Turner and John Turner; son Charles; daughter Anne Sandiford
Exs., son Charles Council and Hardy Pope
D. Oct. 8, 1785   R. Oct. 15, 1790
Wit. Lawrence Joyner, Rebeckah Joyner and Mary Bowing.
                                                        Page 391
COUNCIL, James   Inventory. D. Nov. 13, 1790 Page 392

WELLENS, John. Leg.- son William; son Benjamin; wife Mary; daughter Rebecca Exum and her husband Robert Exum
Exs., sons William and Benjamin Wellens
D. July 16, 1784   R. Dec. 10, 1790
Wit. Thomas Lain, John Wellens, Lucretia Wellens
                                                        Page 393

STEPHENSON, Thomas, Sr.   Estate appraised by Arthur Boykin, John Clayton, Sr. and Arthur Doles   Signed, Thomas Stephenson
D. Dec. 10, 1790   Page 394

READ, John. Leg.- daughter Patience Swet; son Cordall; wife Sarah; children, - Tabitah Byrd, Priscills Byrd; Mason Read; Sally Read.
Exs., friend Willie Francis and James Swet.
D. Aug. 23, 1790   R. Dec. 10, 1790
Wit. Cordall Francis, Hardy Hunt   Page 395

GRIFFIN, Benjamin. Account current. Signed, Micajah Griffin, Ex. Audited by D. C. Barrow, Hardy Pope, Edmund Tyler, Lem. Jones, S. Kello   Page 396

HART, Drewry. Leg.- brother John Hart; to John Webb son of Nathaniel Land; to Elizabeth Daughtrey Carr, daughter of Lawrence Carr.
Exs., brother John Hart and Nathaniel Land
D. Oct. 4, 1790   R. Jan. 10, 1791
Wit. Nanney Ireland, James Foster   Page 397

Edwards, John. Inventory. Signed Micajah and Newit Edwards.   R. Jan. 10, 1791   Page 398

TAYLOR, James. Account current. Audited by John Wright, James McNeil and Mark Nicholson.
R. Jan. 10, 1791   Page 401

WELLENS, John. Inventory. Signed, William and Benjamin Wellons. R. Feb. 10, 1791.   Page 402

WILLIAMSON, Celah. Inventory. Signed, John Crumpler, Adm.   D. Dec. 16, 1790   R. Feb. 10, 1791   Page 402

TURNER, Thomas. Estate appraised by Ledbetter Lowe. Levi Lane and Joseph Wright. Signed, Ann Turner Extx.
R. Feb. 10, 1791   Page 403

UNDERWOOD, John. Account current. Signed Thomas Edmunds and Thomas Vaughan, Exs.   Among items, paid Mathew Underwood his part of estate; paid the two chil-

dren their part of their grandfather's estate; paid John
Underwood his part of the estate, paid his eight children
their part of their grandfather's estate; paid Sally Williams
her part of the estate, paid her five children their part of
their grandfather's estate; paid Thomas Pope his part of estate; paid Thomas Pope, Sally Pope's part of her grandfather's estate; paid Henson Pope his part of his grandfather's
estate; paid William Pope, guardian of John Pope.
Audited by Arthur Foster and John T. Blow.
R. Feb. 10, 1791   Page 404

JOHNSON, Giles. Account current. Signed, David Barrow
and John Johnson, Exs. Paid the widow her proportion; paid
Benjamin Johnson, ditto; Sarah Johnson, same; reserved money
for schooling the orphan Penelope Johnson.
Audited by Edmund Tyler, David Barrow and Arthur Foster
R. Feb. 10, 1791   Page 405

BLOW, Richard. Estate appraised by Arthur Foster, Thomas
Edmunds and Samuel Edmunds.
D. March 15, 1786   R. Feb. 10, 1791   Page 406

PERSON, Philip. Estate appraised by Richard Harrison,
Richard Clifton and Benjamin Harrison. R. Feb. 10, 1791
                                                       Page 409

EVANS, Hannah. Of St. Luke's Parish. Leg.- grandson
William Evans; granddaughter Hannah Thompson Evans; grandson
Benjamin Moseley Evans; daughter Mary Pope; daughter Martha
Pope. Ex., John T. Blow.
D. June 27, 1785   R. Feb. 10, 1791
Wit. George Blow, Henry Briggs   Page 410

BRADSHAW, Martha. Leg.- daughter Penelipa Griffin;
daughter Rody; to Joseph Bradshaw.
Ex., Edward Griffin.
D. Oct. 8, 1786   R. Feb. 11, 1791
Wit. Arthur Turner, Joshua Whitney, Chasey Bradshaw
                                                       Page 411

HOWELL, Hartwell. Account current. Signed, Elizabeth
Howell, Admtx. Audited by Thomas Vaughan and Thomas Edmunds
R. Feb. 11, 1791   Page 412

WILLIAMS, Nicholas. Leg.- son Cowper; son John; daughter Lucy Joyner's negro not to be liable for debts of Lewis Joyner or any man she might hereafter marry; daughter Mary Parker; daughter Martha Buxton; daughter Ann Pitt, profits of my land in N. C., with reversion to her eldest son; daughter Elizabeth Peirce.
Exs., sons Cowper and John Williams.
D. March 4, 1791   R. April 14, 1791
Wit. J. Vick, John Davis, William Williams.   Page 413

IVEY, Henry. Leg.- wife Winney; son Adam when twenty one land adjoining Joshua Thorpe; son Peterson; son Wyke; daughter Charlotte Knight; daughter Elizabeth Newsum; daughter Sally; daughter Rhode Ivey
Exs., sons Peterson and Adam Ivey and John Williamson.
D. Jan. 26, 1791   R. April 14, 1791
Wit. Howell Harris, Joseph T. Thorpe, John Williamson
Page 416

LUNDY, John. Estate appraised by Fran^s Branch, Richard Gilliam and James Lundy   R. April 15, 1791   Page 418

HART, Drewry. Estate appraised by Samuel Maget, Andrew Cheatham and John Gilliam.   R. April 15, 1791
Page 419

MANN, Sarah. Leg.- Ephraim Bryant; brother Jonas ----
Ex., brother James Bryant.
D. March 8, 1791   R. April 15, 1791
Wit. Thomas Channell, Polly Pope, Winee Pope   Page 420

WILLIAMS, Isaac. Estate appraised by Jo. Vick, Demcy Cotton and Lewis Joyner.
D. Dec. 22, 1788   R. April 15, 1791   Page 421

THORPE, Captain Timothy. Account current with Timothy Thorpe, Jr. decd._ Paid William Andrews in right of his wife Maney; paid John Simmons in right of his wife Lucy; paid Dr. Annanias Randal in right of his wife Temperance; paid Martha Ridley; paid Jordan Richardson in right of his wife Silvia.   Signed, Jordan Richardson.
Audited by A. Madele and John Goodwyn.
R. April 15, 1791   Page 423

POPE, Hardy. Leg.- wife Mary, items bought of Joseph
Scott; Molly Pope, widow of my son Henry Pope; son Hardy,
when twenty one; granddaughter Nancy Pope; friend David
Barrow; trustees of will, Daniel Simmons, Shadrack Lewis,
John Johnson and James Clark
 Exs., wife and David Barrow. D. Nov. 30, 1789
Wit. Alex Sanders, Joseph Harris, James Clark
 Codicil: If son Hardy or granddaughter Nancy Pope die with-
out issue, reversion to my near kinsman, John son of Joseph
Pope and David Barrow to be used toward the support of the
Gospel of Christ.
D. Nov. 30, 1789 R. April 15, 1791
Wit. Joseph Harris, James Clark   Page 425

JONES, Martha. Account current with Jordin Richardson,
Adm. of the estate of Timothy Thorpe, Ex. of said Martha.
D. 1781 Audited by Alex Madole (or Madell), John Goodwyn
R. May 15, 1792   Page 426

TAYLOR, Charlotte. Leg.- my mother Temperance all my por-
tion of my fator's estate
 Extx., mother Temperance Taylor
D. Nov. 30, 1790 R. April 15, 1791
Wit. Robert Taylor, John Taylor   Page 427

HARRIS, Henry. Of the Parish of St. Luke. Leg.- daughter
Nancy with reversion to the children of my four brothers,
Benjamin, Abraham, Meshaland and Hardy Harris
 Exs., friends Lawrence and Henry Smith
D. Feb. 6, 1791 R. June 9, 1791
Wit. William Drewry, Elizabeth Harris, Coalia Council
            Page 428

PARKER, Drewry. Estate appraised by William Chambless,
William Myrick and Joel Newsum.
D. March 3, 1789 R. June 9, 1791   Page 428
Account current. Signed, Randolph Newsum, Ex.
Audited by Edward Fisher and John Taylor, Jr.
R. June 9, 1791   Page 430

TURNER, Pass. Leg.- wife Ann; all my children, Polly,
Nathan, Rebeckah, John, James and Josiah
 EXS., friends David Barrow and John Johnston.
D. March 23, 1791 R. June 9, 1791
Wit. Samuel Johnson, Samuel Corbett, John Luter,
   Pettaway Johnson   Page 431

BARHAM, Charles. Leg.- son Robert; granddaughter Milley Barham; daughter Mary Harris; daughter Lucy Deloach; Drewry Parker with reversion to all the children he had by my daughter Elizabeth; grandson Joel Newsum; grandson Barham Newsum; son James Barham
  Exs., son James and grandson Joel Barham
  D. Sept. 17, 1783   R. June 9, 1791
  Wit. James Battle, Moses Foster, Elizabeth Holding,
     John Simmons Sr.
  Edward Fisher qualified as Ex. James Barham being
dead and the other refusing   Page 432

BARHAM, James. Of the Parish of St. Luke. Leg.- son Joel; daughter Martha Harris; daughter Sarah Fisher; daugh- Rebecca Holleman; son James; daughter Mary; daughter Susanna Meacom; son Judkins; son Samuel; son Timothy Thorpe Barham; son John; granddaughter Phebey Barham, daughter of Judkins.
  Exs., sons Joel, James and Samuel Barham and sons-in-law
     Edward Fisher and William Holleman.
  D. Feb. 26, 1791   R. June 9, 1792
  Wit. John Simmons, Jr., William Butts,
Edward Fisher qualified as Ex.   Page 434

FORT, John. Estate appraised by John Taylor and Mark Nicholson. R. June 9, 1791   Page 435

TAYLOR, Etheldred. Leg.- wife Elizabeth; daughter Elizabeth when eighteen.
  Exs., brother John Taylor and my relative Mr. Charles
     Taylor.
  D. Feb. 20, 1791
  Wit. Edward Fisher, William Ellis, Henry Taylor
  Codicil; to Ann Milton, alias Ann Bowser, with reversion of bequest to Patsey Milton, so called daughter of Ann Milton, Jr.
  Wit. Thomas Ridley, William Wright, William Newsum,
     R. July 14, 1791
  Exs., refused to qualify and executorship was granted
     John Taylor, Jr.   Page 437

WRIGHT, David. Estate appraised by Joseph Scott, Jr., Richard Beal and Joshua Beal.
  D. Feb. 19, 1791   R. July 14, 1791   Page 439

PORCH, James. Estate appraised by Jesse Cooper, William

Harris and Lewis Harris.   D. Feb. 6, 1788
   R. July 14, 1791   Page 441

   POPE, Henry. Account current. Signed Mary Pope, Admtx.
Audited by John Thomas Blow and William Crichlow
   R. July 14, 1791   Page 442

   FOSTER, William. Leg.- wife Edith; son John; son William;
daughter Nancey; daughter Rebecca; unborn child.
   Exs., Robert Goodwyn, Micajah Ellis and John Simmons, Sr.
   D. Jan. 20, 1791   R. July 15, 1791
   Wit. John Simmons, Jr. Miles Cary, Jesse Arrington, Thomas
         Hollcome, Micajah Ellis.
         Robert Goodwyn qualified.   Page 443

   HARRIS, Hardy. Estate appraised by John Blunt, James
Turner and Edmund Turner.
   D. Dec. 21, 1790   R. Sept. 8, 1791   Page 444

   FERGUSON, Robert. Estate appraised by James Maget, Micajah
Edwards and Saml. Maget.
   D. Sept. 1790   R. Sept. 8, 1791   Page 446

   THORP, Moses. Estate appraised by J. Harris and George
Ivey.   R. Sept. 8, 1791   Page 447

   PORCH, James . Account current. Signed, Moses McKenny
Audited by Jesse Cooper and Arthur Applewhite.
   R. Oct. 13, 1791   Page 447

   IVEY, John. Estate appraised by Moses Thorp, Rich'd
Gilliam and James Lundy
   D. Jan 8, 1790   R. Oct. 13, 1791   Page 450

   CALTHORP, John. Leg.- son John; son James; son Henry;
son Nowell.
   D. April 14, 1783   R. Oct. 13, 1791
   Wit. Patience Turner, Thomas Turner, Jordan Bass
                                                  Page 451

DAVIS, Thomas. Leg.- uncle Henry Davis, Sr., two negro girls in Northampton County, N. J., if he will bring them to Virginia and manumit them at age of twenty one; brothers Etheldred and James Davis
Ex. uncle Henry Davis.
Wit. Joel Davis, Philip Davis
D.   R. Oct. 13, 1791   Page 452

SPEED, Robert. Estate appraised by James Edwards, Henry Briggs and Richard Johnson.
D. Dec. 14, 1790   R. Oct. 13, 1791   Page 453

TURNER, Henry. Parish of St. Luke. Leg.- son Jacob, land adjoining Capt. Nicholas Maget and Arthur Whitehead; daughter Mary Parker; granddaughter Patience Turner; son Jacob and his children now living, Henry, Etheldred, Rebecca, Patience, Milly, Susannah and William Turner.
Ex., son Jacob Turner.
D. Dec. 15, 1789   Proved Sept. 9, 1790   R. Oct. 13, 1791
Wit. John Whitehead, James Maget, Elizabeth Turner
                                          Page 454

BENNETT, John. Leg.- daughter Mary Rose; daughter Martha; daughter Holland Screws; son William; son Samuel; son Moses; son Lemuel and son Elias; daughter Rebeccah
D. March 21, 1788   Oct. 13, 1791
Wit Richard Doyel, Henry Bools; Lem'l. Jones.   Page 455
Exs., son William and friend Edmund Johnson

POPE, Hardy. Estate appraised by Henry Jones, Mathew Charles and John Johnson. Signed, Mary Pope Extx.
D. Sept. 20, 1791   R. Oct. 13, 1791   Page 456

WILLIAMS, Epaphroditus. Leg.- son Ephraim land being part of Robert Bryants' patent, adjoining Jacob Williams, Joel Edwards, Robert Fargason and Edmond Barret, Sr.; son Jacob; daughter Sarah Bryant; daughter Elizabeth Worrell.
Exs., sons Ephraim and Jacob Williams.
D. April 8, 1791   R. Dec. 8, 1791
Wit. Lewis Bryant, Joel Edwards.   Page 459

MARTIN, James. Leg.- wife Amey; son Kinchen; daughter Lucy Gurley. Exs., wife and son-in-law George Gurley.
D. Oct. 18, 1791   R. Dec. 8, 1791
Wit. George Gurley, Thomas Newsum, Jr., John Newsum
                                          Page 460

BRADSHAW, Benjamin. Estate appraised by Arthur Bowing, Richard Doyel and John Worrell. Signed Jacob Bradshaw and Benjamin Bradshaw. R. Feb. 9, 1792 Page 461

THORPE, Joshua. Leg.- nephew Lewis, son of John Thorpe; sister Elizabeth Pritchard; neice Lucy, sister of aforesaid Lewis Thorpe. Ex., nephew Lewis Thorpe.
D. Jan. 22, 1792 R. Feb. 9, 1792
Wit. Charles Maclemore, Adam Ivey, L. Mason, Fred'k Horn
Page 462

SIMMONS, John. Estate appraised by Jos. Vick, Benj. Kerby and Rice B. Pierce. R. Feb. 9, 1792 Page 463

RICKS, Ann. Estate appraised by John Davis, Jos. Vick, and Lem'l Hart. D. Nov. 19, 1791 R. Feb. 9, 1792
Page 464

SIMMONS, John. Account current. Signed, Daniel Simmons. Audited by Robert Taylor and Daniel Butts.
D. Nov. 9, 1792 R. Feb. 9, 1792 Page 467

BRITT, John. Leg.- son William; daughter Tamer; four youngest sons Benjamin, Joseph, Beasent and Arianton; wife Priscilla; my seven children - Sarah Johnson, Mary and above named sons.
Exs., Benjamin Britt and John Crumpler
D. Feb. 8, 1786 P. Jan 8, 1791 R. Feb. 9, 1792
Wit. John Pursell, Edmund Crumpler, William Crumpler
Brittain Britt qualified, Exs., refusing. Page 468

DRAPER, Thomas. Leg.- daughter Mourning; son Jesse; son Jeremiah, land bought of John Worrel; son Ephraim; son William; son Thomas; daughter Sarah Jordan.
D. 19th of 4 mo. 1788 Ex., son Jesse Draper
Wit. Thomas Ricks, Robert Ricks and Richard Ricks
Codicil. - son Ephraim Draper also to be an Ex.
D. 11th of 2 mo.
Wit. Lemuel Jones. R. Feb. 9, 1792 Page 470

TURNER, Henry. Of the Parish of St. Luke. Leg.- son John; daughter Elizabeth Bittle Turner when twenty one or married; son Benjamin; unborn child; my store in Northampton

N. C., known as William and Henry Turner and Company, to be
continued if he choses, with my son John living with him and
my son to inherit my part; son Benjamin my lot in Princetown
Exs., friend William Turner and Will Turner the son of
Benjamin to manage the store in this place.
D. Dec. 13, 1791   R. March 8, 1792
Wit. Nicholas Warren, Nathaniel Edwards, William Bittle
Page 472

DARDEN, Holland. Leg.- wife Pheribe; son Jacob; son
Jonathan; son James; son John; wife to have all of the es-
tate that fell to her from her first husband; son John,
land adjoining Robert Fisher; son Holland; daughter Anne;
daughter Edith; son Jonah; daughter Julia; my mother to
have my part of my father's estate.
Exs., sons Jacob, Jonathan and James Darden and friend
John McCabe. D. Feb. 23, 1792   R. March 8, 1792
W. James Carr, John Birdsong, Robert H. Disher
Son Jonathan land adjoining Joshua Gardner.   Page 474

THOMAS, Henry. Estate appraised by Benjamin Blunt, Jr.
Henry Harrison and Cordey Clifton
D. April 17, 1789   R. March 13, 1792   Page 477

GRAY, Anna. Estate appraised by Thomas Turner, John
Mundell and Benjamin Blunt, Jr.
D. April 20, 1789   R. March 13, 1792   Page 478

HILL, Reubin. Estate appraised by Samuel Maget, Newit
Edwards and Etheldred Everett.   Page 479
D. 1789   R. May 10, 1792

HOLT, Thomas. Account current. Signed, Nathan Holt.
Audited by John Judkins and Ribert Andrews.
R. May 10, 1792   Page 480

VICK, William. Account current. Signed, Lewis and
Pilgrim Vick, Exs. Audited by John T. Blow and Thomas
Edmunds. D. 1784   R. May 10, 1792   Page 481

DAVIS, Thomas. Inventory. Signed, Henry Davis, Ex.
D. May 28, 1792.   R. June 14, 1792   Page 482

DRAPER, Thomas.   Signed, Ephraim Draper, Ex.   Appraised
by Micajah Griffin, Charles Council and William Wills.
D. June 14, 1792   Page 483

ELLIS, Hezekiah. Estate appraised by Randolph Newsum,
R. Clements and Joel Newsum.
D. Jan. 20, 1791   R. June 14, 1792   Page 484

HART, John. Of the Parish of Nottoway. Leg.- wife Jane;
son Samuel; daughter Rebecca; son John; son Charles; son
Lemuel ; son Henry Hart.
Exs., sons Henry and Samuel Hart.
D. March 12, 1792   R. June 14, 1792
Wit. Jesse Womble, Thomas Washington, Jesse Washington
                                               Page 485

BARNES, Peninah.   Estate appraised by Lemuel Hart, George
Washington and David Washington. Signed, Jacob Barnes, Adm.
D. March 3, 1791   R. June 14, 1792   Page 486

BENNETT, William.   Estate appraised by John T. Blow,
William Cricklow, Benjamin Edwards.   R. June 14, 1792
                                               Page 487

TYLER, Jeremiah.   Estate appraised by John T. Blow,
Benjamin Edwards and Amos Stephenson.
D. Dec. 16, 1789   R. June 14, 1792   Page 489

DAVIS, Thomas.   Account current. Signed, Henry Davis.
Audited by Thomas Edmunds and John Taylor
R. June 14, 1792   Page 491

TAYLOR, Etheldred. Estate appraised. (not signed)
D. Aug. 10, 1791   R. June 14, 1792   Page 492

VICK, Mathew, Sr.   Estate appraised by John Johnson,
William Cricklow and James Butts. Signed, Joseph Vick.
D. Dec. 6, 1788   R. June 15, 1792   Page 494

HINES, Howell.   Estate appraised by Abraham Mitchell,

William Edwards and Mathew Wills. Signed, Josiah Vick, Ex.
R. June 15, 1792   Page 496

HUTCHINGS, Daniel. Of Norfolk Borough. Leg.- wife
Elizabeth; provision for unborn child, with reversion to
brother Robert Moseley, alias Hancock.
Exs., wife and brother-in-law Thomas Wilson
D. May 27, 1756
Wit. Joseph Holt, Ann Miller
Codicil: The house bought of Capt. Pulloyal to be dispos-
of and divided as in above will   March -, 1766
Wit. William Godfrey, John Livingston.
Proved by Alenader Guthrie, who testified that the said
Hutchings was a Captain of a Packet from Norfolk to
Burwell's Ferry. William James qualified as Elizabeth
Hutchings was deceased.   · R. July 12, 1792   Page 498

HELLWIG, John. Leg.- wife Mary; children George and
Polly, land purchased of Charles Hancock Birdsong, now in
possession of Miriam Birdsong, reversion to wife at death
of said Miriam Birdsong; Neice Lucy Lane.
D. May 29, 1791   R. July 12, 1792
Exs. friends Benjamin Ruffin, Thomas Gray, Joseph Ruffin
Wit. John Cobb, Sarah Ruffin, Benjamin Ruffin, Jr.
                                                      Page 500

THORPE, Joshua.   Estate appraised by Thomas Peete,
Arthur Applewhite and John Reese. R. July 12, 1792
                                                      Page 501

PHILLIPS Moses. Leg.- Mary Cocke, the wife of William
Cocke of Surry County; to friend Samuel Kello
Ex., Samuel Kello   D. Sept. 30, 1789
Wit. Benjamin Drew, Francis Young, Jr.
Codicil. Mary Cocke is deceased and her child, above
bequest to Samuel Kello. D. Nov. 1, 1791
Wit. John Hausmann, Edward Griffin R. July 13, 1792
                                                      Page 503

DARDEN, Holland.   Estate appraised by Joshua Gardner,
John Lee, Henry Gardner.   R. July 13, 1792   Page 504

VICK, Samuel. Account current. Signed, George Gurley
Audited, George Gurley Jr. and Nathan Barnes.
R. Aug. 9, 1792   Page 509

TURNER, William. Audited by John Blunt and John
Wilkinson. R. Aug. 9, 1792   Page 507

TURNER, Pass. June 1791. Estate appraised by Simon
Johnson, John Luter and Henry Jones. R. June 13, 1792
Page 509

HARRIS, Nathan. Inventory. Signed, Mary Harris.
R. Sept. 13, 1792
Page 509

BLAKE, Thomas. Account current. Signed, John and
Benjamin Blake. D. March 25, 1789
Audited by John Barrow and Jesse Cooper.
R. Sept. 13, 1792
Page 510

MURFEE, Richard, Sr. D. Dec. 15, 1789 Appraised by
David Edwards, William Edwards and James Edwards
R. Sept. 13, 1792
Page 512
Account estate. Signed, William Murfee, Ex. Matt Murfee
named as one of the family. Audited by Henry Briggs and
James Edwards. R. Sept. 13, 1792
Page 514

WILLIAMS, Nicholas. 1791 Inventory. Signed, John
Williams. R. Sept. 13, 1792
Page 516

ARRINGTON, Jesse. Estate appraised by John Simmons,
Micah Ellis and Lewis Knight.
D. July 19, 1792 R. Sept. 13, 1792
Page 517

GRIZZARD, (Grizard) William. Account current dated
July 15, 1779. Signed Moses Johnson. Bills paid for
Huling Grizard, Tabitha Grizard and Jeremiah Grizard.
Audited by John Wilkinson and Cordall Bynum.
R. Oct. 11, 1792
Page 518

CRENSHAW, John. Estate appraised by Samuel Maget, James
Maget, Howell Whittington. R. Oct. 11, 1792
Page 518

COKER, Nathaniel. Sept. 1781. Account estate. Signed,
Richard Kello. Paid fo schooling for Salley Coker; paid
Wison Coker one seventh part of the slaves. Audited by
Beverley Boothe, Edmund Tyler. R. Oct. 11, 1792
Page 519

DAY, Edmund. Account current. Signed, William
Whitehead, Ex. D. Jan. 22, 1783. Audited by Nicholas
Maget and Thomas Ridley R. Oct. 11, 1792 Page 522

MURRAY, Mary. Leg.- daughter Elizabeth Smith, land
bought of Benjamin Barham; bequest to daughters (not named)
son William Alexander Smith; residue of estate to be divid-
ed between Mary Harwood and Sarah Maget.
Exs., John Harwood, William Maget and Elizabeth Smith
D. Jan. 17, 1791 R. Oct. 11, 1797
Wit. Edward Fisher, Benjamin Barham, William Holliman
Page 529

WILLIAMSON, Burwell. Leg.- wife Lucy; daughter
Wilmouth Jordan; daughter Nancy Williamson
Exs., wife, son-in-law Joseph Jordan, daughter Nancy and
friend Samuel Kello
D. May 22, 1792 R. Nov. 8, 1792
Wit. Micajah Holleman, John Nelms, George Summerell
Page 530

COBB, John. Parish of Nottoway. Leg.- son Exum; son
Michael; son Jeremiah; son Benjamin; son Thomas and son
George Blow Cobb; daughter Rebecca Mecome, if she does not
live with Samuel Mecome; grandson Mathew Mecome when twenty
one; granddaughter Polly Mecome; Captain Charles Briggs to
be paid 90 L to maintain my four youngest sons, Jeremiah,
Benjamin, Thomas and George until they are fifteen; daugh-
ter Elizabeth Wootten; granddaughter Jane Exum Wootten at
twenty one.
Exs., William Hines (Sheriff), son Michael Cobb and
Thomas Gray
D. Oct. 1, 1792 R. Nov. 8, 1792
Wit. Lucy Lane, Richard Pond, Sr., Drewry Pond.
Page 531

BRADSHAW, Benjamin. Leg.- son Jacob, the plantation
bought of Joseph Jones; son Benjamin, tract bought of
Arthur Williams, adjoining Joseph Bradshaw and Ephraim
Spivey; son Philip, land bought of Moses Joyner, adjoining
Sampson Pitman, Charles Cosby and Charles Powers; son
William; son Richard; daughter Gelina; daughter Ridley;
daughter Lucy Stephens; wife Mary Bradshaw
Exs., sons Jacob and Benjamin Bradshaw
D. March 20, 1790 R. Feb. 10, 1791
Wit. Francis Young, Jr., William Bradshaw, Philip
Bradshaw Page 536

WESTBROOK, John. D. Dec. 21, 1785. Estate appraised

by James Lundy and William Claud   R. Nov. 9, 1792
                                        Page 538

IVEY, Henry. D. May 27, 1791 Appraised by John
Williamson and John Reese, Sr. R.   Page 540

LAWRENCE, Thomas. Leg.- daughter Rhoda; daughter Susannah;
son William; wife Margaret; children of my deceased daughter
Elizabeth
   Exs., wife and son William Lawrence.
   D. Feb. 12, 1790   R. Feb. 14, 1793
   Wit. Josiah Murfee, Francis Murfee, William Edwards.
                                        Page 541

JONES, James. Leg.- son James; wife Lucy; son Jordan; son
Anselm; daughter Lucy West; daughter Molly Kitchen and Rebecca
Sebrell.
   Exs., sons Anselm, James and Jordan Jones.
   D. Aug. 15, 1787   R. March 14, 1793.
   Wit. Charles Briggs, Jr., Allen Rogers.   Page 543

TAYLOR, Colonel Henry. Account current. Signed,
Etheldred Taylor. Paid John Taylor's legacy; paid board for
Charlotte and Henry Taylor; paid for linens for my mother;
paid for Elizabeth Taylor's wedding clothes; paid James Taylor
for William Taylor's estate; paid Col. Gray for Lucy Taylor's
estate; paid my mother for H. Taylor and the three girls in
1782; paid Mary, Martha and Charlotte Taylor; paid William
Taylor's legatees.   Etheldred Taylor, deceased.
   Audited by John Wright, Thomas Ridley, Thomas Peete.
   R. Feb. 14, 1793   Page 543

BARHAM, James.   Inventory   R. Jan. 10, 1793
                                        Page 547

BARHAM, Charles. Appraisal. (not signed)
R. Jan. 10, 1793   Page 549

HAISTY, Moses.   Inventory.   D. Feb. 6, 1792
R. Jan. 10, 1793   Page 550

COCKE, Hartwell. Leg.- wife Sarah; William Urquhart my
case of bottles presented me by Redmond Hackett, Esq.; John

Clements; four sons of Edward Archer,- John, William,
Richard and Samuel Archer; Thomas Fearn, John Fearn and
Drewry Andrews.
    Exs., wife Sarah, brother Robert Cocke, Col. Richard
        Cocke, Sr., Col. Samuel Kello and friend William
        Urquhart.
    D. Oct. 28, 1792   R. Jan. 10, 1793
    Wit. Thomas Fearn, Thomas Gray, Francis Clements, John
        Andrews, Solo. Holmes, John Fearn.   Page 551

JOYNER, Arthur. Leg. son Robert; son Kemp; son
Theophilus; daughter Mary Green Joyner.
    Exs., friends John Davis and Burwell Rawlings
    D. Sept. 20, 1792   R. Jan. 11, 1793
    Wit. Lewis Joyner, Thomas W. Clements, John Smith
                      Page 553

COUNCIL, John. Of the Parish of Nottoway. Leg.- son
Amos land adjoining John Worrell, Giles Johnson and William
Mackey; son Jesse; daughter Lydda; daughter Tabitha; daugh-
ter Sarah; daughter Temperance; son John Council
    Exs., sons Amos and Jesse Council
    D. Jan. 2, 1785   R. April 11, 1793
    Wit. David Barrow, Giles Johnson, Stephen Johnson
                      Page 554

SPEED, Robert. Leg.- son Edwin; son George; son Robert;
daughter Milly; wife Ann Speed.
    Exs., friends John Johnson and Josiah Vick
    D. Sept. 14, 1790   R. Dec. 10, 1790
    Wit. Jo. Vick, Hardy Doyel, Lucy Pledger.   Page 556

JOHNSON, Josiah. Of St. Luke's Parish. Leg.- wife
Hannah, with reversion ro all my children.
    D.   R. June 13, 1793
    Wit. Newit Claud, Nancy Johnson, Nancy Harrison
                      Page 558

THORPE, Jeremiah. Of Parish of St. Luke. Leg.- wife
Martha; son Timothy land in N. C.; son Hardy; son Willie;
daughter Olive Thorpe; son Joshua: son Harry; daughter Sarah
Check; grandchildren, the orphans of my deceased daughter
Mary Spence; daughter Lucy Long; daughter Polly Long; grand-
daughters Martha and Polly Long.
    Ex., son Joshua Thorpe.
    D. Dec. 18, 1792   R. June 13, 1793
    Wit. John Atkinson, Aron Smith, Lewis Harris,
        Lucy D. Duprea   Page 558

GILLIAM, Robert. Leg.- son John; daughter-in-law Penelope
Gilliam; grandson John, son of Joseph Gilliam when he is
eighteen. Exs., son John and Jacob Turner.
D. March 11, 1787   R. June 13, 1793
Wit. Jacob Barrett, Exum Everitt, Nathan Britt.
                                                        Page 561

COUNCIL, John. Estate appraised by Arthur Bowing, John
Carstarphen, Jacob Bradshaw. Signed, Amos Council and Jesse
Council, Exs.   R. June 13, 1793   Page 562

HELVEY, John. Estate appraised by William Mellone and
William Spivy. R. May 11, 1793   Page 564

JONES, Mathew. Parish of Nottoway. Leg.- son Albridgton
land left me by my father; daughter Sarah; daughter Ann;
daughter Elizabeth; sister Mary Jarrell.
Ex. brother Albridgton, also to be guardian of my children
D. July 26, 1793   R.
Wit. Lewis Joiner, George Camp, Joshua Joiner Jr.
                                                        Page 566

LAWRENCE, Robert. Leg.- wife Priscilla, land formerly in
Nansemond, but now in Southampton; son Josiah; son Jesse; son
Jacob land adjoining Nicholas Maget; daughter Sarah Williams,
negroes in possession of Isaac Williams; daughter Mary Foreman
negroes in possession of John Foreman; son-in-law Benjamin
Ellis; daughter Priscilla Allen, negroes in possession of
Richard Allen; to Lawrence Ellis.
Exs., sons Josiah and Jacob Lawrence.
D. Dec. 29, 1791   R. Sept. 12, 1793
Wit. Samuel Maget, John Bishop, Nath'l Land, Lawrence
     Williams   Page 566

JONES, William. Leg.- Nancy Simmons, daughter of Mason
Simmons; Henry J. P. Westbrooke, son of Parson Westbrooke,
deceased; Mason Simmons Westbrooke, daughter of aforesaid;
Richard H. Simmons, son of William Simmons; mother with re-
version to my brother Edwin Simmons and to his children; bro-
ther William Simmons.
Exs., brothers william and Edwin Simmons
D. July 22, 1793   R. Sept. 12, 1793
Wit. James Butts, Jo. Vick, Robert H. Fisher, Edwin
     Simmons   Page 568

HART, Henry. Leg.- son Benjamin; daughter Elizabeth;

daughter Ann; wife Lucy Hart.
Exs., Joseph Hart, Sr., Benjamin Hart.
D. Aug. 17, 1792   R. Sept. 12, 1793
Wit. Jesse Womble, Robert Hart, John Hart.   Page 569

HART, Samuel. Leg.- brother Henry; sister Rebecca my
plantation, if she will pay Richard Andrews for the said
land; brother John; brother Charles Hart.
Exs., brother Henry Hart and Thomas Washington
D. Aug. 2, 1793   R. Sept. 12, 1793
Wit. Benjamin Bailey, William Atkinson, John Andrews.
                                                  Page 569

MOODY, Philip. Estate appraised by Lewis Joyner, Jr.,
Benjamin Williams and George Washington
Ex., John Andrews.
D. March 26, 1783   R. Sept. 12, 1793
Account current, audited by William Urquhart and
Arthur Boykin.   Page 570

COCKE, Hartwell. Estate appraised by Sol. Holmes, John
Andrews, Timothy Atkinson. R. Oct. 10, 1793
Appraisal in Brunswick by Benjamin Johnson, William Thomas
Pennington and William Johnson   Page 573

CROCKER, Arthur. Estate appraised by William Bailey,
Thomas Brock and Harmon Harris.
D. Jan. 10, 1793   R. Oct. 10, 1793   Page 574

DREW, Dolphin. Account current. Signed, S. Kello,
Adm. Audited by Will Hines and Thomas Ridley
R. Oct. 10, 1793   Page 575

WHITEHEAD, John. Leg.- wife Meriam, the plantation on
which I live bought by my grandfather of William Powers, adjoining Arthur Whitehead, after death of my mother; sons
(all under age) Maximillan, Lewis Augustus, Jack Anthony,
Arher Meade, Adolphus and Lemuel Murder Whitehead; my land
in Gates County, N. C.; which I bought of James Parke and
Benjamin Harrell to be sold, also the land patented by my
father in July 1774; daughter Sally, daughter Mitildy;
daughter Lucindy; daughter Harriet
   Exs., wife, Robert Jordan, Sr., Hansel Bailey of Surry Co.
      John Maget, Samuel Maget.

D. July 8, 1791   R. Dec. 8, 1791
Wit. Jacob Lawrence, Samuel Maget   Page 576

REESE, Olive. Leg.- son John; son Joseph; son Edwin; son
Lewis; daughter Rebeccah; daughter Silvia Reese.
Ex., Benjamin Blunt, Jr.
D. May 15, 1793   R. Oct. 10, 1793
Wit. Benjamin Williamson, Edwin Bass, John Williamson
                                                    Page 578

BARNES, Nathan. Leg.- wife Martha; son John; son Britain;
son Cordall; daughter Jeansy; sister Mary Barnes.
Exs., wife, son John Barnes and David Barrow
D. June 15, 1790   R. Oct. 10, 1793
Will proven by James Wilkinson, Benjamin Drew and
William Vick, Jr.   Page 578

TAYLOR, Robert. Leg.- neice Patsy Woodlief, daughter of
Thomas and Martha Woodlief; reversion to my five relations,
William Browne and Ann Browne, descendants of William and
Ann Browne decd.; Samuel Browne, Martha Browne and Mary
Browne, children of Benjamin Edwards and Mary Mason Browne;
sister Mary Mason Browne, the plantation on which William
Gilbert is overseer; Aunt Temperance Taylor a mare I had of
Mr. John Taylor
    Exs., brother-in-law Benjamin Edwards Browne and cousin
        Etheldred Taylor
D. Jan. 3, 1789   R. Nov. 14, 1793
Wit. Etheldred Taylor, Thomas Blow, John Taylor
                                                    Page 579

LAWRENCE, Thomas. Estate appraised by A. Mitchell,
Simon Murfee, James Edwards.   R. Nov. 14, 1793
Paid legacies to William and Susanna Lawrence.   Page 580

EXUM, Benjamin. Account current. Signed, John and
Exum Cobb, Exs.   D. 1785   Paid John Elvin, who married
the widow, paid Ann Salter for her legacy from John Cobb's
estate; paid John Cobb a legacy.   Audited by Benjamin
Ruffin, Benjamin Kirby and Thomas Butts.
R. Nov. 14, 1793   Page 582

BRIEF, John. Estate appraised by Arthur Boykin, West
Tynes and John Pursel. R. Dec. 12, 1793   Page 583

GILLIAM, Thomas. Leg.- wife Cala; daughter Lucy Johnson;

son Thomas; daughter Mary Tucker; Jemimah Sorsberry to
live on my plantation during her single life, or as long
as my wife lives or her brother Henry.
  D. Sept. 27, 1793
  Proved by Robert Tucker, John Rochell, William Butts and
  Thomas Gilliam
  Wit. John Simmons, Sr., Levy Rochell, Peter Simmons.
  Cala Gilliam's refusal to accept the will, witnessed by
  Mary Sorsberry, Henry Sorsberry.
  Thomas Gilliam Jr., qualified   R. Ded. 12, 1793
                                                Page 584

  GARDNER, Joshua. Leg.- wife Ann; my surviving chil-
dren,-Henry, John, James, Jesse, Ann, Betsey, Rhoda, Polly
and Peggy; son Henry the tract bought of Moses Darden; son
Jesse land bought of Mathew Jones, adjoining John McCabe;
daughter Ann Jones; daughter Betsey Carr; daughter Polly
Darden Gardner.
  Exs., wife and son Henry Gardner
  D. Feb. 4, 1793   R. Dec. 12, 1793
  Wit. Jacob Darden, Sr., Jacob Darden, Jr. Jonathan
       Darden   Page 586

  PRETLOW, Mary. Leg.- Ann Ricks, wife of Robert Ricks;
Rebecca Hunnicutt, widow of James Hunnicutt; Sarah Bailey,
wife of Lemuel Bailey; Barnaby Nixon of Prince George;
Peter Peebles, Jr.; James Peebles; remainder of estate to
Thomas, Robert, Richard, Joseph, Mary and Milicent Ann
Ricks, the children of my brother Robert Ricks; Elizabeth
and Sarah Bailey, daughters of my sister Elizabeth Scott,
deceased.   Ex., nephew Robert Ricks.
  D. July 28, 1792   R. Dec. 12, 1793
  Wit. Thomas Pretlow, Ann Pretlow, Thomas Taylor
                                                Page 587

  GARDNER, James. Leg.- son James, land adjoining James
James Daughtrey, Col Benjamin Baker, Mathew Gardner and
John Daughtrey; to three of my grandchildren, sons of my
son John Gardner, deceased, viz.- Jesse, David and John
the land bought of Thomas Sharp, adjoining Nicholas Cobb;
son Jesse, land adjoining Robert Darden Sharpe, the land
granted Robert Bryant; son Joseph; daughter Juda, wife of
Thomas Holland; daughter Mary, wife of James Vaughan;
daughter Sarah, wife of William Fowler; daughter Margaret,
wife of Josiah Vick; daughter Martha, wife of Abenezer
Buxton, reversion of bequest to her son Joseph Buxton;
daughter Penelope; daughter Honour; wife Sarah, land purchased of John Lawrence.
  Exs., wife Sarah, brother Joshua and son Jesse Gardner.
  Joshua Gardenr, John Carr and Henry Gardner to divide
  my estate.

D. Aug. 23, 1784   R. Dec. 12, 1793
Wit. Joshua Gardner, Mathew Gardner, Henry Gardner,
    John Carr   Page 598

CALTHORPE, James. Leg.- Aggy Cursey; Mary Black; Joshua
Cursey, son of Aggy Cursey; provision for unborn child of
Aggy Cursey.   Ex., Joshua Claud
D. Jan. 31, 1793   R. Dec. 12, 1793
Wit. John Claud, Turner Person, Sterling Francis
                                                 Page 600

BARNES, Peninah. Account estate. Signed, Jacob Barnes,
Adm. William Barnes, guardian.   Audited by Jo. Vick and
Lem. Hart.   R. Dec. 13, 1793   Page 601

MOUNTFORD, Thomas.   Account estate.   Signed, Wade
Mountford, Adm.   Audited by Daniel Simmons and Henry
Jones.   R. Jan. 9, 1794   Page 601

SIMMONS, Benjamin.   Account estate.   Signed, John
Simmons, Adm.   Audited by Zebulon Lewis, John Wright and
Mark Nicholson.   R. Jan. 9, 1794   Page 602

BRANTLEY, James.   Estate appraised by James Wilkinson,
Howell Edmunds, Jr. and Nath'l. Edwards.   R. Jan. 9, 1794
                                                 Page 604

THOMAS, Henry.   Account estate. Signed, Mary Thomas,
Admtx.   D. 1789   Audited by Robert Mabry, Thomas Turner,
John Williamson and James Lundy.   R. Feb. 13, 1794
                                                 Page 604

BAILEY, Mary.   Account current. Signed, Jordan Judkins,
Adm.   D. 1787   Paid Celia Barlow; paid the children of
Ann Coker, deceased a legacy left them by Barnaby Bailey;
paid Elizabeth Hay her legacy; paid J. Harrison his one
third part of the sale of the land.   Audited by Sam. Kello
and John Haussman. R. Feb. 13, 1794   Page 605

LAWRENCE, Robert. Inventory.   Signed, Jacob Lawrence.
R. Feb. 13, 1794   Page 606

REESE, Olive. Estate appraised by James Lundy, George
Ivey and John Thorpe.
D. Dec. 17, 1793   R. Feb. 13, 1794   Page 606

GARDNER, James, Sr. Estate appraised by Jacon Darden,
Sr., Mathew Gardner and William Edwards.
Signed, Jesse Gardner.
D. Dec. 21, 1793   R. Feb. 13, 1794   Page 607

CLAUD, John. Leg.- wife Sally to have the north side of
the land adjoining Hailey Foster, Dunn's Branch and Walden
Kersey; daughter Polly Claud Francis; daughter Lucy; daugh-
ter Fanny Claud Francis
Exs., John Barrow and Henry Barrow.
D. April 3, 1793   R. Feb. 13, 1794
Wit. Aaron Smith, Benjamin Miller, Philip Claud,
    Joshua Westbrooke   Page 608

KELLO, Richard. Account current. D. 1789. Signed,
S. Kello, Ex. Among items, - account as guardian of Presly
Barrett and of John Mecom. Paid John Kerby his proportional
part of the estate of John Mecome, deceased. Account as ad-
ministrator of Nathaniel Coker. Audited by William
Urquhart and M. Holleman   R. Feb. 13, 1794   Page 610

RIDLEY, Jack Edwards. Leg.- wife Jane and my brother
by law William Wright.
Exs., wife and William Wright.
D. Feb. 26, 1793   R. Feb. 13, 1794
Wit. Matt Figuers, Mary Figuers, L. Mason,
    Fil. Washington   Page 611

POPE, Jesse. Leg.- son Nathaniel land adjoining Nathan
Barnes, Amos Joyner and Evans Pope; daughter Jinny; daugh-
ter Mary; son David; daughter Hannah Beal; remainder of
estate to be divided between John, Zedekiah, Jesse, Hannah,
Jinny and Mary Pope.
Exs., son Nathaniel Pope and Asa Beal
D. Oct. 22, 1791   R. Feb. 13, 1794
Wit. Nathan Barnes, Amos Joyner, Evans Pope   Page 612

THORPE, John, Jr.; Account current. Signed, Martha
Thorpe and Hardy Harris. Paid Hardy Harris his wife's

120

proportional part of the estate of John Thorpe, Sr.
D. Aug. 6, 1793   R. Feb. 13, 1794
Audited by Robert Mabry, John Williamson and James Lundy
Page 612

THORPE, John, Sr. Account current. Signed, Martha
Thorpe and Hardy Harris, Exs. of John Thorpe, Jr. decd.,
who was the Ex. of John Thorpe, Sr. The following were
paid equal sums of their father's estate:- Mildred Spence;
Aaron Thorpe; Moses Thorpe; Jeremiah Thorpe; Olive Reese;
Mary Reese; Sarah Harris; Drucilla Thompson; John Thorpe, Jr.
Audited by Robert Mabry, John Williamson and James Lundy
R. Feb. 13, 1794   Page 614

KINDRED, Benjamin. Leg.- mother Ann Kindred; brother
John; brother Elisha; sister Mary Edwards.
Ex., friend George Blunt.
D. Feb. 9, 1793   R. Feb. 13, 1794
Wit. Drew Powell, Hosea Newton, William Newton.
Page 614

COOPER, Jesse. Estate appraised by A. M. Neil, Henry
Adams and William Crichlow   D. Feb. 4, 1794
Account current. Signed Robert Speed and John Johnson,
Exs. D. 1790.   Audited by Jo. Vick and Joseph Scott
R. Feb. 14, 1794   Page 616

CLAUD, John.   Estate appraised by Aaron Smith, Jesse
Holt and Burwell Westbrooke.   R. March 13, 1794
Page 617

MOORE, Mrs. Sarah.   Account current. Signed, John
Simmons.   D. 1785   Audited by Thomas Ridley and Joseph
Wright. R. March 13, 1794   Page 618

MERCER? John.   D. 1776   Signed, John Pursell surviving Ex. Paid funeral expenses of Patience Mercer; paid
Betsey Mercer's legacy; paid Grace Mercer's legacy; a receipt from Henry Levy for a legacy from Robert Mercer's
estate. Audited by Solomon Holmes and William Urquhart.
R. March 17, 1794   Page 619

DRAPER, Thomas. Account current.   Signed, Ephraim

Draper, Ex. D. 1792. Paid legacies to the following, Thomas, William, Jesse and Jeremiah Draper; Edmond Jordan his wife's legacy and my own. Audited by Lemuel Jones and J. Denson. R. April 10, 1794 Page 619
Signed Ephraim Draper, Ex.

SPIVEY, WILLIAM. Appraised by John Adams, William Wellons and Benjamin Andrews. Signed, Charles B. Briggs
D. April 29, 1793 R. April 10, 1794 Page 620

SPIVEY, John. Estate appraised by John Spratley and Henry Simmons. Signed, Charles Briggs, Adm.
S. Dec. 14, 1793 R. April 10, 1794 Page 621

ROCHELLE, John. Of the Parish of St. Luke. Leg.- wife Judeth; all my children, land and property in North Carolina.
Exs. brother Levi Rochelle and friend James Butts.
D. Feb. 30, 1794 R. April 10, 1794
Wit. George Curley, Jeremiah Drake, Stephen Handcocke
Page 621

JOHNSON, Josiah. Inventory. Signed, Hannah Johnson
R. April 10, 1794 Page 622

EVANS, Hannah. Inventory. Signed, John Thomas Blow Sr.
D. Feb. 26, 1791 R. April 10, 1794 Page 623

HELVEY, John. Signed, Mary Helvey, Adm. Audited by Benjamin Ruffin and Charles Briggs
R. April 10, 1794 Page 623

Jones, Mary. Parish of Nottoway. Leg.- cousin Mary Williams Ex., Elisha Whitney
D. June 1, 1783 R. April 10, 1794
Wit. Joshua Whitney, Jemima Hatfiedl, Ann Whitney
Page 623

HARRIS, West. Leg.- wife Julia, land adjoining William Harris; son Hardy when twenty one
Exs., friends Henry Thorpe, Arthur Applewhite, John Richardson.

D. Feb. 14, 1794   R. April 10, 1794
Wit. Morris Dunn, Mabel dupree, John T. Richardson.
                                        Page 624

WILLIAMS, Isaac.   Signed John Davis, Adm.   D. 1789
Account current. - paid Jordan Denson for maintaining Edwin
and Elizabeth Williams; paid Joseph Denson for maintaining
Sally and Joseph Williams; paid Josiah Vick his account as
Ex., of Benjamin Williams decd.   Audited by Samuel Calvert
and James Bonnot.   R. May 8, 1794   Page 626

HINES, Richard.   Signed Charles Briggs, Adm.   Paid
the widow Hines.   Audited by Samson Stanton and Benjamin
Ruffin.   D. 1789   R. June 11, 1794   Page 627

COUNCIL, John.   Signed, Amos Council and J. Council Exs.
Paid seven legatees.
D. Jan. 24, 1794   R. June 12, 1794.   Page 627

POPE, John.   Account current.   Paid legacy to Henson
Pope; bonds delivered to the orphans.
Audited by Thomas Edmunds and Samuel Edmunds.
D. Feb. 11, 1793   R. June 12, 1794   Page 628

IVEY, Henry.   Signed Peterson Ivey.   Paid Winna Ivey,
widow of Henry Ivey decd., by virtue of a marriage contract.
D. 1791   R. June 12, 1794.   Audited by Kin Turner,
Solomon Cooper and Benjamin Blunt, Jr.   Page 629

CLAUD, Joshua.   In account with Byrd Lundy, decd.
1777, by clothes sold at Harrisburg.   Signed Lewis Thorpe
Ex. of Byrd Lundy.   Paid Henry Tiller for orphans of
Byrd Lundy decd.   Audited Robert Mabry and James Lundy
R. July 10, 1794.   Page 630

LUNDY, Byrd.   Account estate dated 1778.   Signed,
Lewis Thorpe, Ex.   Paid Phebe Lundy, part of her legacy;
Paid Mary Lundy, part of her legacy.   Paid each of follow-
ing the same amount, - Mary Lundy, Henry Tiller, Phebe
Lundy, Edwin Lundy, Byrd Lundy, Joshua and James Lundy,
when they come of age and Jabez Morris; paid Francis Branch

and wife as per decree; to Henry Morris the balance of
his wife's legacy.   Audited by Robert Mabry and James
Lundy.   Signed, Lewis Thorpe, Ex.   R. July 10, 1794
Page 631

BRYANT, Lewis.   Account current.   Audited by Simon
Everett and Charles Birdsong.   R. July 10, 1794
Page 631

SPIVY, William.   Leg.- daughter Sarah; son Benjamin;
son Britain; daughter Mary Powers; daughter Martha Kitchen;
to John and Mary Spivy, children of William Spivy, one
share of estate.
Exs., sons Benjamin and Britain Spivy
D. June 21, 1793.   R. July 10, 1794.
Wit. Thomas Lain, Joseph Lain.   Page 632

DREW, Jeremiah.   Account current.   Signed, William
Myrick and Randolph Newsum, Exs.   D. 1785
Paid Thomas Fitzhugh's legacy; paid Ansclomn Harris' legacy;
paid Newit Edwards for the Drew orphans; to Henry Thorpe
his wife's legacy; Newit Drew's legacy.
R. July 10, 1794.   Audited by John Wright, John
Simmons and Edward Fisher.   Page 633

HOLLEMAN, Micajah.   Of Nottoway Parish.   Leg.- wife
Mary; son Arthur at twenty one; son Exum at twenty one.
Exs., friends Jesse Williamson, Samuel Kello and William
Urquhart.
D. Dec. 24, 1788   R. June 12, 1794
Wit. Benjamin White, Jr., Absalom Williamson
Page 635

JONES, James.   Account estate.   Signed, Anne Harris,
Extx.   Paid Theophilus Scott a judgement obtained by him
and Mary his wife in the court of Southampton County versus
the Exs.   Audited by William Thomas, Thomas Fitzhugh and
John Gurley.   R. July 10, 1794.   Page 636

JONES, William.   Account current.   Legacies paid to
Nancy Simmons, Mason L. Westbrook, Henry J. P. Westbrook,
Richard H. Simmons, Mary Jones, Leisa Simmons, Edwin Simmons.
by James Edwards, Ar Mitchell and James Butts, Auditors.
D. Nov. 27, 1793   R. Aug. 14, 1794
Page 637

MARTIN, James.   Inventory.   Signed George Gurley, Jr.
R. Sept. 11, 1794   Page 638

PCPE, Jesse.   Inventory.   Signed Nathaniel Pope, Ex.
R. Sept. 11, 1794   Page 638

BEAL, Benjamin, Sr.,   Account current. Signed, William
Williams, Adm.   Audited by A. Jones, Wm. H. Baker
D. Feb. 17, 1787   R. Sept. 11, 1794   Page 639

TILLAR, John.   Of the Parish of St. Luke.   Leg.- wife
Rebecca, with reversion to son Jack Tillar Westbrook, alias
Tillar when twenty one; sister Polly Tillar and sister-in-
law Sally Westbrook.
Exs., friends Thomas Westbrook and Ben. Avent.
D. Feb. 11, 1794.   R. Sept. 11, 1794
Wit. John Atkinson, William Holleman, John Mecom.
                                                Page 640

THORP, Martha.   Leg.- John Harris son of Edward Harris
until my son Joseph Thorp is twenty one; to my four youngest
children, Pamelia, Fanny Sally and Joseph Thorp.
Exs., friends John Harris and James Harris.
D. April 21, 1794   R. Sept. 11, 1794
Wit. Aaron Smith, Newit Claud, James Smith, Lucy Long
                                                Page 640

CLEMENTS, Benjamin, Jr.   Account current. Signed by
Thomas Peete, the surviving Ex.   D. 1788
Paid Thomas Gilliam, Jr. guardian of Thomas C. Gilliam as
by decree of the Southampton Court; to John Rochelle as
per decree; to William Urquhart, Ex. of Thomas Clements Jr.
R. Sept. 11, 1794   Page 641

VAUGHAN, William.   Leg.- wife Ann; son William; son
Thomas; son James land bought of Samuel Nicholson; son
John; son Howell; son Henry.
Exs., brother Thomas Vaughan and friends Thomas Turner
        and Thomas Ridley.
D. Dec. 10, 1793   R. Oct. 9, 1794
Wit. William Edmunds, Etheldred Brantley,   Page 643

PEIRCE, Elizabeth. Parish of Nottoway.   Leg.- daughter

Elizabeth; daughter Martha Cobb; son Peter; son Bolton;
son Spencer; son Nathaniel
 Exs., Robert Goodwyn and Joseph Vick
 D.   R. April 28, 1794
 Wit. Jo. Vick, Josiah Cashiel (?), Benjamin Andrews.
               Page 644

 JONES, Mary. Estate appraised by Joseph Denson, Henry
Jones and Toomer Joyner. Signed Elisha Whitney
 D. April 1794   R. Oct. 9, 1794. Page 645

 BOOTH, Moses. Parish of Nottoway. Leg.- wife Diana;
son Peter land purchased of Benjamin Phillips, Phillips
Booth and Henry Blow; son John land bought of Moses Booth;
daughter Martha Warren.
 Exs., sons Peter and John Booth
 D. Aug. 5, 1794   R. Oct. 9, 1794.
 Wit. Peter Bailey, H. John Burgess, Charles Bailey.
               Page 645

 TAYLOR, Robert. Estate appraised by Mark Nicholson,
John Taylor, Sr., Miles Cary, James Miller.
 R. Oct. 9, 1794.   Page 646

 LUNDY, Edward, Sr. Account current. Signed William
Lundy, Ex. of Edward Lundy, Jr., decd. Audited by Robert
Mabry, Thomas urner and John Williamson.
 R. Nov. 13, 1794   Page 648

 REESE, John, Sr. Parish of St. Luke. Leg.- wife
Mary; son Randolph; son Rogers; son Rivers; son Reuben;
son Rowell; son John; son Joseph; daughter Patty, wife of
Mathew Morgan; daughter Mary, wife of John Thorpe; daugh-
ter Selah, wife of Benjamin Adams, Jr.; daughter Lucy
Johnson; daughter Sally, wife of Benjamin Ivey; daughter
Sucky, wife of Philip Ivey.
 Exs., son Randolph and Roger Reese and friend Henry Thorp
 D. Dec. 1, 1792. R. Nov. 13, 1794.
 Wit. William Grizzard, Randolph Millton, Thomas Pate
               Page 649

 GARDNER, James, Sr. Account current. Signed, Jesse
Gardner, Ex. Audited by Henry Gardner, James Darden and
Jacob Darden, Jr. R. Dec. 11, 1794   Page 650

COBB, John.   Account current.   Signed William Hines
and M. Cobb, Exs.,   Audited by Charles Briggs, J. Vick
and John H. Pond.
D. 1792   R. Dec. 11, 1794   Page 650

ANDREWS, Ann.   Inventory
D. Oct. 24, 1793   R. Dec. 11, 1794   Page 651

ANDREWS, William. Sr., Account current.   Signed William
Andrews and John Andrews.   Paid legacies to John, Thomas
and Drury Andrews.   Audited by William Urquhart and John
Urquhart.   D. 1772.   R. Dec. 11, 1794
                                               Page 652

ANDREWS, Ann.   Account current.   Signed John Andrews,
Adm.   Audited by William Urquhart and John Urquhart.
R. Dec. 11, 1794.   Page 653

PORTER, James.   Leg.- wife Ann; son Jacob; son James;
son Nathan; daughter Edith Vick; daughter Priscilla Vick;
daughter Penina Parten; daughter Leddice; daughter Lucy;
daughter Polly when eighteen.
Exs., sons Jacob and Nathan Porter.
D. Oct. 6, 1791   R. Dec. 11, 1794
Wit. Benjamin Blunt, Benjamin Faircloth, Ephraim Faircloth
                                               Page 654

RICKS, Ann.   Account current.   Signed William Crichlow,
Adm.   Audited by Alexander M. Neil, John P. Blow, Henry
Adams.   D. 1792   R. Dec. 11, 1794   Page 655

VICK, William, Sr.   Leg.- son Thomas, who has removed
to Georgia; daughter Sarah wife of Howell Dugger; granddaugh-
ter Patsey Dugger; granddaughter Polly Dugger; daughter
Rachele, wife of James Pennington; daughter Dorcas, wife of
John Boykin; son Nowit; daughter Patience, wife of Daniel
Browne; son William; son William, land on which Holloway
Denson formerly lived, adjoining William Whitehead and Mary
Pope; daughter Charlotte; wife Martha.
Exs., wife and sons William and Newit Vick.
D. Aug. 8, 1794   R. Dec. 11, 1794
Wit. Jo. Vick, Ann Barnes, John Fennel   Page 656

LAND, Bird. Leg.- son Littleberry; son Lieuallen;
daughter Lucretia, wife of Britton Bowers; son Lewis Land.
Ex., son Littleberry Land.
D. Aug. 22, 1794   R. Dec. 11, 1794.
Wit. Mathew Gardner, Jr., William Fowler, Edwin Beal.
                                                    Page 657

THORP, Susanna. Leg.- George Edwards my nephew by
marriage   Ex., George Edwards.
D. Nov. 6, 1791   R. Dec. 11, 1794
Wit. Richard Wren, William Wren.   Page 658

Ivey, John. Account current. Signed Phillip Ivey.
Audited by John Williamson, James Lundy, John Thorpe.
D. Jan. 1790   R. Jan. 8, 1795   Page 658

WESTBROOK, John. Leg.- son Jarret; son Zachariah;
daughter Betsey; daughter Dolly Westbrook.
Exs., Howell Scarbrough and Robert Murrel (Preacher)
D. Dec. 22, 1794   R. Jan. 8, 1795
Wit. Henry Warren, William Marks, Ann Westbrook.
                                                    Page 659

TURNER, Benjamin. Leg. - wife; son Walter; son
Mathew; daughter Sally; daughter Elizabeth Turner.
Exs., friends William Boykin, Joel Boykin, John Urquhart
D. Nov. 6, 1794   R. Jan. 8, 1795
Wit. Britain Britt, Mathew Shereman   Page 661

JOHNSON, John, Sr. Of Parish of St. Luke. Leg.-
son John land adjoining John T. Blow, Benjamin Williams
and Thomas Williams; wife Ann and my five children.
Exs., son John Johnson and son-in-law William Pope
D. Jan. 30, 1779   R. Dec. 11, 1794
Wit. John Thomas Blow, Mary Blow, Sally Jarrell.
                                                    Page 662

PETERSON, Gomer. Estate appraised by Samuel Maget
and James Barnes
D. Oct. 1791   R. Jan. 8, 1795   Page 663

VICK, Jacob. Estate appraised by John Jackson, Jacob

Bailey and Giles Vick.
    D. 1st of 2 mo, 1790   R. Jan. 8, 1795.   Page 664

THORP, Susanna.   Inventory. Signed George Edwards.
R. Jan. 8, 1795   Page 665

DARDEN, James. Leg.- wife Ann; son Elisha, with rever-
sion to my sister Julia Darden and Jacob Darden's Children.
Exs., Jacob Darden, Sr. and Jacob Darden, Jr.
D. Dec. 5, 1794   R. Jan. 8, 1795
Wit. Robert H. Fisher, Stephan Pope, Zerobabell Stakes.
                                                    Page 665

DARDEN, James.   Inventory.   R. Jan 15, 1795
                                                    Page 669

BOOTH, Moses, Sr.   Inventory.   Signed Peter Booth
R. Feb. 12, 1795   Page 669

THOMAS, William.   Of Parish of St. Luke.   Leg.- son Henry
the land adjoining my land called Sarah Carter's; son William
when twenty one; son John when twenty one; daughter Lucy; my
sister Elizabeth; son John land known as Betty Edwards';
granddaughter Charlotte Pretlow; son George Gurley Thomas
when twenty one.
Exs., Son Henry Thomas and George Gurley, Jr.
D. Dec. 29, 1794   R. Feb. 12, 1795
Wit. William Newsum, John Gurley, John T. Blow, Sr.
                                                    Page 670

VICK, Robert.   Account current.   Audited by Charles
Birdsong, William Vick and Newit Vick.
    D. May 15, 1794   R. Feb. 12, 1795   Page 672

BLUNT, Elizabeth.   Leg.- daughter Frances Briggs Lucas,
land bought of Lewis Griggs in the County of Greensville;
son Benjamin William Blunt, with reversion to friends
William Lucas of Mecklenburg County and Rebecca Raines, wife
of Hartwell Raines.   Ex., husband, Samuel Blunt
    D. Sept. 26, 1794   R. Feb. 12, 1795
Wit. Benjamin Blunt, George Blunt.   Page 672

BLUNT, George.   Leg.- father Benjamin Blunt.

Ex., father Benjamin Blunt
D. Dec. 2, 1794   R. Feb. 12, 1795
Wit. Sam. Blunt, Ben Edwards, William Blow

Page 673

APPLEWHITE, Ann. Leg.- son William; son Thomas when
twenty one; daughter Mary Barham; son John; son Hardy; to
the four children of Jesse Cooper; to my eleven children;
son Benjamin; daughter Sally Dashoil (?); daughter
Priscilla Jordan; daughter Jean; daughter Rebecca; daughter Nancy Applewhite. Ex., son John Applewhite.
D. Feb. 3, 1795   R. Feb. 12, 1795
Wit. Josiah Dashiele, Thomas Peete, Lucy Waller.

Page 674

CHARLES, Mathew. Of the Parish of Nottoway. Leg.-
wife Mary; granddaughter Margaret Joyner; son Jethro;
grandson William Charles.   Exs., son Jethro and wife Mary
D. Feb. 21, 1794   R. Feb. 12, 1795
Wit. Joshua Miniard, Robert Council, James Clark

Page 673

POWELL, James L.   Estate appraised by Henry Adams,
Richard Ricks and William Crichlow
D. June 28, 1794   R. Feb. 12, 1795   Page 675

ADAMS, Benjamin. Leg.- daughter Sally Ivy; daughter
Priscilla Prince; wife Margaret; daughter Charlotte; daugh-
ter Nancy; son Arthur; daughter Betsey; granddaughter Sally
Adams. Exs., wife and son-in-law Joseph Prince.
D. Oct. 30, 1794   R. March 12, 1795
Wit. Herbert Pate, Jordan Pate, Richard Mason

Page 676

BITTLE, Robert. Leg.- to my --- Henry Bittle; son
Kirby; daughter Mary Lanier; grandson Henry Barham the
negroes now in possession of his father Benjamin Barham;
son John; daughter Mildred Turner; grandson Benjamin Turner;
grandson Benjamin Bittle; granddaughter Elizabeth Bittle;
to daughter of Mildred Turner; son William Bittle.
Exs., sons Henry and William Bittle
D. Feb. 14, 1795   R. April 9, 1795
Wit. Will Edmunds, Jacob Summerell, Thomas Holladay.

Page 677

JARROTT, Fortunatus. Leg.- brother John Jarrott; my

clothes to be divided between brother John and William
Peoples; to Susanna, daughter of William Peoples; to Henry
Bell, son of George Bell, the land I had of Benjamin
Wheeler; sister Nancy Jarrott.
Ex., John Jarrott.
D. Dec. 13, 1795(?)   R. March 5, 1795
Wit. William Peebles, Wiley Hopkins, Joseph Hopkins.
Joel Lane, Judge of the Court of Wake County, N. Car. to
take the oath of Wiley Hopkins and Joseph Hopkins, that
above signatures are their own.   Page 678

BOYKIN, John, Sr.   Of Nottoway Parish.   Leg.- daughter Cherry, wife of Robert Eley; son Mathew; son John; son
Joel; son Daniel; daughter Patience, wife of Jacob Turner;
daughter Elizabeth; daughter Martha, wife of Thomas Vick;
daughter Ava, wife of William Branch; daughter Keziah;
daughter Sarah, wife of Arthur Sherod; son Ely Boykin.
Exs., son Ely Boykin and Jacob Turner.
D. Oct. 8, 1794   R. April 9, 1795
Wit. Britton Britt, John Cook, Frederick Boykin.
                                               Page 680

WOMMACK, Thomas.   Leg.- son Carter, said son to take care
of his mother Elizabeth Wommack; to John Memore (?) children,
namely James, Elizabeth, Polly and John; to Harris Thomson,
son of Lodowick Thomson; balance of my estate to be sold and
divided between my surviving children.
Ex., son Carter Wommack
D. Jan. 26, 1794   R. April 9, 1795
Wit. William Wright, Byrd Lundy   Page 681

KELLO, Richard.   Estate appraised by A. Exum, R. Exum,
J. ------.   R. April 9, 1795   Page 682

Account current.   Signed Sam Kello Ex.   Audited by Will
Hines, Charles Briggs and J. Denson.
R. April 9, 1795   Page 683

REESE, Olive.   Account current.   Signed John Reese, Sr.
(deceased) Adm.   Audited by Robert Mabry and John Williamson.
R. May 14, 1795   Page 684

CALTHORPE, James Butts.   Estate appraised by Thomas Gray,
Richard Pond and John H. Pond.
D. April 25, 1795   R. May 14, 1795   Page 684

WESTER, William, Jr. Estate appraised by James
Edwards and Mathew Wills.
   D. Dec. 13, 1794   R. May 14, 1795   Page 685

HARRIS, Landon. Estate appraised by Thomas Fitzhugh,
John Taylor, Sr. and Sterling Capel.
   D. Jan. 22, 1793   R. June 11, 1795   Page 686

McNEIL, James. Leg.- freedom to negro slave Molly;
to nephew Alexander McNeil.
   Exs., nephew Alexander McNeil, Thomas Edmunds and Charles
      Taylor.
   D. Oct. 9, 1794   R. June 11, 1795
   Wit. John T. Blow, Jr., John Taylor, Sr., John Chrichlow
      and John Fort.   Page 687

BRISTER, Samuel. Leg.- wife Ann; to my five last chil-
dren, namely John, Benjamin, James, Hannah and Willis. My
other children having been provided for.
   Ex., wife Ann Brister.
   D. Oct. 2, 1794   R. June 11, 1795
   Wit. James Summerell, Thomas Travis, Arthur Doles.
                                 Page 688

RIDLEY, Mathew. Of the Parish of St Luke. Leg.- to
mother Sarah Drew; friend Henry Blunt, son of John Blunt;
to Francis Ridley, son of Thomas Ridley, Sr.; to Thomas
Holladay, son of John Holladay, decd.
   Exs., uncle James Ridley and Henry Blunt.
   D. April 13, 1795   R. June 11, 1795
   Wit. Thomas Ridley, Stephenson Blake, Amey Ridley,
      Maney Blake   Page 689

ATKINSON, Ann. Leg.- daughter Ann; son Elisha; son
Elias; daughter Rachel Williams; daughter Elizabeth Delk.
   D. Feb. 12, 1794   R. June 11, 1795
   Wit. Jesse Johnson, Phebe Atkinson.   Page 689

HALLCOME, Richard. Estate appraised by Thomas Turner,
Arthur Turner & Thomas Fitzhugh. Signed, Charles Briggs.
   D. Dec. 19, 1794   R. June 11, 1795   Page 690

SPIVEY, William. Account current. Signed Charles

Briggs, Adm.   Audited by Benjamin Ruffin, Samson Stanton.
Among items, bond due the father William Spivey's estate
    D. April 28, 1795.   R. June 11, 1795   Page 691

RAMSEY, Catherine.   Estate appraised by Etheldred
Brantley, Henry Blunt, Willie Francis.
    D. Feb. 26, 1795   R. June 11, 1795   Page 692

STEWART, Benjamin.   Leg.- wife Lyddia the use of my plan-
tation and personal estate, at her death plantation to son
Henry, rest of estate to all my children then living and to
my grandson Charles Stewart.
Exs., wife and friend Robert Goodwyn.
    D. March 5, 1794   R. June 11, 1795
Wit. Daniel Butts, Robert Goodwyn, John Scott
                                                Page 693

TURNER, Benjamin.   Estate appraised by Sol Holmes, Arthur
Doles, Timothy Atkinson.
    D. April 4, 1795   R. July 9, 1795   Page 693

WOMMACK, Thomas.   Estate appraised by Francis Branch,
Carter Wommack, John Berryman and Henry Tillar.
    D. April 16, 1795   R. July 9, 1795   Page 696

PORTER, James.   Estate appraised by Littleton Fort,
James Turner, Benjamin Turner.
    D. Jan. 31, 1795   R. July 9, 1795   Page 697

SUTER, William.   Leg.- sister Rebecca; brother Henry; bro-
ther John; brother Arthur Suter.
Exs., brother Arthur and Nathaniel Edwards.
    D. April 28, 1795   R. July 9, 1795
Wit. Aaron Smith Jeremiah Inman, Nathaniel Edwards.
                                                Page 698

STEWART, Samuel.   Inventory. Signed, Humphrey Drewry, Adm.
    D. Dec. 22, 1792   R. July 9, 1795   Page 699

MYRICK, Henry.   Estate appraised by William Chambliss,

Thomas Peete and Hardy Applewhite. Signed William Nyrick,
Adm. D. Feb. 23, 1795   R. Sept. 10, 1795
Page 700

WHITEHEAD, Mary. Leg.- daughter Elizabeth Newby; daugh-
ter Mary Bentel (?); daughter Polly Cotton, **slave** Jesse
Cotton has now in his possession; granddaughter Peggie
Bridger; grandson Alexander Whitehead; grandson Nathaniel
Newby; granddaughter Sally Newby.
   Exs., Joseph Bentel and Jesse Cotton.
   D. July 19, 1795   R. Sept. 10, 1795
   Wit. Jacob Turner, Elizabeth Everett, Mary Jacobs,
          Etheldred Turner   Page 701

THORP, John. Leg.- wife Polly; refers to hogs on
Charles Bass' pond; son Aaron; daughter Elizabeth Reese;
daughter Susanna; son Moses; son John; daughter Polly;
provision for an unborn child; the legacy due by the will
of John Reese for my wife to be sold and invested in a
slave.
   Exs., John Harris, Sr., Randolph Reese, Rivers Reese
          and Roger Reese.
   D. July 7, 1795   R. Sept. 10, 1795
   Wit. John Williamson, Nathaniel Smith, Rowell Reese.
                                              Page 702

SUMMERRELL, Jacob. Leg.- daughter Barbary DeLoach;
daughter Margaret; son Hartwell; son Sam Manning Summerrell
when twenty one; daughter Lucy; daughter Salley Caul (?)
Summerrell and wife Lucy Summerrell.
   Ex., William Bittle.
   D.   R. Sept. 10, 1795
   Wit. William Edmunds, Thomas Holladay, John Turner
                                              Page 703

HUNT, Miles. Estate appraised by Roger Reese, Thomas
Pate, Jr., John Reese.
   D. May 22, 1795   R. Sept. 11, 1795   Page 704

FORT, Olive. Estate appraised by Joel Turner, Mark
Nicholson, Arthur Foster.
   D. Oct. 1794   R. Sept. 11, 1795   Page 704

BRISTER, Samuel. Estate appraised by James Summerell,

Thomas Summerell, Thomas Stephenson.
D. Aug. 1795   R. Oct. 8, 1795   Page 706

JARRETT, Fortunatus.   Estate appraised by Richard Drewry,
Thomas Newsum, Abel Ezell.
Signed by John Jarrett, Ex., of Sussex County
D. April 18, 1795   R. Oct. 8, 1795   Page 707

HART, Samuel. Estate appraised by Robert Hart, Jesse
Womble and Richard Hart.
D. Dec. 1793   R. Oct. 8, 1795   Page 707.

WILLIAMSON, Calia. Account current, signed John
Crumpler, Adm. Paid Sally Fly her part of the estate,
paid Winnie Fly, ditto. Audited by Solomon Holmes and
Jacob Turner
D. Dec. 1791   R. Oct. 8, 1795   Page 708

BEAL, Ephraim. Estate appraised by Joseph Scott, Shad
Lewis and Hardy Johnson.
D. Sept. 27, 1794   R. Oct. 8, 1795   Page 708

LAND, Bird.   Estate appraised by William Beale, Richard
Beale, Richard Beale, Jr.
D. Dec. 20, 1794   R. Oct. 8, 1795   Page 709

ANDREWS, Faithy. Leg.- Britain Britt, son of Britain
and Pamelia Britt, my part of my father's estate, sister
Ex., Britain Britt, Sr.   Parmelia Britt.
D. May 20, 1795   R. Oct. 8, 1795
Wit. Rebecca Turner, Patsey Britt   Page 710

NICHOLSON, Mary. Leg.- son Charles Briggs Nicholson;
rest of estate between all my children, with an equal part
to Polly and Nancy Barham.
Exs. son Charles and Bird Lundy.
D. Sept. 23, 1795   R. Oct. 8, 1795
Wit. John Mccom, James Mccom, Janny Myrick   Page 710

COBB, Michael. Leg.- money after just debts are paid

to be used for the education of my brothers, Benjamin, Thomas and George until they are fifteen, agreeable to my father's will; wife and all my children until my youngest child Jack Cobb is twenty one
Exs., brother Exum Cobb, Spencer Pierce and Charles Briggs, Jr.
D. Nov. 10, 1795   R. Dec. 10, 1795
Wit. Will Hines, George Clements, Rebecca Mecom.
Page 711

BROWNE, Olive. Leg.- friend Thomas Lain; to Lucy Hines, daughter of William Foster; to Polly and Joseph Lain, children of Thomas Lain.
Exs., friend Thomas Lain and his son Joseph when of age
D. Oct. 9, 1794   R. Dec. 11, 1795
Wit. Micajah Ellis, Bolin Ellis
Page 712

TURNER, Willie. Leg.- mother Lucy Turner, with reversion to John Westray Turner; if he should die under age to Lucy and John Little.
Ex., friend Lewis Dupree.
D. April 1, 1794   R. Sept. 11, 1794
Wit. Cordal Francis, John Winddom.
Page 713

PURSELL, Martha. Of Parish of Nottoway. Leg.- son John; to Arthur Crumpler.
Ex., Arthur Crumpler.
D. Feb. 18, 1795   R. Dec. 10, 1795
Wit. John Crumpler, Amos Turner
Page 714

COBB, Henry. Of Parish of Nottoway. Leg.- to my five grand children, Amey, Robert, Ann, Betsey and Henry Grimmer; daughter Milla Grimmer; son-in-law Seymour Vaughan my land; granddaughter Chlotella Cobb; granddaughter Betsey Vaughan at death of son-in-law Seymour Vaughan and daughter my Vaughan to my grand children Henry and Ann Vaughan,
Ex., son-in-law Seymour Vaughan
D. Jan. 5, 1791   R. Dec. 10, 1795
Wit. Asa Beale, Josiah Murfee, Francis Murfee
Page 714

LOWE, Levi. Leg.- wife Sally; son Elias; son Micajah; son Spencer; daughter Sally; daughter Betsey; daughter Cherry; daughter Nancy Lowe
Ex., son Elias Lowe
D. March 12, 1795   R. Dec. 10, 1795

Wit. John Pursell, Mathew Crumpler, John Wright

Page 715

WESTBROOK, John. Account current. Signed Lucy Turner, Adtx. Paid Turner Person for Mary Person's share of a negro. Audited by Robert Mabry and James Lundy.
D. Aug. 27, 1786 R. Sept. 11, 1795 Page 716

FISHER, Mary. Inventory. Signed Robert H. Fisher, Adm.
D. June 23, 1795 R. Dec. 10, 1795 Page 717

HART, Henry. Estate appraised by William Atkinson, Richard Hart and Jesse Womble. D. Dec. 10, 1795
Signed, Joseph and Benjamin Hart, Exs. Page 717

Account current. Paid Elizabeth Hart her legacy; paid Ann Hart ditto; paid Benjamin Hart ditto.
R. Feb. 11, 1796 Page 718

BEALE, Joshua. Estate appraised by Shad Lewis, Stephen Johnson and Lemuel Hart. R. Feb. 11, 1796 Page 718

APPLEWHITE, Ann. Inventory. Signed John Applewhite, Ex.
R. Feb. 11, 1796 Page 720

MURFEE, Simon. Leg.- son Richard, my plantation at death or marriage of my wife; son Simon; son Josiah; son Francis; son Burwell; son Drewry; son Wills Murfee.
Exs., friends Josiah Vick, Samuel Calvert and son Josiah Murfee.
D. March 28, 1795 R. Feb. 11, 1796
Wit. James Edwards, William Edwards, Giles Wester

Page 720

FORT, John. Of the Parish of St. Luke. Leg.- mother; sister Rebecca Barnes' children; sister Temperance; brother Edwin Fort.
Exs., friends William Chambless and Joseph Thorpe
D. Sept. 13, 1795 R. Feb. 11, 1796
Wit. William Capele, Kinchen Jelke, Charles Nicholson
Page 721

ANDREWS, John. Leg.- daughter Elizabeth; daughter Sally; wife Lucy; son James; daughter Nancy Boykin.
Exs., William Urquhart, John Urquhart, wife Lucy Andrews.
D. June 9, 1795   R. Feb. 11, 1796
Proved by depositions of William Urquhart, Jacob Turner, Daniel Butts.   Page 722

BARNES, Jacob. Leg.- son Benjamin, land adjoining James Barnes; son Jacob land on J.Whitehead, James Barnes and Nathan Barnes; daughter Ann; daughter Selah Vick; wife Elizabeth, reversion to sons Josiah and Thomas Barnes; sons Joshua and Thomas Barnes land in Pitt County, N. Car. and son James land in Edgecomb County, N. Car.
Exs., wife Elizabeth and son Josiah Barnes.
D. Sept. 15, 1790   R. Feb. 11, 1796
Wit. Edmund Barrett, James Barnes, Jesse Vick,
      Jesse Barrett.   Page 723

VAUGHAN, Lydia. Nuncupative will, made in the home of Noel Vick, in presence of Milly Porter and Patty Vick.
Dec. 29, 1795   'That I have to be divided between Lydia Porter, Polly Vaughan, Fanny Vick and Betsey Vick. I desire that Milly Porter will see it done according to my desire'
Signed, Jo. Vick, William Johnson.
R. Feb. 11, 1796   Page 723

HART, Jesse. Leg.- son Richard with reversion to my son Moses; son William with reversion to son Samuel; son Moses land bought of Jesse Womble; daughter Mary; daughter Mildred; daughter Jane; daughter Charity; wife Nancy with reversion of the bequest to the following children:- Richard, Olive, Sarah, Mary, Moses, Mildred, William, Jane, Charity and Samuel Hart.
Exs., son Richard Hart and Jesse Womble
D. Dec. 31, 1790   R. Feb. 11, 1796
Wit. Joseph Hart, Benjamin Hart, Jesse Hart.   Page 724

MYRICK, Ann. Leg.- son William; son John; son Howell; grandson Howell Jones.
Exs., son William Myrick and grandson Howell Jones
D. Feb. 18, 1795   R. Feb. 11, 1796
Wit. H. Arrington, John Marks, John Myrick   Page 725

VICK, William. Inventory. Signed, Newit Vick.

D. Dec. ., 1794   R. Feb. 11, 1796   Page 726

COBB, Henry.   Estate appraised by A. Jones, Joseph
Scott and James Edwards.
   D. Feb. 1, 1796   R. Feb. 11, 1796   Page 726

NICHOLSON, Joshua.   Additional account current. Signed,
Howell Edmunds one of the Exs.   Among items, paid Edward
Lundy, Ex.   Audited by John Wilkinson and James Gee.
   R. Feb. 11, 1796   Page 727

BRITT, John.   Account estate. Brittain Britt, Ex.
Among items:- paid Tamor Britt's legacy; paid Benjamin Britt
his part of the land sold, paid Joseph Britt ditto; paid
Benjamin Britt ditto; paid Arrington ditto; paid the following
their part of the personal estate: Sarah Johnson, Tamor Britt,
and Polly Britt; paid the widow's dower.
   Audited by William Urquhart and Sol Holmes.
   D. 1791   R. Feb. 11, 1796   Page 728

CHARLES, Mathew.   Estate appraised by Arthur Bowing, Henry
Jones and James Clark
   D. March 18, 1795   R. Feb. 12, 1796   Page 729

DARDEN, Holland.   Account current. Signed, Jacob Darden,
Ex. Among items:- paid the Doctor's account for the illness
of Jonah and Holland Darden, decd.; paid Ann Darden her share
of the estate; paid Holland, Jr. ditto; paid John ditto; paid
Jonah ditto; paid Ann and Elish Darden, ditto; for schooling
the orphans of Elisha Darden.   Audited by Henry Gardner
and Jesse Carr   D. 1792.   R. Feb. 12, 1796   Page 730

GARDNER, John.   Estate appraised by J. Vick, Josh. Slade
and Jacob Joyner, Jr.
   D. Dec. 21, 1795   R. Feb. 12, 1796   Page 731

COCKE, Hartwell.   Account estate, Signed by William
Urquhart.   Audited by Sol Holmes and John D. Haussman
   D. Nov. 1792   R. Feb. 15, 1796   Page 731

URQUHART, William.   Estate appraised by Kinchen Jelks,
William Chambliss and Richard P. Clements.
D. Feb. 28, 1795   R. April 13, 1796   Page 733

TURNER, Willie.   Estate appraised John Blunt, Henry
Smith and John Person.
D. Oct. 11, 1794   R. April 15, 1796   Page 734

BEALE, Benjamin, Jr.   Leg.- wife Elizabeth a tract in
Roger's Neck; friend Jordan Denson to dispose of certain
parts of my estate and pay the debts I owe Jordan Denson &
Co. and Pretlow and Randolph; son Jeremiah; son-in-law
Solomon Gobb; son Shadrack; my daughters Elizabeth Williams,
Charlotte Carr, Polly Williams, Silvia Beale and Peggy
Beale; the children of my wife by her former husband a
right to what belonged to their father's estate
Ex., wife Elizabeth Beale.
D. Feb. 16, 1793   R. April 15, 1796
Wit. Joseph Scott, James Scott, J. Denson.   Page 736

HARRIS, John Dawson.   Leg.- John Edmunds Dawson; Edmond
Turner; Polly Dawson; William Phillips; John and Bowling
Barnes, sons of Bailey Barnes.
Exs., Edmund Turner and John E. Dawson.
D. April 6, 1796   R. April 15, 1796
Wit. Henry Smith, William Sturgeaon, Henry Brantley
                                                Page 737

VICK, James.   Leg.- wife Sarah Nicholson, land bought
of Lewis Joiner, adjoining Arthur Arrington, William
Crumpler, Thomas Williams and Nathaniel Jones; son Parks
N. Vick; son Richard tract bought of Benjamin Andrews adjoining Samuel Drewet, Charles Briggs; daughter May Worrell;
daughter Tabitha Vasser, with reversion to her children;
son Joseph; son James; to my ---- Sarah Vick, with reversion
to my children Parks Nicholson, Richard and Rebecca Vick.
Exs., friend Micajah Holliman and wife Sarah Vick
D. Sept. 13, 1795   R. April 15, 1796
Wit. Noel Waddell, Josiah Murfee, Thomas W. Clements
                                                Page 739

DRAKE, Cordal.   Leg.- wife Polly, daughter Polly with
reversion of bequest to brothers Silas and Arthur Drake.
Es. wife Polly Drake
D. Sept. 5, 1795   R. June 9, 1796   Page 739
Wit. Bailey Oberry, Eaton Joyner, Elizabeth Lowe

WHITFIELD, Benjamin. Leg.- son Benjamin; son Reuben;
son John; daughters, Elizabeth Crenshaw, Mary Hargraves
and Sarah Revell.
Exs., sons Benjamin, Reuben and John Whitfield
D. Jan. 26, 1787
Wit. Mary Whitfield, Reuben Whitfield, Jesse Vick.
Codicil: Mary Hargrave now a widow to have a home on
John Whitfield's land. D. June 8, 1796
Wit. Jesse Vick, Elisha Whitfield, Stephen Hancock
R. June 9, 1796   Page 740

COKER, Henry. Account current. Signed, Joshua Bailey,
Jordan Judkins, Mark Judkins and John Brittle.
D. Nov. 14, 1790   A. June 9, 1796   Page 742

WILLIAMS, Richard. Estate appraised by William Hart,
Henry Gardner and John Lee. R. June 9, 1796   Page 742

PIERCE, Rice B. Account current. Michel Cobbs, decd.
Adm. Account versus Elizabeth Pierce, decd.
        "   "   Elizabeth Pierce, Jr.
        "   "   Spencer Pierce
Audited by Samuel Calvert and J. Vick.
R. June 9, 1796   Page 743

BLUNT, George. Inventory. Signed, Ben. Blunt.
R. June 9, 1796   Page 744

KINDRED, Benjamin. Estate appraised by Thomas Holladay,
Samuel Edmunds, John Powell. Signed, Benjamin Blunt, Ex.
D. May 10, 1794   A. June 9, 1796   Page 745

COKER, Henry. Further appraisal by Peter Bailey, Benjamin
Branch and Newsum Branch.
D. Nov. 2, 1790   A. June 9, 1796   Page 746

FULGHAM, Mary. Leg.- daughter Martha Joiner; daughter
Ann Turner.
Exs., sons-in-law Thomas Joiner and Pass Turner.
D. March 21, 1736   R. Feb. 12, 1796

BROWNE, Jesse. Account estate with administrators of Samuel Ridley Browne. Among items, paid Martha Jack's representatives; paid Elizabeth R. Kello's children; paid Robert Dickens and wife; paid John Atkinson's representatives; paid representatives of Peter Pelham and wife Parthenia; paid Jesse Browne; paid William Wilkinson and wife Jane; paid John Faulcon and wife Lucretia; paid Samuel Browne. decd. his representatives. All paid the same amount. D. Nov. 7, 1795
Jesse Browne, Anthony Browne, Albridgton Browne, James Browne and John Browne, heirs of Samuel Browne, decd. Ex. of Jesse Browne. Audited by Jacek Williams, Samuel Maget, Miles Everett. R. July 14, 1796   Page 748

JONES, Richard. Account current. Signed, Jacob Barnes, Ex. D. Sept. 1780   Received of John Simmons, Ex. of James Jones, being part of Richard Jones' share of his father's estate. Audited by Alexander McNeil and Mark Nicholson. R. July 14, 1796   Page 749

MURFEE, Simon. Estate appraised by James Edwards, Semour Vaughan and William Lawrence.
D. Feb. 25, 1796   R. July 14, 1796   Page 750

SCARBROUGH, Mary. Estate appraised by James Bennett, Thomas W. C. Clements, J. Bell and Moody Collier
D. Feb. 29, 1796   R. July 14, 1796   Page 752

WILLIAMS, Mathew. Estate appraised by Absalom Joyner, John Williams and David Washington. Signed Lewis Williams, Adm. D. June 27, 1795   R. July 14, 1796   Page 752

WHITEHEAD, Mary. Inventory. D. Aug. 8, 1796
R. Sept. 8, 1796   Page 753

REESE, John, Sr. Estate appraised by Joseph Fort, Newit Claud and Thomas Peete. R. Dec. 8, 1796
                                             Page 754

ADAMS, Benjamin. Estate appraised by Zebulon Lewis, John Applewhite and William Applewhite D. March 19, 1795
R. Sept. 8, 1796   Page 756

ELLISON, Gerard R. Leg.- wife Sarah; son Caleb, land adjoining Jesse and Etheldred Washington; son Edwin; son James when twenty one; my three other children, Dorcas, Cutie and Zachariah Ellison.
Exs, Gideon Ellison and Samuel Cornwell.
D. July 1, 1795   R. Sept. 8, 1796
Wit. Joshua Bailey, Absalom Bailey, Thomas Washington, Charles Sadler   Page 757

THOMAS, Nathan. Estate appraised by Benjamin Blunt, Jr. James B. Womack and Etheldred Turner.
D. July 11, 1796   R. Oct. 13, 1796   Page 759

CALTHORPE, James Butts. Account current. Signed, James Pond, Adm. Audited by Exum Cobb and William Wellons
R. Oct. 13, 1796   Page 760

CALTHORPE, James. Estate appraised by Robert Mabry, Benjamin Blunt and Thomas Turner.
D. April 15, 1795   R. Oct. 13, 1796   Page 761

THORPE, John. Estate appraised by John Williamson and George Ivey. Signed Benjamin Blunt, Jr. D. Oct. 29, 1795 and Dec. 15, 1795   R. Oct. 13, 1796   Page 762

LANCASTER, James. Leg.- wife Rebeckah; refers to mill built with Lemuel Bailey; daughters Mildred and Jerusha one half of the mill built in Isle of Wight County with Lemuel Bailey; daughters Polly and Zilla; granddaughter Elizabeth Champion Bell; friend John Gwaltney to be guardian for my daughter Jerusha; wife Rebecca to be guardian for daughters Polly and Zilla; son-in-law James P. Bell to be guardian for granddaughter Elizabeth C. Bell.
Ex. friend John Gwaltney
D. March 12, 1796   R. Oct. 13, 1796
Wit. Herbert Sledge, John Bryant, David Davis, James Delk.   Page 763

HOLLAMAN, William. Leg.- son John land adjoining Joseph Hart and William Bailey; son William, land adjoining Micajah Holleman; wife Lucy; son Thomas Holleman
Exs., wife and sons John and William Holleman.
Wit. Exum Harris, Joseph Hart, Charles Sadler

D. Jan. 19, 1795   R. Oct. 13, 1796   Page 765

POND, Richard. Leg.- son Drewry; son William; wife
Mary; daughter Nancy Megee; daughter Dianah; son Samuel,
daughter Mary; son Daniel Pond.
Exs., wife Mary and sons Drewry and William Pond.
D. March 5, 1794   R. Oct. 13, 1796
Wit. John Pond, Tabitha Bond, Dianna Pond   Page 766

BLOW, Henry. Leg.- wife Sally, until my two children,
Sally and William Blow come to lawful age.
Exs., brothers Micajah and Thomas R. Blow, brother-in-law
Owen Myrick.
D. May 27, 1796   R. Oct. 13, 1796
Wit. William Chambliss, Michael Blow, Janney Myrick
Page 768

POPE, Simon. Estate appraised. Not signed.
D. Jan. 7, 1796   R. Jan 13, 1796   Page 768

COBB, Michael. Estate appraised Not signed
Signed, William Wellons and John H. Pond.
R. Oct. 13, 1796   Page 769

MYRICK, Henry. Account current. Signed William Myrick,
Adm. Among items;- cash paid William Chambliss, guardian
of Owen Myrick; cash paid for Fanny Myrick to guardian
Henry Myrick; by cash received in the house of Howell
Myrick, decd.
D. Feb. 7, 1796   R. Oct. 13, 1796
Audited by Richard Clements and John Taylor, Jr.
D. Feb. 7, 1796   R. Oct. 13, 1796
Page 772

BEALE, Benjamin. Estate appraised by Shad Lewis,
Joseph Scott and Stephen Johnson
D. May 14, 1796   R. Oct. 13, 1796   Page 772

LUNDY, Elizabeth. Estate appraised by Robert Mabry,
James Harris and James Lundy. Signed, Lunsford Lundy
D. Nov. 17, 1795   R. Nov. 11, 1796
Page 774

TURNER, Pass. Account current. Signed James Clark,
Adm. Paid widow according to will. Audited by Daniel
Simmons and Pettaway Johnson. R. Oct. 13, 1796

Page 775

STEWARD, Lemuel. Account current. Supplies the widow
and children. Audited by John Taylor, Jr. and Newit Drew.
D. June 22, 1793   R. Oct. 13, 1796

Page 776

JOHNSTON, Stephen. Of Nottoway Parish. Leg.- wife Sarah
all the remains of her estate that she brought into my estate;
son John; son William; daughter Polly; son Johnson; daughter
Sally; son Stephen Johnston.
    Exs., sons Benjamin and Mathew Johnston. (Name written in-
       terchangably Johnson and Johnston.
D. Sept. 27, 1796   R. April 17, 1797
Wit. David Washington, Thomas Camp, Joseph Vick.

Page 776

TURNER, James. Leg.- son Edmund at twenty one, reversion
to son Benjamin, when of age; reversion to son Edmund when of
age; daughter Nancy Turner.
    Exs., Henry Blunt, William Blunt, Edmund Turner, Richard
       Blunt.
D. Feb. 14, 1797   April 17, 1797
Wit. William Blunt, Newit Harris, Edmund Turner, Henry
       Blunt, Richard Blunt.

Page 778

HARRIS, Edmund. Leg.- wife Elizabeth; to Penny Carr Harris
and Jinny Harris at twenty one, daughters of Landon Harris; to
my five children, Sterling, John, Peyton, James and Charlotte
Turner.   Exs., sons Peyton and James Harris
D. May 20, 1795   R. Aug. 21, 1797
Wit. Francis Branch, Peyton Lundy, John Williamson

Page 779

DELOACH, Solomon. Leg.- wife Lucy; to Solomon, son of
Richard Deloach decd.; Allen DeLoach Dunn; Thomas DeLoach
Dunn; Williamson Parker; Frederick , son of Drewry Parker,
decd.   Ex., Colonel Samuel Kello
D. Nov. 14, 1795   R. May 16, 1797
Wit. Burwell Long, Lucy Myrick, John Meglamore

Page 780

JONES, Lemuel. Leg.- son Joseph; son Samuel; daughters,

Peggy, Elizabeth, Martha and Ann.
Exs., brothers-in-law Jordan and Joseph Denson.
D. Nov. 23, 1796 R. May 15, 1797
Wit. Henry Butts, Edmund Johnson, Zachariah Doyel
Page 781

BISHOP, Joseph. Parish of Nottoway. Leg. wife Ann,
son Mark, son Daniel; daughter Martha Bishop; daughter
Rebecca Wells; daughter Mary Holt, son William Bishop
Exs., wife Ann and son William Bishop
D. Sept. 15, 1795 R. May 15, 1797
Wit. Henry Davis, Joel Davis
Exs., refused and Edmund Marks qualified Page 782

EDWARDS, Benjamin. Leg.- nephew Benjamin Blunt; re-
mainder of my estate to be divided between the children of
my brothers William and Richard Edwards; the children of my
sisters Elizabeth Edmunds and Ann Blunt.
Exs., brothers William and Richard Edwards.
D. Dec. 17, 1796 R. May 15, 1797
Wit. Richard Blow, John T. Blow, Jr., William Blow
Page 783

DRAKE, Barnaby, Sr. Leg.- son Exum; daughter Sarah,
wife of John Powell; daughter Martha; to Albuin (?) son of
Jacob Jenkins; son Simmons; wife Mary; son
Burwell, when of age; youngest daughters, Milbra and Penny;
daughters Mourning and Martha land adjoining that Samuel
Hart bought of Exum Drake; wife Mary.
Ex., Son Simmons Drake.
D. Dec. 26, 1791 R. May 15, 1797
Wit. Jesse Willeford, Thomas Carlile, John Beaton.
Page 783

JOYNER, Joshua. Parish of Nottoway. Leg.- son John;
son Joshua; son Drewry; son Nelson; son Elisha; daughter
Fereby; daughter Edith; wife Martha. (Refers to eight
children only seven named.
D. Sept. 14, 1783 R. May 15, 1797
Exs., sons John and Joshua Joyner
Wit. Joseph Scott, Jr., Joseph Mountfortt, Joshua Joyner
Page 785

HARRIS, William. Account current. Signed Jo. Vick,
Sheriff.
D. April 13, 1797 R. May 15, 1798 Page 787

DUNNING, John. Estate appraised by John D. Hausmann, John Clayton, Thomas Lane.
D. Oct. 8, 1796   R. May 15, 1798 (?)   Page 787

BAILEY, Captain Hartwell. Estate appraised by Mark Judkins, Peter Booth, James Booth
D. Jan. 16, 179   R. May 15, 1797   Page 788

HICKS, William. Estate appraised. (not signed)
D. Nov. 1796   R. May 15, 1797   Page 790

THORPE, Moses. Account current. Signed John Thorpe, Ex. Audited by Robert Mabry and John Williamson.
D. 1790   R. May 15, 1797   Page 792

LITTLE, William. Estate appraised by James Lundy, James Harris, Lunsford Lundy
D. May 29, 1794   R. May 15, 1797   Page 791

WESTBROOK, Samuel. Account current. Signed, Burwell Westbrook, Ex.   D. 1785   Among items, paid Hannah Westbrook guardian to Turner, David, Joel, Samuel and Pheby Westbrook; paid Sheriff, copy of execution Ann and Rebecca Westbrook, decd., by the amount of that part of the estate sent Mary Westbrook during her life.
Audited by Robert Mabry and James Lundy. D. Dec. 23, 1786
D. May 15, 1797   Page 793

HART, Robert. Leg.- son John; son Robert; son Drewry; wife Sarah; daughters, Avereler, Silvier and Sarah
Wit. Richard Hart.
D. Dec. 22, 1739   R. May 15, 1797
Wit. Joseph Hart, Joseph Hart, Jr., Jesse Hart.
Ex. refused and John Hart qualified   Page 794

BLUNT, Elizabeth. Estate appraised by J. Kindred; Drew Powell and William Newton.
D. Aug. 29, 1796   R. May 15, 1797   Page 795

HART, Jesse. Estate appraised by William Adkinson

Charles Sadler and Joseph Hart.
D. Feb. 23, 1796   R. May 15, 1797   Page 795

APPLEWHITE, Henry.   Account current, signed, by
John Applewhite, Ex.   Audited by Zebulon Lewis and
Thomas Peete, Jr.   R. May 15, 1797   Page 796

HARRIS, Amos. Account current. Signed Arthur
Applewhite the surviving Ex.   Audited by Robert Mabry,
John Williamson and L. Mason.
D. March 12, 1790   R. May 15, 1797   Page 799

. EDWARDS, William. Leg.- son James land bought of
Speed and that of Mills Applewhite, adjoining Jonah
Edwards; son Elias; refers to land which he has sod to
Simon Murfee; son Albridgeton; daughter Sally Wester;
daughter Elizabeth Williams; daughter Lyddy Lawrence;
daughter Mary; wife Priscilla; son William
Exs., sons James, William and Elias Edwards.
D. March 21, 1794   R. Sept. , 1795 (?) Page 800
Wit. (not given)

HARRIS, William.   Account Current. Adm. Arthur
Applewhite, being deceased, presented by John Applewhite
his Adm.   Audited by Robert Mabry, John Williamson and
L. Mason. D. July 19, 1794   R. May 15, 1797
Page 801

APPLEWHITE, Ann.   Account current. Signed, John
Applewhite, Ex.   Among items: interest on money advanced
to Sarah Moore and Henry Applewhite.   Audited by Thomas
Peete and Thomas Peete, Jr.   R. May 15, 1797
Page 802

POWELL, James. Account current. Signed, Samuel
Calvert, Adm.   Audited by James Bennett, T. W. Clements.
R. May 15, 1797   Page 803

BARHAM, Robert. of the Parish of St. Luke. Leg.-
wife Hannah; daughter Peggy; daughter Charlot; daughter
Sally; son Howel; daughter Mary Cooper; to all my children-

Milly Hutchings; Patsey Gilliam; Betsey Gilliam; Peggy; Charlot; Sally and Howel.
Exs. friend John Simmons and Joel Barham
D. March 20, 1792   R. May 15, 1797
Wit. John Simmons, Sr., Levy Rochell, Joel Barham and
      Peter Mannery   Page 803

DAUGHTRY, Elizabeth. Account current. Signed, James Gardner, Ex. D. L790. Audited by James Edwards, William Fowler and William Edwards.
R. May 16, 1797   Page 804

KIRBY, John. Estate appraised by John Simmons, Micah Ellis, Moody Collier.
D. Jan. 30, 1797   R. July 17, 1797   Page 805

FLETCHER, Benjamin. Estate appraised by Sol Homes, Timothy Atkinson, Britten Britt.
D. Aug. 19, 1796   R. July 17, 1797   Page 807

JOYNER, Joshua, Jr. Estate appraised by J. Scott, John Bowers, Willis Bowers.
D. Feb. 1, 1797   R. July 17, 1797   Page 808

ELCOME, Richard. Account Current. D. 1797 Audited by Benjamin Ruffin and Philips Davis.
R. July 17, 1797   Page 809

WILLIAMS, Richard. Leg.- wife Rachel; son George; daughter Elizabeth Williams.
Ex., Charles Birdsong.
D. June 29, 1795   R. July 17, 1797
Wit. Charles Birdsong, Giles Joiner, Mathew Bryant.
                                              Page 811

HURST, William. Leg.- wife Nancy; son William; my eight children, Amy, Abraham, Charles, Cate, Easter, Oliver, Delitha and Write
Ex.; Charles Birdsong.
D. June 20, 1795   R. July 17, 1797

WIT. Charles Birdson, Giles Joyner, Mathew Bryant
Page 812

JONES, James, Sr.. Estate appraised. Signed, James, Anselm and Jordan Jones. Appraisers not named.
D. March 3, 1793 R. July 17, 1797 Page 814

GRAY, John. Account current. Signed Hannah Gray, Admtx. Audited by Thomas Turner and Benjamin Blunt, Jr.
R. July 17, 1797 Page 815

POND, Mason. Estate appraisal. Appraised by John Collier, William Wellons and John Davis
D. June 5, 1797 R. July 17, 1797 Page 816

BEALE, Richard. Leg.- daughter Millia; son Asa the plantation bought of Hardy Pope; son Abia; daughter Jady; son Silah, tract bought of William Ward; son Elijah; son Dickey; son Jacob; daughter Nancy; daughter Alice.
Exs., sons, Asa, Abia and Silah Beale.
D. Jan. 9, 1797 R. July 17, 1797
Wit. Kinchen Edwards, William Fowler, Margaret Joiner
Page 817

DeLoach, Solomon. Estate appraisal. Signed, Fred'k. Parker, Adm. Appraised by William Chambless, Richard Clements, Joel Barham.
D. June 13, 1797 R. July 17, 1797 Page 818

TRAVIS, Pyland. Leg.- wife Lucy; daughters, Tabitha and Patey Travis.
Exs., brother Charles Travis and Drury Lane.
D. Nov. 16, 1795 R. July 17, 1797
Wit. Richard Hargrave, Samuel Hargrave, Catherine Travis
Page 820

BISHOP, Joseph. Estate appraisal. Appraisers, Mark Judkins, James Booth, Britain Travis.
D. April 5, 1797 R. July 17, 1797 Page 820

THOMAS, William. Appraisal. Not signed.
R. July 17, 1797 Page 822

WILLIAMS, Richard. Account current. Signed, Jordan Williams, Ex. Audited by Jacob Darden, Sr. and Jacob Darden, Jr.
D. 1794   R. July 17, 1797   Page 824

COOPER Jesse. Account current. Signed, Cordal Barnes. Among items, to paid the balance of his wife's guardian's accounts. Audited by Jo. Vick and A. M. Neil.
D. Jan 19, 1794   R. July 17, 1797   Page 824

BELL, Richard. Estate appraised by William Fowler, Hincheon Edwards, Willis Johnson.
D. Feb. 19, 1797   R. July 17, 1797   Page 827

CHARLES, Jethro. Estate appraised by James Clark, Charles Council, Arthur B --ing.
D. Nov. 19, 1796   R. July 17, 1797   Page 829

GARDNER. James. Account current. Signed Jesse Gardner, Adm. Audited by J. Denson and John Davis.
R. July 17, 1797   Page 831

LUNDY, Edith. Leg.- son Peyton; daughter Nancy Rivers; daughter Patsey Nicholson; granddaughter Charlotte and grandson Byrd, children of son Peyton; son John Lundy.
Exs., son John and friend Robert Mabry.
D. July 30, 1797   R. Aug. 21, 1797
Wit. Moses Johnson, Robert Mabry   Page 833

DREWRY, Humphry. Leg. daughter Rebecca; daughter Mary Pond; daughter Hannah Simmons; daughter Elizabeth; daughter Rhody Andrews' children.
Exs. friend Samuel Drewry and John Pond, Jr.
D. Aug. 15, 1796   R. July 17, 1797
Wit. J. Vick, Thomas Hallcome, Charles Sandiford
                                              Page 835

Turner, Arthur. Estate appraised by John Crumpler, John Pursell and Arthur Crumpler
D Sept. 1795   R. Aug. 21, 1797   Page 836

EDWARDS, William. Estate appraised by William Fowler,
Kinchen Edwards and Seymore Vaughan. Signed by William
Edwards and Janes Edwards.
 D. May 27, 1797 R. Aug. 21, 1797   Page 837

APPLEWHITE, Thomas. Estate appraisal. Appraisers
not recorded. R. July 10, 1788   Page 339

-------- O -------

WILL BOOK FIVE.

HARRIS, West. Account current. Signed Henry
Thorpe, surviving Ex. Audited by Jamws Lundy and John
Williamson. D. March 1797 R. Aug. 21, 1797
               Page 1

MILTON, Elisha. Leg.- granddaughter Patsey Milton,
daughter of Ann Milton, the deed to be made her by Mr. Eth^d
Taylor; to my three children, Leah, Randolph and Ann Milton
Exs., friends Arthur Turner and Benjamin Barham, Jr.
 D. Dec. 1, 1788 R. Aug. 21, 1797
 Wit. Eth^d. Taylor, William Rose, William Jarrell
               Page 2

ADAMS, Benjamin. Account current. Signed Joseph
Prince, Ex. Audited by Thomas Peete and John Applewhite
 D. 1795 R. Aug. 21, 1797   Page 3.

EDMUNDS, Ann. Leg.- Mary Edmunds Dawson; Rebekah
Turner; my three granddaughters Sall Simmons, Jane Edmunds
Dawson, (3 ?); great granddaughter Ann Northington Turner;
said Ann dies without issue reversion to the children of
Edmund Turner; reversion of Jane Edmuhd's request to Sally
Simmons' children.
 Ex. Edmund Turner.
 D. Oct. 51, 1791 ... Aug 21, 1797
 Wit. Willie Francis, John Francis, Mary Smith
               Page 3

DRURY, William. Of the Parish of St Luke. Leg.- wife

Lucy; son John; son Charles; son Edmunds; daughter to Sally; to Polly Grizzard, daughter of Phebe Grizzard; son John to my brother Richard Drewry to raise; son Edmund to be bound to Humphry Drewry.
Ex., brother Richard Drewry.
D. May 16, 1791   R. Aug. 21, 1797
Wit. Henry Smith, Aaron Smith, Nathan Turner.   Page 4

RAY, John.   Leg.- son William; wife Celah; my children John, Mary, Elizabeth, William and Howell Ray.
Exs., wife and Jacob Barrett.
D. Aug. 22, 1796   R. Aug. 21, 1797
Wit. William Chitty, William Sandifur, Elizabeth Ray,
     Isham Jackson   Page 5

HART, Robert.   Estate appraised by Jos. Hart, Jesse Womble and William Bailey.   Signed, John Hart.
R. Aug. 21, 1797   Page 6

LOWE, Lighborn.   Leg.- my five sons, Jeremiah, Samuel (or Lemuel ?), Cajah, Willias and Wiley; daughter Milly; daughter Patsy.
D. Nov. 16, 1796   R. Aug. 21, 1797
Exs., Britain Boykin and John Crumpler
Wit. Micajah Lowe, John Crumpler, Jr., Benjamin Britt
                                                  Page 8

COBB, Michael.   Account current.   Signed, Exum Cobb, Ex.   Paid legacy due Jeremiah Cobb, son of John Cobb, deceased; paid board and schooling for Benjamin and Thomas; ditto for George B. Cobb.   Audited by Charles Bailey, Sr., Robert Goodwyn, Charles Briggs, Jr., Edwin Gray.
R. Aug. 21, 1797   Page 10

HOWELL, Goodrich.   Leg.- brother Alfred Howell after mother's death.
Ex., brother Alfred Howell.
D. Jan. 3, 1797   R. Aug. 21, 1797
Wit. James Irwin, Aaron Smith, Thomas Vaughan.   Page 12

ELLIS, Henry.   Nuncupative will.. Estate to be divided between his four sisters' children: Miles Everett; Benjamin Ellis, Folly C. Ellis and Suasn Hatfield.   He desired his

sister Martha to have his house.
D. April 14, 1797   R. Aug. 21, 1797
Proved by Mary Vick, Ann Rowland and Dorcy Drake, having
died at the house of Jacob Vick   Page 12

ELLISON, Gerrard. Estate appraised by William Bailey,
Jesse Womble, Rich. Hart.
D. Dec. 3, 1796   R. Aug. 21, 1797   Page 13

SUTER (or Luter), John. Account current. Signed, Henry
Smith, Ex. Audited by Henry Blunt and Nathaniel Edwards.
D. July 19, 1738   R. Aug. 21, 1797   Page 14

HARRIS, Landon. Signed, Ann Harris, Admtx. Audited
by John Taylor Jr., Ran⁴. Newsum
D. L795   R. Aug. 21, 1797   Page 16

BAILEY, Captain Hartwell. Account current. Signed,
Jordan Judkins, Peter Bailey. Among items, paid Jesse
Carrell for taking care of two orphans; artcles bought for
the widow. Audited by James Gray and John Brittle.
R. Aug. 21, 1797   Page 16

BURGESS, Henry John. Leg.- wife Sarah; daughter
Elizabeth Matilda when eighteen; son Albridgton Samuel
Hardy Burgess when twenty one.
Exs., Captain James Gray, Col. Albridgton Jones,
      Gen. Lawrence Baker, Dr. Simmons J. Baker.
I appoint Gen. Baker, guardian to my daughter if her
mother should die and Dr. S. Baker, guardian to my son.
D. Feb. 14, 1797.
Wit. William Kello, Thomas Ridley, William D. Hines.
Codicil: My exs. to repair my house.
Wit. Elizabeth Baker, Willis Wilkinson, Emily Briggs.
R. March 28, 1797   Page 17

LANCASTER, James. Estate appraised by Edward Bailey,
Harmon Harris and John Williamson. R. Oct. 16, 1797
                                              Page 18

TRAVIS, Pyland. Estate appraised by Burrell Barrett,
John Jones and Anselm Jones.

Signed, Drewry Lane, Ex.   R. Oct. 16, 1797

Page 20

CLAUD, Edwin. Leg.- all my children, when son Joseph is
twenty one.   Ex., wife Elizabeth and friend Henry Barrow.
D. July 11, 1797   R. Oct. 16, 1797
Wit. John Barrow, William Fitzhugh, Jr., Joseph Mundell

Page 21

Evans, Hannah.   Signed, John T. Blow, Sr., Ex. Account
current.   Among items, paid heirs to the estate of Martha
Pope, Nathaniel Pope and Ben. C. M. Evans.   Audited by
Thomas Edmunds and Henry Thomas.   R. Oct. 16, 1797

Page 22

JOHNSTON, Elijah. Estate appraised by Thomas Wood,
John Morris, Joel Davis. Signed John Jones.
D. Oct. 16, 1797

Page 22

REESE, John . Account current. Signed Roger and
Randolph Reese. Audited by Zebulon Lewis and Thomas Peete
D. Dec. 1794   R. Oct. 16, 1797

Page 23

POND, Richard, Sr.   Estate appraised by Thomas Gray,
Thomas Wood and Thomas Laine.
D. Nov. 12, 1796   R. Dec. 18, 1797

Page 24

MAGET, Nicholas.   Leg.- son John; son James land purchased of William Bryant; son Samuel, plantation adjoining Arthur
Whitehead and said son; son William, land in Northampton Co,
N. Car., son Nicholas; to Sally Everstt daughter of Etheldred
and Elizabeth Everett; negroes given to John Edmunds, decd.,
to be considered his part of my estate; negroes put in the
possession of Etheldred Everett decd., may be considered his
part of my estate
Exs., sons, John and Samuel Maget.
D. Dec. 10, 1795   R. Dec. 18, 1897
Wit. William Bryant Sr., Exum Everett, Jacob Gilliam

Page 25

VICK, James. Estate appraised by John Davis, James Bell,
Spencer Pierce.
D. Oct. 3, 1796   R. Dec. 18, 1797   Page 27

CLARKE, William.   Leg.- wife Sarah, the land left me
in Surry County by my grandfather Clarke's will.
Extx., wife Sarah.
D. Sept. 8, 1797   R. Dec. 18, 1797
Wit. Humphry Drewry, Harris Johnston, John Blake.
Page 28

HART, John.   Estate appraised by Jesse Carrel, John
Brittle and Newsum Branch.   R. Dec. 18, 1797
Page 28

MERCER, John.   Account estate.- paid John Crumpler for
schooling two children.   Audited by William Urquhart and
and Solo. Holmes.   R. Dec. 18, 1797   Page 30

GARDNER, Joshua.   Estate appraised by William Fowler,
Jonah Edwards, Robert Pebworth.   Signed Martha Gardner.
D. Oct. 28, 1797.   R. Dec. 18, 1797   Page 30

ATKINSON, Ann.   Estate appraised by J. Kindred, Henry
Porter and Thomas Taylor.   Signed, Elias Atkinson
D. Dec. 2, 1796   R. Dec. 18, 1797   Page 31

WESTBROOK, William.   Estate appraisal.   (not signed)
D. Nov. 5, 1796   R. Jan. 15, 1798   Page 32

DAVIS, Henry.   Leg.- son Archibald; son Henry after
his mother's death; daughter Hannah Ray; daughter Jeany;
my negro Samuel a tract of land adjoining Richard Blunt.
Exs., wife Lucy, son Henry and Phillip Davis.
D. Oct. 12, 1797   R. April 16, 1798
Wit. Nathaniel Davis, Sarah Mitchel, Charles Briggs, Sr.
Page 33

WHITEHEAD, William.   Appraisal.   (not signed)
D. Sept. 20, 1796   R. June 15, 17--   Page 34

BROCK, Thomas.   Leg. - wife Lucy with reversion of be-
quest to my three children, John; Thomas Ellis and Polly
McKenny Brock; to Belah Williford's four children, Josiah;
Samuel; Susanna and William when twenty one; son Wiliam;

son Benjamin; granddaughter Susanna Williford.
Exs., Edward Bailey and Solomon Holmes and son William.
D. Feb. 3, 1795   P. Aug. 21, 1797   R. Jan. 15, 1798
Wit. Sarah Bailey, William Bailey, James Butts.
Page 38

WESTBROOK, Henry.   Parish of Nottoway.   Leg.- brother
William Person Westbrook; mother Priscilla Westbrook.
Ex., brother William Person Westbrook
D. Oct. 3, 1793   R. Jan. 15, 1798
Wit. John Simmons, Sr., Sally Westbrook   Page 40

HOLLEMAN, Will.   Estate appraised by Edward Bailey,
William Atkinson, Joseph Hart.
D. Dec. 19, 1796   R. Jan. 15. 1798   Page 40

WILLIAMS, Jacob.   Estate appraised by Henry Branch, Drew
Branch and John Warren
D. Nov. 23, 1797   R. Jan. 15, 1798   Page 42

BLAKE, Ben.   Estate appraised by John Barnes, Harris
Johnson and Joseph Turner.
D. Nov. 30, 1797   R. Jan. 15, 1798   Page 43

CRUMPLER, Beasant.   Parish of Nottoway.   Leg.- son
William; Allen Johnson; son Beasant; Allen Little; Eley
Johnson; wife Sarah; daughter Molly Jones; daughter Betsey
Crumpler; daughter Sally Crumpler.
Exs., son Beasant and friend John Crumpler.
D. Oct. 1, 1795   R. Jan 15, 1798
Wit. William Crumpler, Benjamin Crumpler, West Tyus, Jr.
Page 45

CHARLES, Eleanor.   Leg.- son William; son Charles; daugh-
ter Elizabeth.
Exs., friend Josiah Johnson and Joseph Denson
D. Oct. 2, 1797   R. Jan. 15, 1798
Wit. Thomas Chappell, Joseph Denson, Jr., Caty Joiner
Page 46

LOWE, Lighborn.   Estate appraised by Arthur Crumpler,
Jacob Turner, James Johnson.
D. Oct. 26, 1797   R. Jan. 15, 1798   Page 47

BENNETT, John.   Inventory.   Signed, William Bennett, Ex.
R. Jan. 16, 1798   Page 48

DELOACH, Sarah.   Parish of St. Luke.   Leg.- daughter
Lucy; daughter Polly; son Richard Deloach
Ex., son Richard Deloach
D. Aug. 20, 1797   R. Jan 16, 1798
Wit. Will Barnes, Joshua Johnson.   Page 49

POPE, Nancy.   Orphan of Henry Pope in account with
Samuel Roe.   D. 1796   Page 50

NEWSUM, Sampson.   Account current.   Signed, Robert
Andrews, Ex.   Audited by William Chambless and Richard
P. Clements.   D. 1779   R. April 17, 1798   Page 50

MYRICK, Henry.   Account current. Signed, William
Chambless.   Among items: paid Fanny Myrick balance due
her from her guardian Henry Myrick; paid Henry Myrick ditto;
paid Owen Myrick ditto; paid John Myrick ditto; each paid
the same amount of his estate,- Sally Blow; Nancy Fort;
Fanny Myrick and Owen Myrick; cash paid Owen Myrick, guardian
of Lucy Myrick, cash paid myself as guardian of John Myrick.
Audited by Richard P. Clements and John Taylor, Jr.
R. April 17, 1798   Henry Myrick , grandson of Henry Myrick
                                                    Page 51

BRANTLEY, Etheldred.   Estate appraised by William Edmunds,
William Blunt and John Moore
D. Dec. 22, 1797   R. April 17, 1798   Page 53

WARREN, Benjamin.   Estate appraised by Boaz G. Summerell,
Henry Branch, Henry Summerell.   D. Dec. 8, 1797 R.
                                                    Page 54

KIRBY, Ann.   Leg.- my land to be equally divided between
Moody Kirby, Gideon Bell and Lewis Kirby; rest of estate to
be divided between my brothers and sisters,- William Kirby,
Moody Kirby, Zelby Drake, Gideon Bell, Pamelia Bell and
Elizabeth Bell.   Ex., Moody Cotton.(?).
D.   R. May 21, 1798
Wit. Nicholas Williams Gilas (?) Kirby, James Bell
                                                    Page 55

DAWSON, Tuke. Parish of Nottoway. Leg.- wife Ann; three daughters, Rebecca, Elizabeth and Catherine Denson; son Joseph Dawson. Exs., wife Ann and Peter Denson.
D. Jan 14, 1789   R. May 21, 1798
Wit. Joseph Hill, Mills Denson, Rebecca Denson

Page 56

DREWRY, Humphry. Estate appraised by William Wellons, Arthur Bowing and Jesse Gardner.   R. May 21, 1798

Page 56

DREWRY, William. Estate appraised by William Blunt, John Blunt and Henry Blunt. Signed, Robert Mabry
D. Jan. 8, 1798   R.   Page 57

BARHAM, Charles. Estate account   Signed, Edward Fisher, Adm.   Audited by John Simmons, Sr., Thomas Turner and Mark Nicholson.
D. Feb. -- 1796   R. May 21, 1798   Page 58

BROCK, James. Leg.- wife Hannah; grandson John Chavos, commonly called John Brock, son of my daughter Elizabeth Brock; daughter Sarah Read.
Extx., daughter Sarah Reas
D. Feb. 5, 1798   R. May 21, 1798
Wit. John Day, John Kindred.   Page 58

HASTY, Moses. Account current. Signed, Edward Fisher Audited by John Simmons, Jr., Thomas Turner, Mark Nicholson
D. Feb. 25, 1792   R. May 21, 1798   Page 59

GILLIAM, Arthur. Estate appraised by Moses Foster, Robert Nicholson and William Butts. Signed, Robert Goodwyn. . R. May 21, 1798   Page 60

BARHAM, James. Account current. Legacies paid Joel Barham, James Barham, Judkins Barham, Samuel Barham, Timothy Barham, John Barham, Joel Harris, William Holleman, Bailey Barnes, John Meacome and Edward Fisher. Audited by John Simmons, Jr. Thomas Turner and Mark Nicholson.
R. May 21, 1798   Page 61

ALLEN, Arthur. Account estate. Signed, William
Boykin, Adm.   D. 1777.   Legacies paid James Allen,
Benjamin Allen, Ann Allen, Polly Allen, Holland Allen
Audited by Sol. Holmes, Timothy Atkinson   R. May 21, 1798
Page 62

RANDOLPH, Temperance.   Account current. Signed,
William Brown, Adm.   Audited by William Blunt and Richard
Harrison.   D. 1796   R. July 16, 1798   Page 62

TURNER, Henry. Account current.   Signed, William
Turner, Ex.   Paid Will Turner his legacy; paid widow's
dower. Henry Turner in account with William Turner; refers
to his orphans and expenses paid for John Turner, Elizabeth
Turner and Benjamin Turner.
D. 1792   R. July --, 1798   Page 63

SMITH, Aaron.   Of St luke's Parish. Leg.- estate to
be used for the education of my children until son Thomas
becomes twenty one; wife Rebecca; children, William Turner
Smith; Thomas and Polly Smith.
Exs., friends Thomas Holladay Jr., and Benjamin Blunt
D. Feb. 4, 1798   R. May 21, 1798
Wit. James B. Womack, Burwell Westbrook, David Westbrook
Page 65

CHARLES, Elenor.   Estate appraised by Arthur Bowing,
Henry Jones and Mills Daniel   R. July 16, 1798   Page 67

SPIVEY, William.   Appraisal.   Signed, Britain Spivey
and Benjamin Spivey.   D. March 1794   R. July 16, 1798
Page 68

BROCK, James.   H. Cl. Servents(?), Thomas Jones, Drew
Powell and John Woodward, Appraisers.
D. July 14, 1798   R. July 16, 1798   Page 68

BRYANT, William.   Leg.- wife Sally, with reversion to
son Cordal Bryant the land adjoining Edmund Barrett and
Jacob Williams; another tract adjoining James Vick, Lewis
Worrell, Giles Joyner and Jordan Vick; to Lewis Worrell
Exs., wife Sally and Drewry Bryant.
D. Sept. 20, 1797   R. July 16, 1798

Wit. Lewis Worrell, Nathan Williams, Jacob Williams.
Page 69

WADE, Wilson. Estate appraised by Cordial Row, Mills Daniel and Jacob Corbett.
D. Nov. 9, 1797   R. July 16, 1798   Page 70

CRUMPLER, Beasant. Estate appraised by Britain Boykin, James Johnson and Arthur Crumpler.   R. Aug. 20, 1798
Page 71

BRADSHAW, Thomas. Leg.- wife Susannah; son William; my three children, William, Martha and Edia Bradshaw
Exs., wife Susannah and son William Bradshaw.
D. Sept. 16, 1796   R, Aug. 20, 1798
Wit. Elizabeth Hedgepeth, Micajah Griffin, Jr.
     Elizabeth Griffin   Page 72

ROGERS, Collins. Estate appraised by Thomas Gilliam, Robert Nicholson and Henry Simmons.   Signed, James Guy (?)
D. Jan. 28, 1797   R. Aug. 20, 1798   Page 73

WILLIAMS, Henry. Account current. Signed, Arthur Bowen, Adm. L. 1788. Paid William Boykin, guardian of Sally and Elizabeth Williams; paid Shadrack Corbett for his wife; paid Elisha Whitney for his wife.
Audited by Sam. Kello and Samᴸ. Kello, Jr.
R. Aug. 20, 1798   Page 74

NEWTON, Alice. Estate appraised by Nathan Bryant, J. Kindred, Drew Powell.   Signed, William Newton
D. April 1793   R. Aug. 20, 1798   Page 74

CLIFTON, Cordey. Estate appraised by Henry Harrison, James Lundy and Richard Harrison.
D. May 25, 1798   R. Aug. 26, 1798   Page 75

SUTER, Arthur. Inventory. Signed, John Suter
D. Oct. 20, 1796   R. Aug. 20, 1798   Page 76

TAYLOR, Temperance. Inventory. Signed, John Taylor.
R. Oct. 15, 1798   Page 77

JONES, Sarah. Leg.- mother-in-law my estate received
from my deceased husband, Charles B. Jones; reversion to
Ann Jones and Elizabeth B. Jones, daughters of the said
Elizabeth, Hannah B. Jones, daughter of Thomas Jones,
Rebecca W. Jones, daughter of aforesaid Thomas; Susannah
Drew; Sarah Norfleet Blunt, daughter of William Blunt; my
mother Mary Gee; Lavinia Norfleet Gee, daughter of my
father-in-law James Gee, all the land I am entitled to in
Southampton and Northampton, N. Car., at the death of my
brother to my mother Mary Gee; uncle John Wilkinson.
    Exs., uncle John Wilkinson and father-in-law James Gee
    D. Sept. 21, 1798   R. Oct. 15, 1798
    Wit. Martha Williamson, Henry Coker, James Wilkinson
                                                   Page 77

BITTLE, Robert. Inventory. Signed, William Bittle, Ex.
D. Aug. 19, 1795   R. Oct. 15, 1798   Page 79

NEWSUM, Patience. Parish of St. Luke. Leg.- Isham
Newsum and Sally his wife; to my said daughter Sally Newsum
with reversion to Martha Gilliam and Elizabeth Newsum;
Martha Taylor with reversion to my five granddaughters,
Nancy, Sally N., Betsey, Mary and Lucy Taylor; Patsey G.
Newsum; two daughters, Martha Taylor and Sally Newsum's
children.   Ex., friend Thomas Jones.
    D. June 1, 1798   R. Oct. 15, 1798
    Wit. Thomas Pope, John Barrow, Lucy Barrow   Page 80

BUTTS, Elizabeth. Parish of St. Luke. Leg.- son
Benjamin; daughter Jenny; my four children, namely Benjamin,
Robert, Jenny and Polly Nicholson.
    Exs., friends Zeblon Lewis and Benjamin Lewis.
    D. July 2, 1798   R. Oct. 15, 1798
    Wit. Zebulon Lewis, Richard P. Clements, James Simmons
                                                   Page 81

BYRD, James. Estate appraised by John Blunt and
William Blunt. D. Oct. 28, 1790   R. Oct. 15, 1798
                                                   Page 82

DELOACH, Richard. Estate appraised by Thomas Edmunds,

Eth'd Edmunds and Nathan Pope.
D. Jan. 26, 1798   R. Oct. 15, 1709   Page 82

DELOACH, Sarah.   Estate appraised by Thomas Edmunds,
Eth'd Edmunds and Nathan Pope
D. Jan. 26, 1798   R. Oct. 15, 1798   Page 82

VICK, Joshua.   Appraisal of estate remoining in the hands
of Elizabeth Wilson, the relict of said Joshua at the time of
of her death. Signed, William Vick.   Appraisers:- William
Murfee, Richard Blow and Amos Stephens.   Signed, Jeremiah
Drake as to the negroes.   R. Oct. 15, 1798   Page 83

COBB, Exum.   Parish of Nottoway. Leg.- surviving
brothers and sisters; sister Rebecca Mecom; my negro man to
be hired during the life of Mrs. Mary Norseworthy and the
money to be divided as above.
Ex., Charles Briggs, Jr.
D. Jan 26, 1798   R. Oct. 15, 1798
Wit. James Irwin, Ann Salter, Will Hines   Page 85

BRADSHAW, Thomas.   Estate appraised by Arthur Bowing,
Miles Griffin and John Worrell
D. Sept. 6, 1798   R. Oct. 15, 1798   Page 86

BRISTER, Samuel. Leg.- wife Mary; daughter Polly; daugh-
ter Frances Brister.   Ex., John Urquhart
D. Jan. 29, 1798   R. Oct. 15, 1798
Wit. William Urquhart, Samuel Johnson.   Page 86

VICK, Joshua. Account current of the estate lent to his
wife Elizabeth with William Vick, Adm. and to which is added
the estate of Elizabeth Wilson, formerly Elizabeth Vick, decd.
Audited by George Gurley, Richard Blow and Drewry Beal
R. Sept. 17, 1798   Page 87

REESE, Mary. Account current. Signed, Randolph Reese.
Audited by Zebulon Lewis and Thomas Peete.
D. Feb. 1796   R. Oct. 15, 1798   Page 88

BIRD, James. Account current. Signed, John Wilkinson, Adm.

Audited by William Blunt and Willie Francis
D. Oct. 29, 1791   R. Oct. 15, 1798   Page 88

BROCK, Thomas. Estate appraised by William Atkinson,
Joseph Hart and Richard Hart.
D. 1797   R. Dec. 17, 1798   Page 89

LANCASTER, Rebecca. Estate appraised by Edward Bailey,
John Womble, David Davis.
D. Jan. 1798   R. Dec. 17, 1798   Page 91

JOHSON, Sarah. Parish of St. Luke. Leg.- son Harris;
grandson Jordan Johnson the land on which Hannah Johnson
now lives; granddaughter Rebecca Harrison; Nancy Johnson;
to all my granddaughters, Rebecca Harrison, Nancy Johnson,
Sally Johnson, Martha Johnson and Molly Johnson.
Exs., son Harris Johnson and Joel Johnson.
D. Feb. 2, 1795   R. Dec. 17, 1798
Wit. Stephenson Blake, Lucy Blake, Spratley Stevenson
                                               Page 92

Worrell, Josiah. Estate appraised by James Barnes, Newit
Vick and Micajah Edwards.
D. March 1795   R. Dec. 17, 1798   Page 93

MAGET, Nicholas. Estate appraised by William Bryant, Sr.
William Bryant, Jr. and Exum Everett.
D. Nov. 1797   R. Dec. 17, 1798   Page 94

MYRICK, Ann. Estate appraised by Howell Jones, Richard
Blunt, John Barham and Benjamin Barham.
D. Feb. 15, 1796   R. Dec. 17, 1798   Page 95

NICHOLSON, Charles. Leg.- father, after emancipation
of slaves.
Exs., father Harris Nicholson and Dr. Anselm Bailey, Jr.
D. Aug. 27, 1798   R. Dec. 17, 1798
Wit. Benjamin Hines, John Foster.   Page 97

CLAUD, Edwin. Estate appraised by Burwell Whitfield,

David Westbrook and John Blake.
D. April 19, 1798   R. Dec. 17, 1798   Page 97

JOHNSON, Stephen. Estate appraised by Jo. Scott, Lem[1].
Hart and Absalom Joyner.
D. March 29, 1797   R. Dec. 17, 1798   Page 99

SPEED, Charles. Leg.- grandchildren, Suckey, Dickey and
Milly Speed, children of my son Henry Speed, decd.; son
William; wife Jenny; son Thomas; grandchildren Charles, Rhoda
and Patience, the children of my son William
    Exs., friends, Charles Briggs and Henry Briggs.
    D. Sept. 20, 1798   R. Dec. 17, 1798
    Wit. Joseph Vick, Silas Pledger, Lucy Pledger
                                               Page 100

MYRICK, Howell. Manumits slaves. Leg.- estate to my
children, Evans; William M.; Howell; William and Benjamin;
sister Sarah Evans to live with my children.
    Exs., brother Etheldred Evans and Sally Evans
    D. May 15, 1798   R. Dec. 17, 1798
    Will proved by Anthony Evans and John Applewhite Page 101

WARREN, Benjamin. Leg.- wife Mary Warren.
Extx., wife Mary Warren.
D. Dec. 16, 1794   R.
Wit. Edm. Tyler, Sally Warren   Page 102

RAWLINGS, Edwin. Estate appraised by Clait Clifton,
John Rives and John Lundy
    D. Sept. 1, 1798   R. Nov. 19, 1798   Page 102

CRAFFORD, John. Account current. William Hines, Adm.
Paid Mary Crafford for the benefit of the children, propor-
tional part paid to the following:- Mary Crafford's dower,
Henry Crafford, Elizabeth Craffor and Lucy Crafford.
    Audited by Robert Goodwyn and Charles Briggs.   Page 103
    R. Nov. 20, 1798

WILLIAMS, Benjamin. Account current. Signed, Josiah
Vick, Ex. and Mary Williams Extx. Paid expenses of Polly
and Egbert Williams. States the widow had married John

Williams. (large estate, covering fourteen pages.).
D. 1787   R. Aug 21, 1798   Page 104

JUDKINS, Jordan. Estate appraised by Edward Bailey,
Thomas Pretlow and John Womble
D. Oct. 1798   R. Jan. 22, 1799   Page 118

CALVERT, Christopher. Account current. Signed, Samuel
Calvert, Adm. Paid taxes in the Borough og Norfolk; the
heirs of the estate paid their proportional part; paid
Albridgeton Jones in right of his wife Frances; Mathew
Calvert; Ann Holt Calvert; Cornelius B. Calvert; Samuel
Calvert; Spencer Pierce in right of his wife Mary; heirs of
intestate the proportional part of the estate of Cornelius
B. Calvert's estate; paid Peggy Calvert, widow.
Audited by J. Vick and Thomas W. Clements.
D. 1789   R. Jan. 22, 1799   Page 120

SPIVEY, John. Account current. Signed, Charles Briggs,
Adm. Paid bond to the estate of his father William Spivey
Audited by Benjamin Ruffin and Sampson Stanton.
D. 1794   R. Jan. 22, 1799   Page 126

JOYNER, Mary. Leg.- James Joyner; Ely Joyner, son of
Joshua Joyner; Baker Joyner; Elizabeth Joyner of Jonas
Joyner; Elisha Joyner of John Joyner; Shadrack Cobb; Joshua
Joyner of John Joyner.
D. Oct. 22, 1798   R. Jan. 22, 1799
Wit. Baker Joyner, Elizabeth Joyner, Shadrack Cobb
                                                Page 127

VICK, Simon. Leg.- Andrew Mack Mial; granddaughter Mason
Vick; grandson Littleberry Vick; grandson John Vick; grand-
daughter Lucy Vick; grandson Peterson Vick; son Jacob; son
Jesse; son John Vick
Ex., son Jacob Vick
D. Sept. 26, 1798   R. Jan. 22, 1799
Wit. Thomas Pope, Ben Gray, John Barrow, Jonas Bryant
                                                Page 128

PERSON, Anthony. Leg.- wife Elizabeth; provision for
unborn child; brother John Person with reversion to the
children of Henry Person's present wife.
Exs., John Person and Richard Blunt

D. Aug. 20, 1798   R. Feb. 18, 1799
Wit. William Sturgeon, Henry Harrison, Henry Hayley (?)
Page 128

POND, Richard.   Account current. Signed, Mary Pond
and Drewry Pond.   Paid Daniel Pond, son of Daniel Pond;
Mathew Pond son of Daniel Pond his proportional part of his
grandfather's estate.
Audited by Edwin Gray and John H. Pond.
R. Feb. 18, 1799   Page 129

GRAY, Colonel Edwin.   Account current. Signed, Edwin
Gray Ex.   Paid Edmund Blunt his portion of the estate.
Audited by Benjamin Ruffin, Charles Briggs, Jr. and
Charles Briggs, Sr.   R. Feb. 18, 1799   Page 130

WILLIAMS, Sion   Leg.- wife Mary; son Drewry; son
John; daughter Frances Bun (?); son Burwell; son Jordan;
son Jeremiah; daughter Polly; son Eley land adjoining
Burwell Williams, Amos Council and Hardy Johnson; son Sion
land adjoining John Williams, Titus Fowler and Burwell
Williams. Friends Joseph Scott, Absalom Joyner and Samuel
Rowe to partition land; rest of my estate to my children,
Jordan, Silas, Benjamin and Lucy; the reversion of my be-
quest to my wife to my son George Williams.
Exs., sons Drewry and Burwell Williams
D. Jan. 16, 1799   R. Feb. 18, 1799
Wit. Absalom Joyner, Cordall Rowe, R. Johnson
Page 131

BRITT, Benjamin.   Estate appraised by Joel Edwards,
Thomas Everett, George Edwards.
D. Jan. 23, 1797   R. Feb. 18, 1799   Page 133

TURNER, Arthur.   Account current. Signed, Everett
Turner. Audited by Joel Boykin, John Crumpler, Jacob
Turner.   D. Aug. 1797   R. Feb. 18, 1799   Page 134

THORP, Jeremiah.   Account current, with the Ex. Administrator. Paid Willey Thorp's legacy; paid Hardy Thorp;
paid Lucy Long for her daughter Polly.
Ex., Joshua Thorpe decd.   Balance due the orphan of Mary
Spencer, agreeable to will.   Audited by John Williamson
and James Lundy.   R. Feb. 18, 1799.   Page 134

GARDNER, Joshua. Inventory. Signed, Henry Gardner and Ann Gardner. D. Dec. 16, 1793 R. April 15, 1799
Page 135

CARR, Jesse. Estate appraised by Jacob Darden, Jordan Williams and Semour Vaughan.
D. Jan. 28, 1797 R. April 15, 1799 Page 136

PERSON, John. To be buried agreeable to the form established by the Ancient Freemasons. Leg.- nephew John Anthony Person at twenty one, reversion to surviving children of Henry and Polly Person, namely Rebecca, Elizabeth and Polly Person; neice Marianna Person at twenty one with reversion to Rebecca, Elizabeth, Polly and John Anthony Person; neice Elizabeth Person.
Ex., Henry Person.
D. Dec. 1, 1798 R. April 15, 1799
Wit. Thomas Holladay, William Sturgeon, Peter Blow
Page 137

POND, Mary (The elder) Leg.- daughter Mary Wood; Mary Pond, the wife of my grandson John Pond, Jr,; son John; children of my deceased son Richard Pond.
Exs. John H. Pond and William Wellons
D. May 19, 1798 R. April 15, 1799
Wit. Dianna Pond, Samuel Pond, Benjamin Oney Page 138

TURNER, Ann. Estate appraised by John Suter, Pettway Johnson and Sam. Corbett.
D. Jan. 18, 1799 R. April 15, 1799

JONES, Lem[1]: Appraisal (not signed)
R. April 16, 1799 Signed, Joseph Jones, Ex. Page 140

JONES, Lemuel. Account current. Signed, Joseph Jones Audited by Edm. Tyler and John Clayton, Jr
R. April 16, 1799 Page 141

GARDNER, Joshua. Account current. Signed, Ann Gardner and Henry Gardner, Exs. To cash paid Daniel Webb a legacy left his wife. Audited by Jacob Darden, Sr. and Jacob Darden, Jr. D. 1793 R. April 15, 1799 Page 142

168

DARDEN, Ann.   Estate appraised by Jacob Darden, Seymour Vaughan, Jordan Williams.
D. April 20, 1799   R. May 20, 1799   Page 143

SIMMONS, Henry.   Signed, Charles Briggs, Adm.   Estate appraised by Micajah Ellis, John James and John Applewhite
D. Dec. 19, 1798   R. May 20, 1799   Page 143

BLOW, Benjamin.   Account current.   Signed, James Blow. Audited by James Millar and Jo. G. Blunt
D. 1797   R. May 20, 1799   Page 145

JOINER, Jesse.   Parish of Nottoway.   Leg.- wife Priscilla land left me by Joseph Vick; son Lewis; son Amos land given me by my father, on which Thomas Lowe now lives by rent; son Lemuel; daughter Margaret; daughter Sally; daughter Elizabeth; daughter Martha; daughter Levina Joyner.
Ex., son Lewis Joyner.   D. Sept. 25, 1789
Wit. William Ingram, Lucy Joyner, Lewis Joyner.
Codicil leaving further bequest to son Lemuel Joyner.   1798
Wit. Jos. Scott, Job Wright, George Camp.
R. May 20, 1799   Page 145

MORRIS, Nicholas, Sr.   Leg.- daughter Dizey Booth; daughter Mary Pond; Elizabeth Nash, my housekeeper; son John.
Ex., son John Morris.
D. June 21, 1797   R. May 20, 1799
Wit. William Briggs, Charles Briggs, Sr., Goodrich Wills
                                   Page 147

TURNER, John.   Leg.- uncle Benjamin Turner; cousin Joseph Turner.   Ex., Thomas Holladay, Jr.
D. April 2, 1799   R. May 20, 1799
Wit. Turner Newsum, Nathan Turner, Eliza Turner   Page 147

STEPHENSON, Sally.   Widow.   Parish of Nottoway.   Leg.-son William; daughter Sally; daughter Dizey; son Charles; son Lemuel Stephenson.   Ex., son Charles Stephenson
D. 1799   R. May 20, 1799
Wit. Arthur Holleman, Benjamin White   Page 148

JARROTT, Fortunatus.   Account current.   Signed, John Jarrott, Ex.   Legacy paid John Jarrott; legacy paid Nancy

Jarrott. Audited by John Applewhite and Hardy Applewhite
R. June 15, 1799   Page 149

RIDLEY, John E. Account current. Signed, William
Wright, Ex. Audited by Robert Mabry, Nathaniel Wyche
and Lewis Thorpe.
D. 1794   R. July 15, 1799   Page 149

THORP, Joshua, Jr. Inventory. Signed Hardy Thorp,
Adm. D. Oct. 25, 1794.   R. July 5, 1799   Page 151

SMITH, Aaron. Estate appraised by Benjamin Blunt, Jr.,
Henry Barrow and Jesse Holt
D. Aug. 1. 1798   R. July 15. 1799   Page 151

THORP, Joshua, Jr. Account current. Signed, Hardy
Thorp, Adm. Audited by Benjamin Blunt, Jr. and James Lundy
R. July 15, 1799   Page 152

POND, Mary. Estate appraised by Richard Pond, Sr.,
Drewry Pond and John Morris.
D. May 1, 1799   R. Aug. 19, 1799   Page 152

MYRICK, Ann. Account current. Signed, Howell Myrick,
Ex. Audited by Rand. Newsum and John Wall.
D. 1796   R. Aug. 19, 1799   Page 153

JOYNER, Jesse. Estate appraised by Kinchen Edwards,
William Beal, John Bryant.
D. June 1, 1799   R. Aug. 19, 1799   Page 154

JOHNSON, Stephen. Account current. Signed, Benjamin
Johnson, Ex. Audited by William Crichlow and W. Evans
D. 1797   R. Aug. 19, 1799   Page 154

ATKINSON, Ann. Account current. Signed, Elias
Atkinson, Ex. Paid legacies as follows: to Rachel Williams,

Elisha Atkinson, Benjamin Delk, Ann Atkinson.
Audited by Lazarus Cook and Drew Powell.
D. 1795 R. Aug. 19, 1799 Page 155

PAYN, Thomas. Estate appraised by Michael Warren and
Lt_ (?) Fort. D. Dec. 4, 1796 R. Oct. 21, 1799
Page 156

GARDNER, Ann. Leg.- son James; son Amos Gardner.
Exs., friends Capt. Joseph Vick and Arthur Bowing
D. Aug. 22, 1799 R. Oct. 21, 1799
Wit. Benjamin Vick, John Adams Page 157

TAYLOR, John, Jr. Leg.- sons William and Henry at
twenty one; wife; my children, William, Nancy, Elizabeth,
Hannah and Henry Taylor
Exs., Robert Goodwyn, Ellis G. Blake.
D. Feb. 10, 1799 R. Nov. 19, 1799
Wit. Ellis Gray Blake, Thomas Peete Page 157

HANCOCK, Samuel. Estate appraised by Benjamin Branch,
Joseph Washington and James Johnson. R. Dec. 16, 1799
Page 158

BRIGGS, Samuel. Leg.- half brother Henry Briggs, the
plantation purchased of Richard Blow and Capt Thomas
Chappell, which was given me by my father, my wife to be
allowed her right of dower; sister Martha Edmunds; half
brother William Briggs; nephew David Edmunds; nephew George
Edmunds, rest of estate to wife with reversion to my sister
Edmund's children, namely Susan, Davy and George and my bro-
ther Charles Briggs' two sons, namely Samuel and Duncan.
Ex., father Charles Briggs.
D. Nov. 7, 1799 R. Dec. 16, 1799
Wit. Charles Briggs, Jr., Henry Davis, John Pitmon
Page 159

PURSELL, John. Parish of Nottoway. Leg.- son Arthur
land adjoining Valentine Jenkins and my father's line; son
Peter; daughter Mary Pursell.
Exs., sons Arthur and Peter Pursell
D. Sept. 5, 1799 R. Dec. 16, 1799
Wit. Valentine Jenkins, William Jenkins,
Wilton F. L. Jenkins Page 160

CARSTARPHEN, John. Leg.- my estate to be equally divided between my wife Margaret; son John; David and Margaret Carstarphen.
Exs., wife Margaret, Arthur Bowing, Mica^1 Griffin
D. Nov. 26, 1799. R.R. Dec. 13, 1799
Wit. Jacob Turner, Jr., John Worrell, Jr. John Worrell
Page 161

WORRELL, Richard. Leg.- wife Tabitha, reversion of bequest to son Richard then to Shadrack and William Worrell; Edith Council.
Exs., Arthur Bowing and Mica^1 Griffin, Jr.
D. Oct. 12, 1799. R. Dec. 13, 1799
Wit. Temperance Council, Edwin Council, Robert Council
Page 161

LUNDY, John. Leg.- to John Rivers.
Exs., friend John Rivers and Henry Smith.
Wit. Benjamin Blunt, Jr., James Wilkinson, John McLemore
D. Oct. 18, 1799 R. Dec. 13, 1799 Page 162

WILLIAMS, George. Leg.- son Absalom, land adjoining my son Charles in Hertford Co., N. Car.; son Solomon; rest of my estate to my following children, Absalom. Elisosha Grantham, Janet Story, Elizabeth Darden & Nancy Sandefur
Ex. son Absalom Williams.
D. Aug. 24, 1797 R. Dec. 16, 1799
Wit. Isaac Williams, Josiah Williams, Daniel William, Arthur Carr
Page 162

BOWDEN, Robert. Account current. Signed, Thomas Bowden, Ex. Legacies paid the following, - widow, Betsey Bowden, Sally Bowden, Milly Bowden and William Bowden. Audited by John Crumpler and John Pursell
R. Dec. 13, 1799 Page 163

WILLIAMS, Robert. Parish of St. Luke. Leg.- wife Rebecca, with reversion to grandson Elisha Williams, son Robert Williams.
D. July 14, 1783 R. Jan. 20, 1800
Wit. George Gurley, William Thomas, George Gurley, Jr.
Probation granted Robert Williams. Page 164

JOINER, Jacob, the younger. Leg.- wife Martha; son

Charles; son Jacob, the land bought of Dr. Thomas Peete to the line of land conveyed by me to Jesse W. Moore; son Charles the land devised me by my uncle Bridgman Joiner; son William land devised me by my father and lands purchased of Silas Lowe; daughters, Polly, Sally and Martha Joiner; provision for unborn child.
Exs., wife and brother Jordan Joiner.
D. Sept. 20, 1799   R. Jan 20, 1800
Wit. Samuel Slade, Peggy Powers, Martha Vitching, J. Denson.   Page 164

VICK, William. Leg.- wife Elizabeth until my daughter Polly Boykin arrives to age of eighteen or marries; daughter Polly. My land in Raleigh, N. Car. to be sold and the proceeds to be divided between my daughters.
Exs., wife, friend Benjamin Blunt, Burwell Vick, James Gee
D. June 15, 1799   R. Jan. 20, 1800
Wit. Lazarus Cook, George Gurley, Jr., Holladay Revell
                                                        Page 166

REESE, Olive. Account current. Signed, Robert Mabry, Adm. Paid Nathan Felts his wife's portion of her father's estate; Olive Reese, Admtx. Paid each the same amount, Edwin Bass, John McLemore and Kinchen Turner the guardian of Lewis, orphan of Edward Reese. Bond received of Roger Reese Administrator of John Reese, who was the former Adm. of Olive Reese. Audited by Benjamin Blunt, Jr. and John Williamson. D. April 3, 1795   R. Jan. 20, 1800
                                                        Page 167

LITTLE, William. Account current. Signed, Robert Mabry, Adm. Audited by Benjamin Blunt, Jr., John Williamson
D. May 29, 1794.   R. Jan. 20, 1800   Page 168

VAUGHAN, William. Appraisal. Etheldred Brantley one of the appraisers died before the return was made. Appraised by Jesse Holt and Henry Bittle. Signed, Thomas Vaughan and Thomas Turner, Exs.   R. Jan. 20, 1800   Page 170
D. Nov. 7, 1794

MEGLAMORE, John. Leg.- wife Letty, with reversion to son John; daughter Sally Whitehorn with reversion to her children; daughter Betty Baley; daughter Hetty; granddaughter Nancy Lunday
Ex., son John Meglamore
D. May 15, 1797   R. Jan. 20, 1800
Wit. William Newsum, Peter Simmons, Robert Myrick
                                                        Page 171

ADAMS, Henry. Leg.- wife Mary; daughter Martha Tyler; daughter Julia Adams.
Ex., son-in-law Edward W. Tyler and friend Robert Goodwyn
D. Jan. 7, 1800   R. Feb. 17, 1800
Wit. Jeremiah Cobb, Samuel Kello, Robert Exum

Page 172

JOYNER, Jacob. Estate appraised by John Davis, J. Vick and Burwell Williams.
D. Jan. 29, 1800   R. Feb. 17, 1800   Page 173

MITCHELL, Abraham. Estate appraised by Marthew Wills, James Edwards and Jacob Darden, Jr.
D. Oct. 26, 1798   R. Feb. 17, 1800   Page 174

WOMMACK, Thomas. Account current. Signed, Carter Wommack, Ex. Paid to John McLemore, guardian to Betsey, James, Polly and John McLemore, the legacies left them by the decedent. Audited by Byrd Lundy and James Lundy
D. 1795   R. Feb. 17, 1800   Page 176

LUNDY, Elizabeth. Account current. Signed, Lunsford Lundy, Adm. Audited by Robert Mabry and James Harris
D. 1795   R. Feb. 17, 1800   Page 177

BRYANT, Jonas. Leg.- son Ephrim and his wife the land adjoining Richard Williams, Lewis Bryant, with reversion to my son Bennet William Bryant; wife Sarah land adjoining the line of Lewis Bryant and James Bryant; daughters, Lyddy and Pherebah Bryant.
Exs., brother Lewis Bryant and friend James Maget.
D. Nov. 7, 1799   R. Feb. 17, 1800
Wit. James Bryant, Winna Cook, Elizabeth Stricklin

Page 177

BRACY, Ann. Leg.- brother Francis Bracy; sister Mary Wright; sister Elizabeth Beal; sister Petiance Johnson; sister Miriam Edwards.
Ex. friend Kinchen Edwards
D. Jan. 22, 1800   R. Feb. 17, 1800
Wit. John Fowler, William Fowler, Polly Beal   Page 179

TURNER, Pass. Account current. Signed, Henry Jones,

Adm. Audited by Joseph Denson, Arthur Bowing and Presley
Barrett. D. Dec. 1797   R. Feb. 17, 1800   Page 179

CHARLES, Jethro.   Account current.   Signed, Eleanor
Charles, Extx.   Audited by Daniel Simmons and ARTHUR
Bowing. D. 1797   R. Feb. 17, 1800   Page 180

JONES, James.   Account current.   Signed, Hanselm Jones,
James Jones and Jordan Jones.   Audited by Charles Briggs
and Burwell Barrett.   D. 1798   R. Feb. 17, 1800
                                                    Page 181

NEWSUM, Benjamin. Leg.- daughter Elizabeth, reversion to
granddaughter Dysa Newsum and grandson Crafford Newsum.
Ex. Charles Briggs Nicholson.
D. Dec. 14, 1799   R. Feb. 17, 1800
Wit. Charles B. Nicholson, Crafford Newsum, Hamlin Harris,
      William Applewhite.   Page 181

POND, Drewry. Leg.- My land adjoining John Pond and John
Morris to be sold. Beloved wife with reversion to all my
children.
Exs., brother Samuel Pond, William Wellons and Thomas Wood
D. Feb. 15, 1800   R. Feb. 17, 1800
Wit. Robert Magee, Diana Pond, Nancy Magee   Page 182

SIMMONS, Henry. Account current.   Signed, C. Briggs,
Adm.   Audited by Benja. Ruffin and Phillip Davis.
D. Dec. 19, 1799   R. April 21, 1800   Page 182

BRACY, Ann.   Estate appraised by William Edwards, William
Beal.   Signed, Kinchen Edwards, Ex.
R. April 21, 1800   Page 183

IVY, Henry. Leg.- wife Charlotte; son William; provision
for unborn child.   Ex., father George Ivy
D. Feb. 2, 1800   R. April 21, 1800
Wit. Lunsford Lundy, Edward Bass, Robert Murrell (copied
      by clerk when will was proven, Robert Murry)
                                                Page 184

SEWARD, Edwin. Leg.- nephew Coufield Seward; mother
Sarah Thorpe, with reversion to sister Mary Harris then to
her surviving children.
Exs., nephew Coufield Seward and kinsman Byrd Lundy.
D. Jan. 27, 1796   R. April 21, 1800
Wit. Henry Ivy, Joel McLemore, John McLemore   Page 185

LUNDY, Priscilla.   Estate appraised by James Harris and
Peyton Lundy: (Peyton Harris died before signing)
D. Feb. 9, 1799   R. April 21, 1800   Page 186

WILKINSON, John.   Leg.- son Nathaniel when twenty one
land on the Meherrin River and two lots in Murfreesboro;
son John Lewis Wilkinson land partly in Virginia and N. Car.
with reversion of bequests to my brother James Wilkinson.
Exs., brother James Wilkinson, brother-in-law Benjamin
     Weldon Williamson, friend Ely Eley and Cordall N.
     Bynum.
D. June 11, 1799   R. April 21, 1800
Will proved by James Gee, S. Kello, William Blunt, John
Bynum and Benjamin W. Williamson and Simon Everett.
James Wilkinson and Benjamin W. Williamson   Page 186

BROWNE, John.   Nuncupative will.   Proved by Albridgton
Browne, Margaret Browne, John McLemore and Richard Harrison.
Leg.- wife and her heirs.   Brothers, Jesse and James
Browne to manage his affairs.
D. Jan. 21, 1800   P. Jan. 28, 1800   R. April 21, 1800
                                                    Page 188

M. NEIL, James.   Estate appraised by Lem^1. Hart, William
Crichlow and Robert Ricks.
D. Aug. 22, 1795   R. April 21, 1800   Page 188

HARRIS, Ruth. Parish of St. Luke. Leg.- grandson
Anthony Harris, son of Simon Harris; granddaughter Sally
Harris, daughter of Mary Barrom; grandson William Turner,
son of Thomas Turner.
Ex. John Bynum
D. June 10, 1799   R. Oct. 21, 1799
Wit. Sally Phillips, Rebkah Williams, Henry Turner
                                                    Page 189

CLAUD, Sally. Leg.- son-in-law Hartwell Felts, he to

take my son Nuet Newson to raise; daughter Dority Claud; estate to be divided among Dority Claud and Sally Claud and son Nuet Newsom.
Exs., Humphrey Drewry and Harris Johnson
D. Feb. 15, 1800   R. March 18, 1800
Wit. Isaac Sullivan, Dorcas Tanner, Sally Felts

Page 190

BRANTLEY, Etheldred.   Appraisal (not signed)
D. May 22, 1797   R. June -- 1800   Page 190

McLamre, John. Estate appraised William Champless, Frederick Parker and Richard P. Clements
D. March 7, 1800   R. May 19, 1800   .   Page 192

DREWRY, Humphrey. Account current. Signed, Samuel Drewry. Legacies paid Rebecca Drewry, Joseph Drewry, Charles Simmons in the right of his wife Hannah and the children of Robert Andrews. Audited by Samuel Calvert and Charles Briggs, Jr.
D. Dec. 1796   R. July 21, 1800   Page 194

JONES, Thomas. Leg.- wife Sally if she educates my children, Hannah Briggs Jones and Rebecca Williamson Jones; nephew William Henry Gee, son of James Gee.
Exs., wife and friends James Gee and Sam^1. Edmunds.
D. May 20, 1799   R. July 21, 1800
Wit. Henry Blunt, Nathl. Edwards, John Whitehead

Page 195

SUMMERELL, James. Leg.- son Sikes, land adjoining the line of Lucy Williamson and Thomas Summerell; wife Anna with reversion to son Lemuel Butts Summerell; daughter Lucretia Branch; my three daughters, Diana, Sally and Eleanor Summerell; son James Summerell.
Exs., William Boykin and Silas Summerell
D. Feb. 24, 1800   R. July 21, 1800
Wit. Benjamin Brister, William Holden, Shadrack Boykin

Page 197

WHITEHEAD, Arthur. Estate appraised by Jacob Darden, Jr, James Maget and Holliday Revell.
D. Dec. 23, 1799   R. July 21, 1800   Page 198

WHITEHEAD, William. Account current. Signed John

Whitehead; Adm.   (A merchant)   Audited by James
Wilkinson, James Gee, Will Edmunds (Edmund Turner was also
appointed an auditor, but did not serve)
    D. Dec. 1, 1796   R. July 21, 1800   Page 200

DAVIS, Henry. Inventory. D. Sept. 12, 1798 Page 202
Account current. 'Signed, Henry Davis, Ex. Audited by
Charles Briggs, Sr., Phillip Davis.   R. July 21, 1800
                                                Page 203

JOINER, Molly. Estate appraised by Lewis Joyner and
Amos Joyner. D. Feb. 8, 1799   R. Aug. 18, 1800
                                                Page 204

BRITT, Benjamin. Account current. Among items,
paid to the widow. Audited by Joel Edwards and Thomas
Everett.   R. Aug. 18, 1800   Page 204

POPE, Josiah. Estate appraised by Saml. Edmunds,
Etheldred Edmunds and John Kindred
    D. Jan. 24, 1800   R. Aug. 18, 1800   Page 205

ELLIS, Henry. Estate appraised by George Edwards,
Edmond Barrett, Jacob Barrett.   R. Aug 18, 1800
                                                Page 207

CORBITT, Jacob. Estate appraised by Thomas Camp,
Lemuel Rowe; Joseph Turner.
    D. May 1, 1800   R. Aug. 18, 1800   Page 207

CARTER, Joseph. Inventory. Signed; George Gurley
and Richard Blow.   R. Aug. 18, 1800   Page 208

STEVENSON, Thomas. Parish of Nottoway. Leg.- wife
Nancy with reversion to my three sons, Josiah, Martin and
Bennett; daughter Elizabeth Stevenson.
    D. Aug. 29, 1800   R. Oct. 20, 1900
Wit. Arthur Doles, Edward Hatfield, Mary Stevenson.
                                                Page 208

SUMMERELL, Boaz Guin. Leg.- wife Elizabeth; son Thomas;
son William; daughter Nancy Bools if her husband will pay
twenty pounds to my daughter Milly; son Herod; after sale of
my estate the money to be divided among all my children or
their representatives. I desire that John Clayton, Jr.,
Joseph Jones, William Boykin and Henry Branch, or any three
of them to divide my land
Exs., sons William and Thomas Summerell
D. Feb. 1, 1797   R. Oct. 10, 1800
Wit. John D. Houssman, Joseph Jones, Elizabeth Jones.
      (Joseph Jones was a Quaker)   Page 209

SEWARD, Edwin. Estate appraised by John Williamson,
James Lundy and George Ivy.   R. Oct. 20, 1800
                                              Page 211

WILLIAMS, George. Estate appraised by James Harrison,
Jesse Battle and William Hart.
D. Dec. 23, 1799   R. Oct. 20, 1800   Page 211

BROWNE, Olive. Inventory. Signed Thomas Lane., Ex.
D. Oct. 20, 1800   Page 213.

WASHINGTON, George. Of Nottoway Parish. Leg.- son
William; wife Easter; grandson Henry Johnson, son of Mathew
Johnson and Sally his wife; remainder of estate to be sold
and divided among all my children then living
Ex., son William Washington and David Washington.
D. Oct. 2, 1800   R. Oct. 20, 1800
Wit. Joseph Bracy, Archer Drake, James Whitehead
                                              Page 213

STEWARD, Liddia and Benjamin Steward. Account current.
Signed, James Hosea.   Audited by John Simmons, Jr. and
Micah Ellis   D. 1799   R. Oct. 20, 1800   Page 214

CARSTARPHAN John. Estate appraised by Pressley Barrett,
Benjamin Bradshaw, Charles Councill and Jeremiah Joyner
D. Jan. 2, 1800   R. Dec. -- 1800   Page 215

WORRELL, Richard. Estate appraised by Shadrack Worrell,
Charles Council and Joseph Turner.   R. Dec. --, 1800
D. Dec. 10, 1800   Page 215

COBB, Lazarus, Sr. Leg.- son Josiah, land adjoining William Harcum and the land which was my brother William Cobb's; son Nicholas; son Lazarus, land adjoining my brother Henry Cobb and David Edwards; son Frederick; daughter Mildred Cobb.
Exs., sons Frederick and Nicholas Cobb.
D. Oct. 3, 1800   R. Dec. --, 1800   Page 217
Wit. Jacob Darden, Jr., William Harcum, Victor Eley

FORT, Joshua. Account current. Signed, Lewis Thorp, Ex. Paid Selah Fort one third of the money from Thorp's estate; the following paid the same amount,- Priscilla Fort, Joshua Fort, William Barnes, Elizabeth Fort, Joseph Fort, John Fort, Edwin Fort, Temperance Fort. Credited Joshua Fort's proportional part of the estate of Joseph Thorp.
Audited by James Lundy, Robert Mabry,and Nathaniel Wyche
D. Aug. 1, 1800   R. Dec. 15, 1800   Page 218

ELLIS, Henry. Account current. Audited by Jesse Barrett and Jacob Barrett.   R. Dec. --, 1800   Page 219

PERSON, Anthony. Estate appraised by John Moore, John Blunt and Richard Harrison. Signed, Richard A. Blunt
R. Jan. --, 1801   Page 220

-------- O --------

INDEX

www.ingramcontent.com/pod-product-compliance
Lightning Source LLC
Chambersburg PA
CBHW021901020426
42334CB00013B/423